Sport, Dance and Embodied Identities

Sport, Dance and Embodied Identities

Edited by
Noel Dyck and Eduardo P. Archetti

Oxford • New York

First published in 2003 by
Berg
Editorial offices:
1st Floor, Angel Court, 81 St Clements Street, Oxford, OX4 1AW, UK
838 Broadway, Third Floor, New York, NY 10003-4812, USA

Berg is an imprint of Oxford International Publishers Ltd.

Library of Congress Cataloging-in-Publication Data
Sport, dance, and embodied identities / edited by Noel Dyck and Eduardo P.
Archetti.– 1st ed.
    p. cm.
Includes bibliographical references and index.
    ISBN 1-85973-635-1 – ISBN 1-85973-640-8
    1. Sports–Social aspects. 2. Dance–Social aspects. 3. Identity
(Psychology) I. Dyck, Noel. II. Archetti, Eduardo P.

GV706.5.S7113 2003
306.4'83–dc21

2003004507

British Library Cataloguing-in-Publication Data
A catalogue record for this book is available from the British Library.

ISBN 1 85973 635 1 (Cloth)
        1 85973 640 8 (Paper)

Typeset by JS Typesetting Ltd, Wellingborough, Northants.
Printed in the United Kingdom by Biddles Ltd, Guildford and King's Lynn.

www.bergpublishers.com

Contents

Contents

Notes on Contributors

Sally Anderson is a Research Fellow in the Department of Anthropology, University of Copenhagen. She has conducted ethnographic research in Scandinavia for three decades, including initial work on Saami identity and cultural revitalization. Her book, *I en klasse for sig* (*In a Class of Their Own*) (2000) examines cognitive and interactional models afforded by the organization of ongoing class groups in Danish grade schools. Her doctoral dissertation, *Civilizing Children: Children's Sport and Civil Sociality in Denmark*, explored the political and moral organization of children's sport.

Eduardo P. Archetti is a Professor of Social Anthropology at the University of Oslo. He has written extensively on society and culture in Argentina and Ecuador. He has also investigated the meaning of sport and dance for national representations and identities. His most recent books are *Guinea Pigs: Food, Symbol and Conflict of Knowledge in Ecuador* (1997), *Masculinities: Football, Polo and the Tango in Argentina* (1999) *and El potrero, la pista y el ring: Las patrias del deporte argentino* (2001). He has experience of both playing and coaching football and of dancing tango.

Harald Beyer Broch is a Professor of Social Anthropology at the University of Oslo. He has conducted field research in Indonesia, Canada and Norway and is the author of *Growing Up Agreeably: Bonerate Childhood Observed* (1990), *Woodland Trappers: Hare Indians of Northwestern Canada* (1998), and *Jangan Lupa: An Experiment in Cross Cultural Understanding* (2002). He competed at the national level in Norway in cross-country skiing as a junior and, as an adult, was an elite middle distance runner (800m) in the 1960s.

Noel Dyck is a Professor of Social Anthropology at Simon Fraser University in Canada. The author of several books on relations between Aboriginal peoples and governments, he was drawn to the anthropology of sport through his children's participation and his own subsequent involvement as a coach in youth soccer and track and field. He is the editor of *Games, Sports and Cultures* (2000) and is currently completing a study of adults and the social construction of children's sports.

Notes on Contributors

Hans Hognestad is a social anthropologist and Research Fellow at the Norwegian University of Sport and Physical Education in Oslo. He has written articles on football fan cultures in Norway and Scotland and is currently completing a project on the construction of transnational football identities and processes of hybridization. He has worked as an adviser on culture and development issues for the Norwegian Commission for UNESCO. A knee injury suffered at the age of 17 ended his dreams of a professional career in football, but he has found an alternative way to make a living from the game.

Tamara Kohn is a Lecturer in Anthropology and Human Sciences at the University of Durham. She has conducted field research in the Inner Hebrides of Scotland, East Nepal, England and California. She is the co-editor of *Extending the Boundaries of Care: Medical Ethics and Caring Practices* (1999). Her most recent research has looked at martial arts practice in the US and UK. She is a student and teacher of aikido, and is currently completing a monograph based on her martial arts research as well as an edited volume on 'The Discipline of Leisure'.

Werner Krauss is a Research Fellow in the Institute of Social Anthropology, University of Hamburg. He has conducted research on social and environmental issues in Portugal and Germany. He is the author of *"Haengt die Gruenen!" Umweltkonflikte, nachhaltige Entwicklung und oekologischer Diskurs ("Hang the Greens!" Environmental Conflicts, Sustainable Development and Ecological Discourse)* (2001). Following a sporting youth, his interest in practicing sport was gradually overtaken by a passionate interest in consuming and commenting upon sports news.

Anne Leseth is a Research Fellow at the Norwegian University of Sport and Physical Education in Oslo. She is currently completing a doctorate based upon field research conducted in Tanzania during the 1990s. She is interested in critical perspectives on sport and dance as facets of development as well as in experientially based understandings of body practices. She is the author of 'The use of Juju in Football: Sport and Witchcraft in Tanzania', in G. Armstrong and R. Giulianotti (eds.) *Entering the Field* (1997).

Henrik Ronsbo is a Senior Researcher at the Rehabilitation and Research Center for Torture Victims in Copenhagen. He has a Master's Degree in Cultural Geography and International Development Studies from Roskilde University. He also studied at the Janney Programme for Latin American Studies at the New School for Social Research (USA) and has a Ph.D. in anthropology from Copenhagen University. He possesses a vigorous interest in playing , watching and learning from the game of football.

Heike Wieschiolek is an Associate Lecturer in Social Anthropology at the University of Hamburg. Her research interests include cultural models about work, identity and the economic system in East Germany, as well as the political role of educated elites in West Africa. She is the author of " . . . *ich dachte immer, von den Wessis lernen heißt siegen lernen!" Arbeit und Identität in einem mecklenburgischen Betrieb* (1999) and *Afrika im Spannungsfeld kultureller Einflüsse. Eine Auswahlbibliographie zur afrikanischen Sicht* (1999). Trained in Flamenco, Salsa and Oriental dancing, she is currently conducting research into dance and identity.

Helena Wulff is a Senior Lecturer in Social Anthropology at Stockholm University. Her English-language publications include *Twenty Girls* (1988) and *Ballet across Borders* (1998). She has also co-edited *Youth Cultures* (1995) and *New Technologies at Work* (forthcoming). Her research interests evolved around youth culture and ethnicity, and currently focus upon the anthropology of dance, the arts, aesthetics, visualization, information technology, and transnationality. She is now engaged in a study of dance in Ireland that investigates questions of social memory, modernity, and place.

Part I
Introduction

Embodied Identities: Reshaping Social Life Through Sport and Dance
Noel Dyck and *Eduardo P. Archetti*

Introduction

In a football match staged in a Salvadorean village a team representing the *ladino* elite meets one consisting mainly of the sons of indigenous men killed by *ladino* paramilitary patrols during the civil war of the 1980s. On the dance-floors of Hamburg nightclubs German *aficionados* of *salsa* negotiate the delicate issue of women being obliged to follow the lead of their male partners in an age of other-wise relentless gender equality. When selecting playing partners the boys and girls of an inner-city Copenhagen recreational badminton programme mandated by social policies of inclusion move across the gym towards friends while cutting a swath of non-attention through children from other schools and social classes. What these and other ethnographic scenarios examined in this book serve to highlight are the diverse and complex ways in which sport and dance are implicated in the production and expression of embodied identities. These identities inevitably reflect not only stylized forms of movement and purpose, but also the contexts within which they are nurtured.

Bringing together sport and dance as ethnographically distinctive but analytically commensurable forms of body culture and social practice represents a departure from previous ways of thinking about these two fields within anthropology and other disciplines. Sport and dance are conventionally viewed in the West as residing within separate and even opposed cultural realms. Yet they share not only a common status as techniques of the body (Mauss 1973), but also a vital capacity to express and reformulate identities and meanings through their practised movements and scripted forms. Sport and dance spark widespread participation, critical appreciation and endless interpretation by performers and their audiences. Indeed, the embodied practices of athletes and dancers afford not merely pleasure and entertainment but powerful means for celebrating existing social arrangements and cultural ideals or for imagining and advocating new ones.

The eleven chapters that follow explore a variety of sport and dance forms, activities and relationships in locales that reach from Europe to Africa and North,

South and Central America. They probe the ways in which particular historical and ethnographic settings and undertakings serve to mark sport and dance both as embodied activities and as objects for contemplation, recognition and discourse that give rise to a variety of reworked national, ethnic, class, gender and personal identities. The forms of sport and dance discussed in this volume include those created as expressions of modernity that are directly or indirectly implicated in projects of nation-building. Others exemplify processes of globalization within which forms of embodied practice, such as tango, *aikido* and Riverdance, that are produced in the 'periphery' may be exported, thereby contesting the cultural hegemony of the 'centre'.

As prime sites for not only leisure, but also the production, reproduction and contestation of identities, sport and dance balance precariously between a set of recurring contradictions. Thus, the embodied identities spawned by athletes and dancers are frivolous yet serious; categorical yet personal; ephemeral yet abiding; and, relegated to the field of leisure, supposedly on the margins of everyday life, yet the focus of burgeoning economic industries and formidable political interests. Precisely because sport and dance are performed within these oscillating contradictions, they provide penetrating analytical vantage points from which to apprehend the taken-for-granted arrangements and assumptions of social life.

The volume is organized into three parts. The chapters in the first part examine sport training regimes that work to shape the bodies and selves of child and youth athletes, as well as the ways in which boys and girls pursue their own concerns and exercise agency within these settings. Sally Anderson's chapter presents an ethnographic account in which a group of children, meeting at an inner-city Copenhagen recreational centre for badminton practice, receive instruction not only about how to strike the shuttlecock effectively but also about how to comport themselves appropriately within a situation pervaded by Danish ideals of universality and inclusive social fellowship. Anderson argues that the task of promoting state-mandated ideals of sociality through sport involves rather more than the propagation of inclusive cognitive categories and adult supervisors' exercise of proper moral direction. What her carefully observed account establishes is the manner in which these children construct a highly skilled, intricately coordinated non-verbal performance that satisfactorily enacts the tenets of inclusive sociality without disrupting their preference for playing mainly with their friends. Anderson's analysis highlights the physical and social sophistication with which these young badminton players navigate the moral domain that constitutes recreational sport in Denmark.

Noel Dyck's chapter considers the puzzling but abiding contradiction between the nostalgic Canadian cultural ideal of 'pond' hockey and the regimented realm of organized community sports for children. 'Pond' hockey is an oft-invoked representation of sport and childhood that envisions spontaneously initiated and free-flowing games of ice hockey in which children skate freely, enthusiastically and creatively into a zone of playful exuberance and delight. It stands in marked contrast to the workaday world of adults and the tutelary regime of the schoolroom. Dyck asks why such a vividly imagined set of ideals is, nonetheless, so systematically violated by adult-organized community sport organizations for children. His analysis pursues what this disjuncture tells us about the ways in which understandings of childhood, relations between parents and children, and the shaping of child and adult identities are articulated through sport.

Harald Beyer Broch's chapter investigates gender ideologies and stereotypes in children's handball in Norway. He focuses on the play of 13- to 16-year-olds, since this developmental stage is generally seen as being especially characterized by identity insecurity and experimentation. Broch analyses identity management and presentation as these are revealed through the children's discourses on sport dress, bodies and talent. Paying close attention to the ways in which children actually engage in handball, he treats them not simply as competitors in an athletic contest, but as fully social persons whose engagement in sport is complex and variable. Boys and girls are shown to be equally concerned with their looks and body images and sensitive about discursive depiction of their on-court personalities, aggressiveness and skill as players. Athletes' interactions with their coaches are also shown to figure significantly in the embodied play and gender identities being fashioned by children in competitive handball.

The second part of the volume explores some of the many ways in which engagement with sport and dance may serve to express and reformulate the social and experiential identities of adults. Hans Hognestad's chapter looks into the phenomenon of long-distance support for British football clubs among Norwegian sport enthusiasts. While the popularity of football in Norway reaches back to the early part of the twentieth century, it continues to be categorized culturally as a non-Norwegian pastime. Since skiing remains the key symbol and carrier of Norwegian virtues within nationalist ideology, involvement in football permits its enthusiasts to experiment with identities that fall outside the carefully monitored confines of what constitutes proper ways of being Norwegian. Declaring and enacting one's identity as a fan of one or another British football team affords entry into a liminal zone within which Norwegian men serially escape the confines of national identity and propriety. The remarkable lengths to which Norwegian fans from all sectors of society go in identifying with particular British football clubs and in fulfilling pilgrimages to overseas football grounds speaks to their search for expressive individuality through transnational sport sophistication.

Heike Wieschiolek's chapter examines the *salsa* dancing scene that has recently emerged in Hamburg. Although now a thoroughly globalized style of dancing, *salsa* exhibits an unmistakable Latin American flavour in its music, movements and gender assumptions. In contrast to most social dance forms made popular during the last quarter century, *salsa* is performed by couples and requires body contact. Moreover, its musical structure and steps are sufficiently novel and demanding for German dancers to render it a technique requiring formal instruction. Anchoring her analysis within the anthropology of dance, Wieschiolek traces the ways in which dancing *salsa* enables men and women to take temporary leave of the gender and identity constraints characteristic of German urban life. Ironically, the methodical and disciplined ways in which Germans prepare themselves to dance *salsa* in the proper manner serve to distance them from Latin American couples, who bypass *salsa* dance classes and move directly to the dancefloor in Hamburg.

Tamara Kohn's chapter elucidates the practice of *aikido*, a generally noncompetitive martial art originating in Japan but today practised both there and abroad. *Aikido*, argues Kohn, passes in and out of the realms of 'sport' and 'like sport', depending upon context and intent. The physical training and athleticism central to *aikido*, along with the organizational politics, social relations and sense of commitment generated by participation in a *dojo*, are clearly reminiscent of club structures in sport. But the practice of *aikido*, which features purely defensive techniques, is directed not toward competition but rather toward mastery of physical techniques and, through these, toward an enhanced sense of self and others. Kohn's analysis highlights the attractions of *aikido* as a means of selfdevelopment and personal healing in a fragmented contemporary world. The capacity of *aikido* to generate satisfying embodied experiences and identities rests on the virtually limitless applications to the complexities of everyday life that can be made of knowledge acquired on the training mat.

Henrik Ronsbo's chapter documents the manner in which the game of football has in little more than forty years become a dominant means for embodying male identities and asserting indigenous status in the village of Santo Domingo, Salvador. Ronsbo's ethnography of masculinity proceeds from an insightful reading of earlier anthropological accounts of economic and political structures and processes in Meso-American society. He argues that traditional ethnological concerns with male sociality that were descriptively rooted in the study of religious brotherhoods in this region have been overtaken by the arrival of football as a popular pastime. The first part of Ronsbo's chapter details the everyday practice of football as a means for leisure as well as for the creation, maintenance and dissolution of alliances between young men within the indigenous community. In the second part he analyses a historic and contentious match between ethnically distinct segments of a community that was violently divided during the civil war of the 1980s. In this venue, too, football embodies identities, albeit those that connect their bearers to painful memories and continuing divisions.

The third part of the volume delves into the use of sport and dance as vehicles for expressing and reformulating national identities. Helena Wulff's chapter investigates the moral politics and purposes of national identity in which Irish dance is steeped. Irish bodies have long been subjected to particularly stringent forms of control by church and state, and within this context dancing has been deemed especially problematic. Indeed, in 1935 the state implemented the Public Dance Hall Act as a way of stopping informal dancing at crossroads and in barns and private houses. Today in Belfast it is joked that the Free Presbyterian Church has banned sex because it might lead to dancing, while in Dublin a recent production of the Dance Theatre of Ireland was enthusiastically reviewed by the local media – which, nonetheless, only hinted at the nudity featured in the performance. Notwithstanding the global popularity of Riverdance and other forms of Irish dance, there linger within both parts of Ireland unresolved contradictions regarding dancing, sexuality and touch. Wulff's chapter delineates the complex interconnections between dance, morality, nation-building and identity in Ireland.

Werner Krauss's chapter interrogates the relationship between nation, sport and identity through an account of the German national football team's symbolic and emotional significance in postwar German society. The demoralization and stigma borne by Germans following the Second World War were accompanied by a determination to eliminate any vestiges of cultural practices and postures associated with national socialism. The unexpected victory of the German team in the 1954 World Cup competition staged in Berne suddenly offered Germans a powerful yet legitimate means of experiencing national pride and expressing a renewed and positive German national identity. Krauss locates the essence of what came to be known as the 'Miracle of Berne' in the shift that it signalled from the battlefield to the playing-field and from the martial to the cultural. Krauss's analysis of German football in terms of miracles, heroes, myths and master narratives traces the continuing impact of highly masculine German values upon representations of national identity.

Eduardo P. Archetti's chapter mounts an analysis that compares sport and dance as forms of embodied practice and aesthetic pleasure that serve both as public mirrors and as models of identity. Focusing upon football and tango, Archetti recounts how these two forms of performance have become exemplars of Argentinian movement, style and identity. Football, he notes, constitutes a ritual and a game at one and the same time. While football celebrates males' loyalty to clubs and neighbourhoods, tango engages both men and women sensually. It celebrates the art of seduction under male control and features the exhibition of 'cool' control and the performing of chess-like figures and movements – much like the Argentinian speciality of controlled dribbling of the ball on the playing-field. Both football and tango, argues Archetti, became central to the construction of national narratives in Argentina, not least through the exporting of so many of its footballers and tango dancers to the rest of the world.

Anne Leseth's chapter on dance, sport and politics in Dar-es-Salaam examines the ways in which body practices both reflect and shape the political contexts within which they are performed. She begins her analysis with a critical assessment of conventional social-science categories and boundaries that separate practices such as sport and dance from one another. Tanzanians, she reports, classify various games, athletic contests and styles of dance together under the rubric of *michezo*. While the modern notion of 'sport' is also well known in Tanzania, owing to its instrumental use by both colonial and post-colonial governments as a means for 'developing' and changing people, Leseth argues that 'sport' and *michezo* represent not only different categories but fundamentally different ways of knowing body practices. Leseth's ethnographic account of the use of sport and dance as means for pursuing and celebrating national unity also reveals how hybrid forms of Tanzanian body practice blend imported styles with traditional forms of movement.

This volume has four overlapping objectives. The first is to consider ways in which different forms of sport and dance, as techniques of the body, can be brought into a common theoretical framework. The second aim is to explore how the embodied movements and practices of athletes and dancers are transformed into performances that connect audiences and performers interactionally as well as communicatively. The third task is to trace the ways in which sport and dance give rise to embodied identities that are generated on the fields of play or on dance-floors, but that are also transported to and deployed within other realms of social life. Finally, this volume considers the manner in which the bodies and activities of athletes, dancers and their fans are not only socially inscribed but also socially inscribing. In short, this volume asks how sport and dance fit into and reflect social lives and settings, and how these performative activities and the relationships to which they give rise serve to reshape the larger contexts within which they are enacted.

The traditional reluctance within anthropology to give serious and sustained attention to the study of games and sports resulted in large part from the viewing of these as products of modernity (Archetti 1998). Since sports produce an asymmetry between winners and losers, they were labelled as appurtenances of competitive, industrial societies that, accordingly, belonged outside the purview of ethnology. That particular intellectual tide has been largely reversed in recent years, and ethnographic studies of sport are finding their way into the anthropological literature (for example, Armstrong and Giulianotti 1997; Brownell 1995; Dyck 2000; and Klein 1997).

Although dance has been sporadically reported by ethnographic fieldworkers for a century, the establishment of a more focused and critical anthropology of dance has been a relatively recent development. The once near-exclusive focus upon non-Western cultures, along with a long-standing, but not especially fruitful, attempt to arrive at a universal definition of dance have given way over time to more fully comparative and processual approaches (Blacking 1985; Spencer 1985; Wulff 1998a). The roughly concurrent emergence of dance and sport as parallel fields of study that are not only provoking innovative and exciting insights into the social uses of the body and the nature of embodied performance, but are also linking these forms of body practice to broader contexts of social and cultural life, makes this a propitious time to begin to explore interconnections between the two.

Sport, Dance and Techniques of the Body

Marcel Mauss, a pre-eminent figure of early twentieth-century anthropology, characterized techniques of the body as the ways in which from society to society people know how to use their bodies (1973: 70). Proceeding from the concrete to the abstract, he retraced the steps by which, through the reading of ethnology and observations taken from his own life, he had come to recognize the body as being 'man's first and most natural instrument. Or more accurately, not to speak of instruments, man's first and most natural technical object, and at the same time technical means, is his body' (1973: 75).

The training procedures human beings apply to animals, noted Mauss, they voluntarily apply to themselves and to their children. Recalling the manner in which he had been taught by a gymnastics teacher to run with his fists close to his chest, 'a movement completely contradictory to all running movements' (1973: 73), Mauss had had to see professional runners in action before realizing the necessity of running in a different manner. Moreover, lying ill in a hospital in New York, Mauss wondered where he had previously seen girls walking as his nurses did. He realized that it was at the cinema. Returning to France, he noticed how common this particular gait was, especially in Paris. That American female walking fashions had begun to cross the Atlantic, thanks to the cinema, was an idea that Mauss could generalize.

Identifying the body as a social as well as a psychological and biological phenomenon, Mauss nominated education (or training) as being dominant among all elements of what he termed the art of using the human body:

> The notion of education could be superimposed on that of imitation. . . . What takes place is a prestigious imitation. The child, the adult, imitates actions which have succeeded and which he has seen successfully performed by people in whom he has confidence and who have authority over him. The action is imposed from without, from above, even if it is an exclusively biological action, involving his body. The individual borrows the series of movements which constitute it from the action executed in front of him or with him by others (1973: 73).

It was precisely the notion of the prestige of the person who performed the ordered, authorized, tested action *vis-à-vis* the imitating individual that, for Mauss, encapsulated the social element in techniques of the body. Cases of invention, of laying down principles were, in his view, rare. While cases of adaptation might be an individual matter, in general Mauss thought these to be 'governed by education, and at least by the circumstances of life in common, of contact' (1973: 85–6). Summing up the social dimensions exhibited by different styles of walking, Mauss concluded that there was perhaps no 'natural' way for an adult to walk, but only one or another socially mediated and transmitted form of perambulation.

Mauss's penetrating and inventive analysis of techniques of the body prefigured central aspects of Foucault's (1977, 1978, 1985, 1986) writings on the body as a site of discipline and power and of Bourdieu's (1984, 1990) explorations of sports as markers of taste and distinction in class-based societies. Moreover, Mauss enlisted the Latin word *habitus* as the appropriate one for referring conceptually to 'habits' that 'do not just vary with individuals and their imitations, . . . [but] vary especially between societies, educations, proprieties and fashions, prestiges. In them we should see the techniques and work of collective and individual practical reason rather than in the ordinary way, merely the soul and its repetitive faculties' (Mauss 1973: 73). What Mauss bequeathed to those curious about the complex social workings and salience of body techniques was an analytical scheme within which ethnographic observations about the differing ways in which people use their bodies might be linked theoretically to larger social processes and purposes.

What can anthropological studies of sport and dance take from the work of Mauss? To begin with, his recognition of running, swimming, games and dancing as appropriate and significant matters for social analysis dismisses prejudices that would marginalize these as trivial matters. Although he did not identify sports arenas and dance-halls as privileged loci for the initiation of an anthropology of techniques of the body, he did include dance and athletics in this discussion. Furthermore, his general theorization of techniques of the body readily accommodates comparative analyses of sport and dance, both with one another as well as with 'non-leisure' activities. The priority that Mauss placed upon the transmission of body techniques suggests a logical starting-point for ethnographic accounts of the actions of athletes and dancers. Most important, perhaps, is the clarity and boldness with which he sketched the possibilities for further investigation within this area.

Each of the chapters in this volume revolves at least implicitly, and in some cases quite explicitly, around the physical enactment of techniques of the body associated with a particular game, sport, martial art or form of dance. The intricate actions and coordinated movements that together constitute, for instance, not only the kicking of a ball but the playing of a football game or the dancing of a tango all depend upon the transmission of particular techniques of the body. Some performers may demonstrate an ability to use their bodies so skilfully that their movements appear to be almost entirely unrehearsed and 'natural' ways of functioning. But how do the talented and not-so-talented learn how to use their bodies in any given performative situation?

Formal instruction is a prominent feature of the way in which Germans learn to dance *salsa* in Hamburg. Students of *aikido* acquire the ability to perform this martial art under the watchful tutelage of their *Sensei*. Similarly, organized community sports programmes for children in Denmark, Canada and Norway provide more or less extensive technical training to boys and girls, many of whom may be participating in a given sport for the first time. The degree to which systematic and continuing instruction remain prominent features of these activities varies, not least in terms of the intensity and seriousness of the level of competition or performance being pursued. But whatever the level of participation, the formal disciplining of bodies that occurs within sport and dance involves not only the transmission of knowledge about, and the shaping of competence with, given techniques of the body, but also the proselytizing of particular schemes of preference, valuation and meaning.

The line that separates formal training in sport and dance from the learning of body techniques through observation, imitation and what Mauss termed 'the circumstances of life in common' (1973: 85–6) is sometimes a very fine one. Athletes and dancers do, indeed, learn from watching and listening to one another. Individual performers may adapt or reinterpret conventional moves or, more rarely, may even devise novel steps or plays. The assessing and proclaiming by students, team members or dance partners of the limits of the technical competence of a coach, official or instructor is a matter that does arise in sport and dance from novice to professional levels. The point is that while the teaching and learning of techniques of the body involves the transmission of physical knowledge that may not be readily translated into verbal terms, nevertheless, these and other embodied processes of sport and dance occur within thoroughly social settings and are subject to being noticed and discussed both in gestures and words. To understand better the ways in which athletes and dancers come to know how to use their bodies, ethnographers of sport and dance must take account of both the kinaesthetic and social action that takes place within formally organized coaching and instructional regimes as well as in informally convened situations where people seek to acquire and perfect the rudiments of one or another particular form of body practice.

Embodied Practices and Selves

The acquisition and refinement of techniques of the body that are central to sport and dance involves a recurring process that links doing, experiencing and then reflecting upon that action. In the course of attending formal or informal training sessions, lessons or rehearsals, athletes and dancers experience varying combinations of sensations. These may range from pain to boredom, fatigue, frustration and/or satisfaction that, on occasion, might even border on elation. What they also experience is self-consciousness. These bracketed times for acquiring embodied understandings of what to do with one's body and how to do it within the context of any given sport or form of dance feature not only acute physicality but also various levels of reflection upon one's attempts to accomplish particular movements and actions in particular ways. In these settings physical action is subject to continuing assessment and correction that seeks to replicate recognized and valued patterns of movement. Whether this is initiated and conducted primarily by the individual dancer or athlete, by coaches or instructors, or in company with fellow participants, it invariably activates the self-consciousness of individual performers.

In sport and dance, techniques of the body connect and operate in concert with techniques of the self (Hughes-Freeland 1998: 3). Who one is and what one does, what one cannot do or, at least, cannot yet do satisfactorily may be readily conflated, either in the reflexivity of a dancer or athlete or in the comments and treatment extended by coaches, instructors or performing partners. Among other things, what physical action produces on playing-fields or dance-floors is selves. As Rapport (1998: 179) argues, just as the self is embodied in performance, so is any performance an embodiment of selves.

Given the decidedly social nature of most forms of sport and dance practice, these processes of embodiment tend to unfold in the presence of larger or smaller aggregations of fellow participants. Privacy, let alone anonymity, is not really possible in venues of practice and performance, locker rooms or backstage dressing-rooms. Yet for many athletes and dancers, one of the most dreaded and difficult adjustments that accompanies retirement or even temporary withdrawal from an activity is the loss of the intense sociality that goes along with being a member of a team, club, company or 'scene'. But the social element in sport and dance goes far beyond the mere exchange of casual chit-chat before and after training sessions to the heart of the ways in which one learns, not just how to use one's body, but also how to enjoy the use of it.

The progressive achievement of 'body discoveries' that informs learning processes within sport and dance is individually experienced but socially mediated. The confirmation, identification and labelling of 'newly' experienced actions or movements requires specific vocabularies of movement that may be either gestural or verbal in nature, as in the case of *aikido*. The movements and actions of sport and dance are ephemeral creations that are experienced and forgotten or that live on through being reflected upon, witnessed, named, remembered and, quite possibly, repeated. An individual's embodied discoveries or achievements cannot be readily verified or discursively celebrated without the assistance of knowing witnesses. Nor can embodied selves be easily generated or sustained in sport or dance without the presence and assistance of co-participants. For the sake of argument, one might devise an illustrative exception: possibly a solitary individual who runs entirely by him- or herself and yet achieves a new or transformed sense of self as a result of doing this. But could one be confident that the ostensibly singular race being run was not sustained in some part by imagined or remembered co-participants or witnesses? What one knows of one's own performances relies to a greater or lesser extent upon how these may be may read in the responses offered, or withheld, by significant and knowing others. The line between 'my' and 'our' embodied discoveries and accomplishments may, therefore, become moot.

What sport and dance also entertain, alongside socially mediated self-consciousness, is expressive and imaginative creativity that must take account of the inherent sociality of these embodied activities. From an anthropological perspective, the significance and meanings attached to the physical performances of dancers and athletes are not textually prescribed but socially constructed within these corporeal fields of interaction (Schieffelin 1998). They depend upon collaborative forms of agreement about what a particular play or movement means and how it might best be produced, as well as on collusion about what remains unsaid and undone. The latter is nicely illustrated in Sally Anderson's account of how badminton-playing children in Copenhagen silently accommodate principles of social inclusivity without allowing these to jeopardize their preferred ways of playing. The entraining of moving bodies to perform either 'set plays' and choreographed steps or improvised and spontaneously coordinated movements demands awareness of the disposition of others and some degree of shared anticipation and imagination. The grace and innovation evoked within Canadian images of 'pond' hockey depend upon the manifestation of such forms of cooperative contrivance.

Doing sport and dance is particularly pleasurable when it involves performing recognized forms of movement in proficient, yet relaxed, and even playful, ways. At its very best, this experiential territory is likened by athletes to an unusual zone or episode within which one's performance unaccountably zooms beyond normal limits and attains some aspect of the highest ideals for a particular sport or game. Wulff identifies the emic term for similarly extraordinary experiences in ballet art as 'ballet revelations' that are remembered as 'a heightened state of mind that resembles a religious conversion. They can be a source of unprecedented empowerment. . . . The point is that they make a lasting impression that cannot be outshone by later experiences of ballet art; ballet revelations are formative and may be the force that makes a ballet pupil decide to become a professional dancer . . .' (1998b: 116–17). Zones and revelations such as these are, by definition, not frequently encountered. They are, however, mimicked by somewhat less intense, but nonetheless absorbing, occasions where athletes and dancers contrive to 'play' with forms of embodied practice. Within these settings dancers and athletes may perform with excitement, passion, a deep sense of release and boundless stores of energy. These liminal times and spaces, located between the monotonous routines of everyday life and the exacting ideals and physical requirements of sport and dance, can afford athletes and dancers pleasurable experiences and embodied selves that transform the time, effort and sacrifices invested in these activities into resources well spent. Tango and *salsa* dancers, along with village football players in Salvador, slide easily into environs such as these.

On the other side of the intrinsic pleasures and accomplishments available to dancers and athletes stand the risks that also await those who choose to pursue these activities. The incidental physical injuries and pain that may accrue from participation in sport and dance represent one set of risks. But the potential dangers posed to the selves of participants may prove even more threatening. To attempt to dance or play a game of football or hockey, for instance, at any level is to open oneself to potential public humiliation. To be revealed to be a person with a demonstrably awkward or uncoordinated body or to be the child who is typically selected last when sides are chosen for impromptu games is to suffer more or less keenly felt injuries to one's dignity and sense of self. But even highly experienced amateur or professional performers are constantly confronted by the unpredictability of sport and dance and the realization that they are, perhaps, only one misstep way from embarrassment and ridicule. This concern with both the external and performative aspects of 'how one looks' is clearly apparent amongst youthful handball players in Norway.

Ensconced in the company of fellow performers, a shared appreciation of such risks might serve to mitigate the sting of embarrassment, although this is by no means an ensured outcome. Competitiveness can prompt a distinct lack of compassion both in sport and dance. But when performing for audiences that comprise more than merely fellow participants and the occasional coach or instructor, one presents one's body, one's movements and oneself for critical appraisal. What is made of such performances by spectators and fans lies beyond the control of athletes and dancers.

Watching Sport and Dance

Ethnographers of sport and dance must be reflexive about how they are positioned in relation to the particular activities, relationships and meanings they seek to investigate. On the one hand, sport and dance can be observed and analysed from the 'outside' in terms of their structural components, composition and effects. The language and concerns employed within this approach are, as Tamara Kohn notes, those of the analyst. The selection of this way of proceeding is to some extent enabled by the embodied and substantially non-verbal nature of sport and dance, for dancers and athletes are neither trained nor, perhaps, inclined to reflect upon their embodied practices in terms of social theory. Treating forms of embodied practice as objects for inquiry remains the preferred analytical stance in the sociology of sport, a field of scholarship that has paid considerable attention to the ways that sport has been applied instrumentally in order to advance or shore up state, class and gender interests (cf. for instance Elias and Dunning 1986; Gruneau 1999; Horne 1987).

On the other hand, the prospect of getting 'inside' the activities and experiences of athletes and dancers has long attracted fans and journalists alike. Although it might be predicted that ethnographers would generally prefer this approach, to classify this as simply a matter of disciplinary and methodological inclination would be to overlook one of the key features of most anthropological work conducted in this field thus far. If the experience of contributors to this volume is any guide, then one would have to conclude that most ethnographers of sport and dance bring to their academic investigations some previous experience and sometimes ongoing personal involvement in these activities. Our problem is less that of negotiating entry to the activities, subjectivities and relationships of selected forms of sport or dance than that of obtaining the degree of separation necessary for conducting critical analyses of situations we frequently tend to know in personal terms .

Ethnography offers a means of combining both 'inside' and 'outside' approaches to sport and dance. The insights, vocabularies and questions that may be afforded by prior personal participation in one form or another of sport or dance may provide the impetus for initiating nuanced ethnographic projects and pursuing innovative lines of analysis. Once launched, investigations such as these fall subject to the usual practices of ethnographic inquiry.

What warrants acknowledgement, however, is the manner in which the vividness and certainty of personal, embodied experience of a specific form of sport or dance may not only shape how we interpret that form but also lead us to suppose that we have similar insights into forms of practice with which in fact we have no such familiarity or understanding. It would be ludicrous to imagine that one's love and understanding of English (or German, Argentinian or Salvadorean) football would afford one special insight into the dynamics and experiences of long-distance running or of a martial art such as *aikido*. Similarly, *salsa* and ballet are two quite distinct forms of dance, neither of which can be simply subsumed in terms of the ostensible presence or absence of the practices of the one within the other.

'Sport' and 'dance' are, as Anne Leseth notes, culturally constructed categories for assembling highly specific sets of activities. What is and isn't 'sport' or 'dance' can be classified in markedly differing ways from one locale to another. Caution must also be exercised in conducting contrasts, not least in the case of those sometimes drawn between sport and dance. The proposition that dance entails

aesthetic expression and is, thus, fundamentally unlike sport, which is corresp-
ondingly reduced to mechanically structured forms of embodied competition, tells
us nothing useful about either of these realms of body practice. Indeed, Eduardo
P. Archetti (1999, and in this volume) has explored the ways in which aesthetics
interpenetrate both football and tango, just as Helena Wulff (1998a) has elucidated
the quite considerable presence of competition in ballet.

Ethnographic analysis must respect the specificities of particular forms of sport
and dance, even those invoked only for the purpose of framing contrasts and
proclaiming definitional boundaries. Nevertheless, the scope of ethnographic
analysis can be powerfully extended through informed comparison and the posing
of common questions. For instance, what types of participation occur in conjunction with sport and dance? A comprehensive list of those involved in sport and
dance reaches well beyond athletes, dancers, coaches and choreographers to
include spectators (or fans) and sometimes journalists and other representatives of
the mass media.

Relations between performance and spectating as well as consideration of fans
and their involvement in sport and dance feature prominently in this volume. The
discussion earlier in this chapter of sport and dance as techniques of the body
underscored the sociality of these activities. To the extent that techniques of the
body are practised in the company of others, there is inevitably a performative
dimension attached to these. Athletes and dancers know that their actions and
movements can be observed at close hand and with greater or lesser amounts of
empathy and criticism by those with whom they train. The practitioners of *aikido*
studied by Tamara Kohn fashion their participation in this martial art in terms of
cooperation and non-competitiveness. Yet in the process of training together they
commit themselves to the exacting discipline of seeking cumulative mastery of the
moves of *aikido*. The state of one's individual progress towards this goal is
apparent to all those with whom one trains.

The young athletes described by Harald Beyer Broch are manifestly aware of
their individual appearance and performance on the handball court. In competition
they are visible to other players as well as to onlookers, who mainly consist of
family members and friends. But the imagined gaze of television cameras, which
in recent years have popularized and sexualized the appearance of elite women
handball players, also enters into the ways in which girls experience and structure
their involvement in handball at the community level. The frequently presumed
separation between performers and spectators becomes highly problematic in
Noel Dyck's report on community sports for children and youth in Canada. The
premium placed by parents upon organized sport as a medium for embodying the
success of their sons and daughters as athletes and of themselves as dutiful and
effective fathers and mothers renders their presence and participation an essential
feature of these activities.

Whether fans watch from the immediate sidelines of a football field, the edges of the dance-floor, seating areas in a theatre or stadium or in front of their television sets, the precise nature of their engagement with any given form of sport and dance deserves careful ethnographic attention. While the Norwegian language may not have a word that directly identifies sport fans, Hans Hognestad's chapter recounts the activities and interests that make being a Norwegian fan of British football an energetically demanding and complex, yet satisfying pastime. In this case, the core activities of watching and talking about a sport, its teams and leading players are conducted from a considerable distance. But this involves far more than the consumption of newspaper and television coverage of British football matches. The discursive relations enjoyed by these football fans underpin their regular social gatherings in Norway, occasional pilgrimages to British football grounds and active involvement in web-based football discussion groups.

What these fans seek from their engagement with British football is quite different from what German fans have obtained from supporting their national football team in the postwar period. It also differs from what the indigenous community in Santo Domingo received from its courageous but defeated team in its historic match against the *ladino* elite. But what each of these and other contributions to this volume further serve to demonstrate are the ways in which sport and dance combine techniques of the body, social practices and cultural imagination in ways that fuel the generation of embodied identities that reflect and address issues that do not necessarily begin or end on the dance-floor or field of play.

Embodied Identities and the Reshaping of Social Life

The focal points of sport and dance are the performances presented by athletes and dancers. Spectators, including other performers, may watch a given football match or demonstration of tango with more or less expert eyes. They bring to these occasions varying amounts of personal experience of practising these forms and differential knowledges of their particular rules, patterns of movement and ideals. They also possess differing levels of familiarity with the styles and accomplishments of particular athletes or dancers and how these might compare with those of their predecessors. Equipped with larger and smaller amounts of these resources, those who pursue an active interest in one or another form of sport or dance are ready to engage in the never-ending and all-absorbing tasks of interpretation, appreciation, and identification that are such central parts of these embodied forms of practice and expression.

Offering one's views about what is transpiring on the playing field or stage and judging whether it is a good, bad or mediocre rendering of a form of sport or dance clearly constitute interpretation. What they also entail is making disclosures about oneself. The utterances and gestures of a commentator, or their absence at any given moment, can be read as evidence of one's level of sophistication with respect to sport or dance, and may also provide further clues concerning one's social and personal identity. Even the most limited forms of commentary – for instance, the offering of polite but less than fulsome applause at the end of a performance – make statements about both the performer and the commentator.

The sharing of interpretations and verbal or non-verbal expressions of appreciation or disgust constitute not only communication, but also modes of social interaction that connect performers and spectators in various ways. Professional athletes sometimes claim to have developed a capacity to block out their awareness of the crowd and its commentaries. But the prospect of playing a match in an empty stadium with few or no onlookers is not an especially appealing one for professional players, nor for many child athletes. For fans the exchange of opinions on any and all facets of a sport or dance, including the merits of individual players or dancers, sports teams or dance companies, provides a medium for the negotiation and maintenance of social relations. This may be confined to a brief conversation struck up with a stranger during the interval between the halves of a game or sections of a performance or, alternatively, may serve as the basis for a friendship that endures for decades. Werner Krauss reports that being identified as a German *and* a football fan helped during earlier fieldwork in Portugal to introduce him as a person and, thereby, to pave his way as a field researcher.

Interpretation and appreciation in sport and dance are accompanied by processes of identification that may operate at a variety of levels and with reference to all manner of factors. The moving bodies of performers, which could be scientifically described and categorized in kinesiological terms, are just as likely to be identified in terms of stereotypical images of gender, age, race, class, ethnicity, religion or nationality. The potential for the drawing of invidious distinctions between 'us' and 'them' always exists within these situations. But there are also ample opportunities for fans who are inclined to establish discerning understandings of the mechanics and aesthetics of performance. Fans may also create narratives that record and celebrate memorable performances first and foremost in terms of the individuality and talent of those who created these moments. Explanations proffered in Ireland of distinguishable Protestant and Catholic types of bodies and ways of moving must, therefore, be read cautiously to establish where kinesiological observation begins and where purposes of social dichotomization take over. This may not be a simple matter to determine. Since techniques of the body are socially and culturally mediated, it can be argued that bodies subjected to formal and informal programmes of training in particular places and times are both inscribed and inscribing.

This reprises the matter of the extent to which sport and dance may be distinguished in terms of their respective instrumentality and expressiveness. That sport can be marshalled for decidedly instrumental purposes is established in Sally Anderson's chapter on children's sport in Denmark and Anne Leseth's account of the use of sport to facilitate, at first, colonial compliance, and later the project of nation-building in Tanzania. Helena Wulff's analysis of the attention devoted to dance by church and state in Ireland identifies this as a means of exercising social control over sexuality. Tamara Kohn's chapter indicates that many practitioners of *aikido* are persuaded to carry on with this form of practice not so much by its exotic trappings as by the immediate psychological and physiological benefits it provides them.

The aesthetic attractions of both sport and dance are examined in Eduardo P. Archetti's chapter. Henrik Ronsbo reports the sustained appeal within a Salvadorean indigenous community of a stylized and individualistic manner of playing football, notwithstanding its tactical shortcomings. Heike Wieschiolek's depiction of how an appreciation of style enters into *salsa* dancing in Hamburg is not far, if at all, removed from the findings of Archetti and Ronsbo. Moreover, even the cultivation of an aesthetic ideal may foster a certain instrumentality. Hans Hognestad's account of the devotion of Norwegian football fans to a decidedly non-Norwegian form of sport practice and Heike Wieschiolek's underlining of the ironic popularity of a male-dominated form of dance in a social environment featuring otherwise obligatory norms of gender equality suggest that devotees of both of these forms of embodied practice quench more than merely aesthetic tastes through their participation in these activities.

Sport and dance share a capacity to engage the imagination and to foster creativity among both performers and fans. This occurs socially as well as aesthetically. The dancing of tango or *salsa* and the playing or watching of football occur outside the confines of routine, everyday life. Through a common commitment to specific techniques of the body and forms of practice proffered by different types of sport and dance, men and women may be enabled to experience a liminality that permits not only temporary escape from the realities of life but also opportunities to contemplate and experiment with new visions and possibilities. The sense of *communitas* (Turner 1969) that is frequently triggered by performance and absorption in sport and dance can suddenly and viscerally connect individuals who would otherwise be unlikely to associate with one another in any manner, let alone in these ways. It is hardly surprising that sport and dance are frequently likened to forms of social, if not religious, ritual. Like ritual, sport and dance serve to connect people in ways that are not otherwise readily available to them in contemporary social worlds.

Conclusion

Do sport and dance serve as mirrors within which societies and individuals can view themselves? Or do they provide models that can be employed instrumentally to shape and control bodies, habits, inclinations and polities? Our answer would be that attempts have been made to use them in both ways, albeit with varying success. What German soccer fans experience when their national team occasionally fails in international competitions suggests that sporting mirrors can provide ambiguous and worrying reflections as well as more flattering images. The capacity of child badminton players to sidestep the serious purposes of the Danish state, much like that of the dancers who playfully perform at National Liberation Day celebrations in Tanzania, suggests that we ought not to underestimate the abilities of performers to steer around the attempts of those who would endeavour to control social life through sport and dance.

A more nuanced and comprehensive view of sport and dance would identify them as ingenious and compelling means for reflecting, commenting and acting upon existing social, political, moral and national arrangements. In their capacity to embody identities that can be celebrated and consumed in the immediate environs of the playing-field or dance-floor, but that may also be taken 'home', so to speak, and employed to rethink and modify prevailing assumptions and arrangements, sport and dance present exciting and subtle forms for reshaping social lives.

References

Archetti, Eduardo P. (1998), 'The Meanings of Sport in Anthropology: A View from Latin America'. *European Review of Latin American and Caribbean Studies*, 65: 91–103.

—— (1999), *Masculinities: Football, Polo and the Tango in Argentina*. Oxford/ New York: Berg.

Armstrong, Gary and Richard Giulianotti (eds) (1997), *Entering the Field: New Perspectives on World Football*. Oxford/New York: Berg.

Blacking, John (1985), 'Movement, Dance, Music, and the Venda Girls' Initiation Cycle', in *Society and the Dance: The Social Anthropology of Process and Performance*, ed. Paul Spencer, pp. 64–91. Cambridge: Cambridge University Press.

Bourdieu, Pierre (1984), *Distinctions: A Social Critique of Taste*. Cambridge: Cambridge University Press.

—— (1990), 'Programme for a Sociology of Sport', in P. Bourdieu, *In Other Words: Essays Towards a Reflexive Sociology*, pp. 156–67. Stanford, CA: Stanford University Press.

Brownell, Susan (1995), *Training the Body for China: Sports in the Moral Order of the People's Republic*. Chicago: University of Chicago Press.

Dyck, Noel (ed.) (2000), *Games, Sports and Cultures*. Oxford/New York: Berg Publishers.

Elias, Norbert and Eric Dunning (1986), *Quest for Excitement: Sport and Leisure in the Civilising Process*. Oxford: Basil Blackwell.

Foucault, Michel (1977), *Discipline and Punish: The Birth of the Prison*. New York: Pantheon Books.

—— (1978), *The History of Sexuality, Volume I, An Introduction*. New York: Pantheon Books.

—— (1985), *The History of Sexuality, Volume II, The Use of Pleasure*. New York: Pantheon Books.

—— (1986), *The History of Sexuality: Volume III, The Care of the Self*. New York: Pantheon Books

Gruneau, Richard (1999), *Class, Sports and Social Development*, revised edition. Champaign, IL: Human Kinetics Press.

Horne, John (ed.) (1987), *Sport, Leisure and Social Relations*. Sociological Review Monograph, 33.

Hughes-Freeland, Felicia (1998), 'Introduction', in *Ritual, Performance, Media*, ed. Felicia Hughes-Freeland, pp.1–28. London/New York: Routledge.

Klein, Alan M. (1997), *Baseball on the Border: A Tale of the Two Laredos*. Princeton, NJ: Princeton University Press.

Mauss, Marcel (1973), 'Techniques of the Body'. *Economy and Society*, 2(1): 70–88 (originally published in French in 1935).

Rapport, Nigel (1998), 'Hard Sell: Commercial Performance and the Narration of Self', in *Ritual, Performance, Media*, ed. Felicia Hughes-Freeland, pp.177–93. London/New York: Routledge.

Schieffelin, Edward L. (1998), 'Problematizing Performance', in *Ritual, Performance, Media*, ed. Felicia Hughes-Freeland, pp.194–207. London/New York: Routledge.

Spencer, Paul (ed.) (1985), *Society and the Dance: The Social Anthropology of Process and Performance*. Cambridge: Cambridge University Press.

Turner, Victor W. (1969), *The Ritual Process: Structure and Anti-Structure*. London: Routledge and Kegan Paul.

Wulff, Helena (1998a), *Ballet Across Borders: Career and Culture in the World of Dancers*. Oxford/New York: Berg.

—— (1998b), 'Perspectives Towards Ballet Performance: Exploring, Repairing and Maintaining Frames', in *Ritual, Performance, Media*, ed. Felicia Hughes-Freeland, pp.104–20. London/New York: Routledge.

Part II
Training Children's Bodies and Selves

Bodying Forth a Room for Everybody: Inclusive Recreational Badminton in Copenhagen
Sally Anderson

Introduction

Two moral maxims, 'we all have to be able to be here' (*vi skal allesammen kunne være her*) and 'there has to be room for everybody' (*der skal være plads til alle*) are used in Denmark to remind people to think, speak and act inclusively. They are commonly pronounced in public forums and institutional and family settings, and thus are part of every child's public moral upbringing. The maxims refer to abstract understandings of inclusive egalitarianism while simultaneously making very concrete demands on verbal and physical behaviour. They are used repeatedly to express dissatisfaction with excessive or exclusive behaviour: 'Your loud quarrelling is bothering everyone here'; 'If you continue to say things that hurt Sara's feelings, she won't feel she can be here'; or 'Stop shoving and move over; there has to be room for all of us.' The maxims thus point to a morality of shared physical space, suggesting social, physical constraints on co-occupiers of this space. No one person should take up so much verbal or physical space that others feel excluded, i.e. feel that they literally cannot *be* in the room. In this moral universe, inclusion refers to actual spatial relations and embodied interaction.

While ideal reminders point toward a preferred morality of sociospatial inclusion, they say little about how inclusiveness, recognized as such despite conflicts and contradictions, is actually embodied and enacted by groups of people in specific settings. In this chapter, I shall explore interactional practices negotiated by a group of children and their trainer in a recreational sport setting. Recreational sports in Denmark are generally pervaded by ideals of universality and inclusive social fellowship. These ideals are particularly foregrounded in sport settings for children. Recreational sports should ideally be open to all children and should provide all participants with a sense of being a part of the group. In what follows, I analyse how a group of inner-city children, meeting on Wednesday afternoons for badminton[1] practice, negotiate 'room for everybody' by bodying forth a particular style of play and mode of spatial relation. I argue that the preferred inclusive sociality involves more than inclusive cognitive categories and proper moral direction; it is a highly skilled, intricately coordinated, non-verbal performance.

Before opening this discussion in more detail, I want to provide background that may help explain why children's recreational sport has become a moral domain of universal ideology and inclusive sociality in Denmark.

'Going to Something' in the Public Sphere

'Going to something' (*at gå til noget*) is an idiom used by Danish children when talking about taking part in specific, organized after-school activities. Among the activities children choose to 'go to' are art, drama, music, dance, scouts and sports of all kinds, provided by a variety of public and private institutions. Many Danish children (aged 10–14) are also members of government-subsidized 'leisure-time clubs'. Extensions of government day-care provision, these clubs are not seen as 'something' children 'go to' but rather as institutions children are 'in'.[2] For children who 'go to' sports, leisure-time clubs fill out the hours between school and sports, which often do not start until 4.00 or 5.00 p.m., when volunteer trainers get off work.

Danish children 'go to' sports organized by local voluntary sport associations, which are funded in part by membership fees and in part by municipal subsidies and facility-provision (Ibsen and Ottesen 1996). Developed in Denmark during the latter half of the nineteenth century, association sport is now considered a traditional, Danish way of 'going to' sports. Voluntary sport associations are also a salient feature of national self-understanding, positively associated with grass-roots organization and a healthy, democratic civil society. Indeed, the Danish anthropologist Karen Lisa Goldschmidt Salamon suggests that associations serve as a metaphor for the nation, in which all Danes are considered members (Salamon 1994).

Traditionally, voluntary sport associations were for adults and young adults. Indeed, schoolchildren (aged 7–14) did not have general, uncontested access to sport associations until after the Second World War (Jørgensen 1998). Historical sources show that early sport associations periodically debated minimum age limits for participation in competitive sports. Organizers and educators, who were against children's participation, felt that the competitive aspects of sports were physically, psychologically and morally unsuitable for growing children's bodies, minds and spirits (Trangbæk 1995a: 159–62). However, as more children and youth became members of sport associations from 1900 to 1930, some authorities began to see the socializing potential of sport and sport associations.

With welfare state development in the 1930s, politicians and private educators alike looked to sport associations to promote physically and civically active youth with strong national identities. Shortly after the Second World War, as political focus shifted from wartime issues of national identity to peacetime issues of democracy, voluntary sport associations were promoted by youth leaders aiming to instil democratic values and practices in children and youth (Korsgaard 1997b: 348–74). In 1948, the Danish government established a Gaming Service and channelled its proceeds into national organizations promoting association sports. As the service developed and expanded in the ensuing decades, substantial increases in proceeds directed political attention to how sport organizations used public resources. This development gained sports a place on national political agendas from the mid-1970s to the turn of the century. Critical debates emphasized the societal and social benefits of grass-roots, recreational sport, while harping on the ills of growing professionalization and commercialization in elite competitive sports (Korsgaard 1997a). Growing participation in recreational sports and unorganized sports among the population at large lent impetus to political arguments for increasing subsidies for these areas of sport to benefit a broader spectrum of citizens (Bøje and Riiskjær 1991). In the last three decades of the twentieth century, issues of civil society and community integration were added to more established issues of health and democracy used to legitimize sport subsidies.

In summary, as children and youth began 'going to' association sports, gradually at first in the 1920s and 1930s, and then with greater momentum in the postwar period, political interest in children's recreational sports increased accordingly. Present policies advocating sports for children and youth argue that sports are 'good for children' because they promote health, instil 'Danish' democratic values and develop children's social networks in a local community. Politically speaking, children's association sports are sites of voluntary participation in activities outside the home, and thus sites of civil gathering and community integration (Ibsen 1995).

Postwar suburbanization led to a dramatic increase in the construction of sport facilities across the country (Mortensen 1999). Growing political support for children's participation in association sport also manifested itself in favourable municipal policies. Sport associations with organized children's sections received municipal subsidies based on numbers of child members. Because subsidies helped sustain reasonable fees for all members, children became an attractive economic resource for many associations. Child membership in associations grew significantly from 1950 to 1970 (Trangbæk 1995b: 26). By the late 1990s, approximately seven out of every ten children were members of sport associations (Larsen 2000), while nine out of ten children had been members of sport associations at some time during their childhood (Ibsen and Ottesen 1996: 102). These high levels of sports participation are generated by multiple factors. Children are genuinely interested in sport, local sport organization is usually well established, municipalities provide subsidies and facilities for children's sports, and, at the state level, sports are an integrated part of national cultural provision. Furthermore, government cultural policies bestow on all children the right to express themselves through sport.

Despite high levels of participation, public health studies in the 1990s indicated a decline in children's physical fitness (Holstein 1997). At this time, the government initiated a national campaign to increase children's participation in sports, particularly in urban areas, and to address issues of children's physical fitness, 'social fitness' and integration in local communities. The government warned of subsidy cutbacks if sport organizations did not take on the 'social responsibility' of providing sport activities for 'resource-weak' people such as urban children and the elderly, and 'marginalized' people such as invalids, immigrants of all ages and youth from socially burdened families (Idrættens vilkår i København 1997).

Government campaigns to incorporate a broader range of children in sport activities coincided with the commencement of extensive urban renewal projects and more localized 'neighbourhood lifts' to revamp community identity and promote local social integration. With these projects came coordinated efforts to revitalize local sports and sport associations for urban children, who – statistics had shown – did not participate in sports as often as provincial age-mates (Idrættens vilkår i København 1997). The case of children's badminton, discussed below, was part of a larger project to bring more sport to children and more children to sport in an inner-city neighbourhood of Copenhagen. It may thus be seen as a consequence of accumulated sport debates, sport politics and policies in modern Denmark.

Neighbourhood Sport Priorities

The city district of Vesterbro has been known as a rough and ready working-class neighbourhood sporting a well-developed bar culture and Copenhagen's main red-light district. As traditional working-class families moved to the suburbs, Vesterbro's run-down, cheap housing provided homes for students and other low-income categories such as substance abusers, eccentrics, immigrants, single mothers and grass-roots activists. Urban renewal has now added 'yuppie' and middle-class families to this categorical agglomeration of residents. The city awarded a defunct slaughterhouse site, situated where Vesterbro runs into Copenhagen's main railway yard, to The Danish Gymnastics and Sports Associations (DGI)[3] to build an unconventional facility for sport and culture. When the new facility, DGI-City,[4] opened in the autumn of 1997, DGI's local branch organized *Projekt Vesterbro*, to introduce DGI-City to Vesterbro residents and encourage them to join existing, or to start new, sport associations in order to access the facility.[5] The project coordinator worked with a local network of physical education teachers, sport association volunteers, social workers and police, all engaged in revitalizing association sports and encouraging local, so-called 'sport-less' and 'association-less' children to join sport associations,

In this same period, the municipality reserved prime time (4.00 to 8.00 p.m.) access to Copenhagen sport facilities for children's sports. In accordance with municipal policy, associations with children's sections were, in principle, allotted better time-slots than those without. The children's badminton group discussed below was a direct result of this transparent political effort to increase sport opportunities for children by persuading adults in urban sport associations to organize children's sections and volunteer as trainers. When Settlement Ball Club (SBC), a Vesterbro club, applied for weekly time-slots in the spacious new facility for its adult badminton group, access policies forced the club to establish a children's badminton section. SBC aligned itself with *Projekt Vesterbro*, which funded the hiring of a temporary trainer, a young student teacher, to set up a free badminton activity for neighbourhood children. Once the activity was up and running, the trainer was to hand the group over to volunteers from SBC.

The cooperative badminton project had three main aims. It was designed to establish a new sport activity in the neighbourhood, to channel local children into association sports and to attain legitimate access to DGI-City facilities for SBC's adult badminton players. A 12-year-old girl attending the new badminton activity imagined the project like this: 'It was probably that some people decided it could be fun to teach children without it costing anything – to teach them to play badminton. They should learn something, I think, to bring Denmark up in sports. I think they really wanted to have some children' (Camilla). In their quest to promote physical health, social health, and neighbourhood integration, and perhaps even to 'bring Denmark up in sports', DGI, DGI-City, and SBC 'wanted some children'. I suggest that these organizations also needed children to legitimate their own expansionist activities in the current political climate.

Ideal Associational Sociality

In many end-of-the-century projects set up in Denmark to encourage 'sport-less' urban children to join associational sport, sport organizers generally portrayed voluntary sport associations as Simmel might – as sites of *Vergesellschaftung* or 'sociation'. With *Vergesellschaftung*, Simmel introduced an analytical view of social life as 'forms of sociation', or 'forms of being with and for one another . . . in which individuals grow together into a unity and within which their interests are realized' (Simmel 1950: 41, 1971: 24). This perspective focuses our attention on processes of human interaction, on how people create and maintain relationships and how they enact and mutually engage with particular social forms.

In some English translations, *Vergesellschaftung* has been glossed as 'sociality' as well as 'sociation' (Simmel 1971). For analytical purposes, however, it is useful to distinguish between these two terms. In what follows, I will use 'sociation' to refer to general actions, forms and processes of human interaction and 'sociality' to refer to historically constructed understandings and forms of sociation. Sociality encompasses a particular emphasis a group puts on certain combinations of forms of sociation, and thus refers to salient forms and processes of sociation that appear particularly important in distinguishing and transforming peoples and places (see Monaghan 1995).

As is implied above, Simmel's analytical concept of 'sociation' resonates with Danish understandings of social connectedness growing out of 'associational life'. Associations bring individuals together in the public sphere on a voluntary basis to pursue an activity of interest. The 'being of and for one another' (*socialt samvær*) that ensues ideally leads to understandings and practices of group solidarity and belonging (*socialt fællesskab*). I suggest that both Simmel's theoretical model and the *emic* Danish model view sociation as reciprocal relations of mutual dependence based on notions of common interests, face-to-face relations and feelings of mutual belonging. The models both invoke interacting individuals with 'faces', 'interests' and 'senses of commitment', but neither addresses in any detail embodied aspects of social proximity. While the Danish associational model of sociation stresses common activity in sport associations, it does not address how social actors embody social connectedness in a *socialt fællesskab*. Intriguingly, both the *emic* and the *etic* theories are equally silent on the bodywork of sociation involving close social proximity. The analysis presented in later sections brings body movement to the fore to explore how children use their bodies to communicate social inclusion and exclusion in the association form of sociation.

Voluntary Sport Associations

In a Danish context, associations are salient forms of sociation and prototypical sites of preferred sociality. The high value placed on associational sociality lends associations political legitimacy. Sport associations bring people together to pursue their interests actively; associational decision-making processes are purportedly democratic, and associations ideally promote a sense of group belonging that cuts across other common axes of social differentiation. *Socialt fællesskab* that ideally grows from 'associational life' implies a moral relation between individuals and collectives that is widely mediated as proper public sociality. Rarely contested at the abstract level, associational sociality is generally considered good for individuals and good for society. Project workers from DGI, DGI-City and SBC regarded sport associations as proper sites of public 'upbringing'. They viewed this form of sociation as an individual process of 'becoming social' and a collective process of 'bringing individuals into society' (as with children and other novices).

By joining voluntary associations, children bring themselves into active, face-to-face relation in a public sphere of interaction, and, in doing so, actively engage in being 'brought up', or instilled with certain habits and understandings of this form of social interaction as moral public sociality.

Public debates on the future of sport associations held in DGI-City resounded with idealized and essentialized assumptions about different kinds of sports and organizational forms. Organizers attributed 'ways of being together' to particular forms of organization. Voluntary sport associations were preferred sites for bringing children into alignment with the public sphere, because associations are thought to promote social engagement and inculcate democratic practices. Organizers also attributed different forms of sociation to different forms of sports. In public forums, recreational sports, focused on inclusive play, usually had a moral edge over competitive sports, thought to focus narrowly on results.

Public debate forums generated abstract, idealized versions of 'ways of being with and for each other' understood as association sociality; but rarely did I hear details of how children and adults actually managed to create a *socialt fællesskab* by mutual engagement with each other. The intriguing silence regarding details of interaction in the physical domain of sports, perhaps a function of the cultural and political value put on association sociality, prompted my study of sociation in children's recreational sports in Vesterbro.[6] Two questions guided the study: how do children interact when they 'go to' a recreational sport 'open to everybody', and what characteristic patterns of sociation do their interactions produce? To investigate these, it was necessary to attend closely to embodied actions in various gyms and training-rooms. I contend that bringing people of any age into relation in the public arena of recreational sports is clearly about bringing people's bodies into relation and foregrounding communication of a non-verbal, physical nature.[7] Observing seasonal practices in different sport associations, I focused on how children accessed these public arenas and how they negotiated corporeal fields of recreational sport as body-selves. I will now turn to SBC's children's badminton to discuss how a particular group of children negotiated recreational sport for all.

Recreational Badminton for Everybody

As was mentioned earlier, SBC's children's badminton was set up in coordination with *Project Vesterbro* to attract children who did not normally go to sports or join associations. To attract this category of children, the activity was kept at a recreational level. Unlike other Copenhagen badminton clubs that held children's tournaments, posted match winners and displayed individual standings in club locales, SBC did not rank its players. At weekly practices, Katrina, SBC's temporary trainer, emphasized 'learning to play the game' and 'having fun' rather than training in special techniques or learning game tactics. She encouraged children to participate in recreational meets for fun and for the experience of playing with other children; but participation was always optional.

Inclusive, non-competitive sport was in keeping with SBC's profile as a neighbourhood club accommodating all categories of Vesterbro residents. Katrina described SBC as a 'social' club, 'typically Vesterbro' with its relaxed, informal atmosphere and *ad hoc* form of organization. Katrina characterized club members as easy-going people, neither career types nor ambitious badminton players. She noted that: 'There's room for everyone in this club. Anyone who wants to can join. New people are received well by all as long as they feel like being here.' As temporary trainer in SBC, Katrina found she was left to her own devices with regard to how to run the children's badminton programme. Compared to a 'normal' badminton club, there was less structure and fewer of the traditional forms usually associated with sports.

> It would have been perfectly okay if I only had the children play badminton for half an hour, instead of using the full hour and a half. This wouldn't work in other clubs, where they'd expect more tempo and planned structure, more exercises, matches and diplomas. But then, too much form wouldn't have worked with this group of kids because they come with such uneven qualifications (Katrina).

The club's idealistic, inclusive and laid-back approach to badminton was not upset by the pedagogical line Katrina adopted. As a teacher-in-training, Katrina was well versed in Danish educational practices, which are remarkably group-inclusive and non-competitive in orientation (Anderson 1996, 2000a). Because of this pedagogical congruency, I argue that children's badminton in SBC may be understood as a prototypical, if somewhat exaggerated, site of inclusive social interaction homologous to that found in Danish schools and day-care institutions.

The group of children who joined SBC badminton remained quite constant throughout the season (September–April). Only a small number of children dropped out, and attendance patterns were stable, unlike the sporadic, and discontinuous attendance patterns I experienced in other Vesterbro associations. This stability suggests that the group of children attending badminton were comfortable and satisfied with the inclusive recreational framing of this activity. Indeed, badminton practices generally proceeded in an overall relaxed, non-competitive fashion.

I have argued that an inclusive form of sociality was intended by Settlement Ball Club, a socially oriented club, and by their temporary trainer, as a practitioner of inclusive pedagogy. I have also argued that the children's stable attendance patterns indicated that a certain level of social comfort was attained. It is important, however, that recreational sports should not be analysed merely as social fields accommodating, more or less elegantly, a broad spectrum of categories of children. Weekly sport practices are more specifically corporeal fields of interaction, producing categories of children, as well as accommodating them through inclusive framing. To shed light on the embodied nature of this form of sociation, I turn to the interactive characteristics of badminton practices. Focusing on relational issues of importance to the children, I will discuss how they and their instructor accomplish a communicative frame of 'badminton for all', by moving their bodies competently through the intersubjective corporeal field. I argue that the inclusive frame remains stable despite a clearly visible co-production of children who 'stand alone', children who 'withdraw' and children who embody 'slackness'. I shall also argue that this form of sociation may be recognized as 'inclusive', as 'fun', and, thus, recognized as a preferred sociality that is 'good for children'.[8]

Not Knowing Anybody

Joining a recreational sport association, open to all, is an exercise in bringing one's physical person into a closed sphere of public interaction. One of the social risks Danish children identified with this exercise was the risk of not knowing anyone, which, according to many of them, led to being all alone and not having any fun.

What it would be like if I didn't know anybody? I wouldn't like that, because firstly it might be a little boring. It is just a lot more fun if you have somebody to keep to right from the start. Otherwise, all the others are friends already and you sit very much alone if you just come directly in – where they all know each other, right? Kind of like changing schools. So it was kind of like – they were very kind and all that, but it was like – it was 'Aww, we don't want to be together with her' (Zoë).

It is a lot of fun if there are some you know, right? But there are always some you don't know so well, so sometimes it's not much fun to be together with them. It's much more fun to be together with the ones you know. Because then it's like – like you have more fun (Bitte).

This here is much better than soccer. That's because I didn't really have any friends at soccer. Here I've got my class, you know. So it's a little more fun (Tore).

I only went to handball practice twice. Then I stopped because I didn't know anybody. I didn't know a single one of them. I really think you have to know at least one (Aylia).

Well, there are some things where you – if you start going to something new, then it can be very good to be alone, because then it is easier to get to know some of the others, right? But I stopped going to table tennis after about 5–6 years, because I didn't have any friends.

– 31 –

The children quoted above were all members of SBC's children's badminton, whom I had asked to compare their experience of 'going to badminton' in SBC with their experiences of going to other sports in other associations. 'Not knowing anybody', was a strong experiential factor guiding their decisions to join or drop a sport activity. For most of the interviewees, experiences of 'not knowing anybody' were coupled with expectations of not having anybody to 'keep to', to 'be together with' or to 'talk with', and consequently not having any fun. Moving one's body alone, without a friend attached, into public interactional spheres could apparently lead to corporeal and social non-relation uncomfortable enough to motivate some children to drop out and try another sport or association.

Children characterized sport activities as 'fun' or 'cozy' (*hyggelig*) or 'no fun' and 'boring' with reference to their experiences of social access. The widely used Danish notion of *hyggelig* implies social connectedness within a bounded group. It refers to pleasant, warm and friendly interaction, ideally making all present feel physically and socially comfortable and snug (see Hansen 1980: 58–87 and Schwartz 1985: 9–10). The data suggest that the social dilemma of not knowing anybody entailed the uncomfortable physical dilemma of standing out as a 'lone body'. Further data provided by the children show that they worked to avoid this uncomfortable condition by actively recruiting other children they already knew.

Recruiting 'Ones You Know'

To establish badminton as an activity and recruit neighbourhood children to play, Katrina (herself recruited for the job by a former schoolmate) ran a badminton camp in DGI-City during the autumn vacation. The camp, open to all, attracted only two children from Vesterbro. Most of the children attending badminton camp came from Christianshavn, a middle-class neighbourhood in a more fashionable part of town. Five boys in the initial group were classmates at a Christianshavn school; the other two boys attended different Vesterbro schools. When Katrina asked this small group of seven children (male, aged 11–12) if they would like to play badminton once a week for free, they agreed to give it a try.

Badminton practice was held once a week, from 16.00 to 17.30 p.m. in DGI-City's largest gym. As the season progressed, the seven boys proceeded to recruit others they 'knew' and, as one put it: 'There was a real chain reaction.' The Christianshavn group grew from five to eleven. Nine were present classmates, and one a former classmate who had changed schools due to problems in this particular class. One boy brought his younger brother along. Tore described the group in this way: 'I go to badminton with all of my friends and four girls.'

The close correlation between friends and classmates is commonly produced in Danish schools, where children are organized in home classes that ideally continue as a school-group throughout nine years of comprehensive schooling (see Anderson 1996, 2000a). Children are expected to find their friends within the bounds of their school class, and they often do. This particular group of classmates had earlier gone to swimming together, and several of the boys had played football in the same club. Upon hearing about vacation sport camps in school, they collectively chose between a gymnastics and a badminton camp:

> I probably really wanted to try gymnastics – vaulting gymnastics might have been fun – but the others said they would rather try badminton, and I'm happy with this. First, it was me and Tore and Steffan. And then right after that, Andreas. And then Erik, and then a couple of the girls came (Mark).

Camilla, the first girl to join, said she had heard about badminton from the boys.

> The boys from my class, they all went to it and then they asked me if I maybe felt like coming to it because they thought it could be *hyggelig*. At first it was just me, and then it began to be a bit . . . I wanted there to be another girl . . . I asked different girls in the class but they had something else on Wednesdays, but Frannie said yes (Camilla).

As Frannie tells it:

> I asked Camilla what she was going to do that day and she told me she was going to badminton. I hadn't heard that she had started badminton, so I asked where it was and then she asked if I wanted to come with her and try it, and I said I'd like that. So I got to come along (Frannie).

When Zoë complained about her Wednesday activity, Frannie and Camilla told her about badminton, saying it was 'really super fun' (*helt vildt sjovt*).

> They said the instructor was really nice and that they learned a lot. The instructor wasn't afraid to teach them, she didn't just show a lot of things and then go off and drink coffee – she was very attentive. So I decided in a matter of minutes to go with them and try it and I got a really good impression. It was really fun. So I went home and told Sara: 'Hey, you should try and come with us – it's really fun.' And she did (Zoë).

Vesterbro children also began recruiting friends and classmates, not from any sense of rivalry with the Christianshavn group, but in a similar fashion. Eigil and Anders, the two original Vesterbro members, came from classes in two different schools, so they recruited more broadly. Anders, one of the few who did not think that coming alone was a problem, told of bringing his friend Alan along soon after badminton started. Eigil invited two classmates, Eske and Henrik, who, in turn, brought in two others, one, an old family friend and one, a former classmate who had recently changed schools. Henrik explained it thus:

We had agreed that I would go over to his place after school. Then Eigil asked me if I wanted to come down here with him and I said OK. When we got down here, I saw what it was and was allowed to try. I thought it was a lot of fun, so I decided to go to it (Henrik).

One girl came with her mother, but found other children from her school already there. A group of girls, classmates in yet another Vesterbro school, joined after a badminton instructor had visited their school. One of these girls brought her younger brother along. In general, Vesterbro children came in smaller groups of no more than 3–4 classmates from four different local schools.

There were twenty-three children in all; eight girls and fifteen boys aged 11–12. The two younger brothers were 10 years old; a boy and a girl who joined later were both 14. Eleven of the children were from Christianshavn, twelve came from Vesterbro. As a whole, these children appeared to be a group of 'regular kids'. By this, I mean that, although the children came from a variety of socioeconomic backgrounds exemplified by residency in two different neighbourhoods, socio-economic differences were not overtly accentuated by clothing styles, ethnicity or other visible markers.

I have tried to show some of the motivations and relations that led children to join Wednesday afternoon badminton. Recruiting children into badminton began with adult initiatives, but, once it had started, children took over, pulling in chains of friends and classmates to create their own fields of accessible mates within the larger group of potentially non-accessible strangers.

Ability Matters

While most all children I interviewed pointed out that it was 'fun' being together with 'ones you know' (usually classmates), some said they preferred badminton to team sports, because it was less violent and other children did not get as angry. For example, boys who had played football without success spoke of rough play and a lack of tolerance from other players:

The best thing about badminton is that when you play at a meet, your mates back you up. That's the most important. That's why I didn't like football. I am not very good at it, so the others just got mad at me (Anders).

When I went to football, I was the worst one on the team, which wasn't very much fun. The best thing about badminton is that you don't get knocked about. No one ever comes and tackles you from behind, pulls your shirt half off or breaks your finger, and I think that's good (Eigil).

One of the girls liked the way the game itself ordered a relationship to another person: 'I just like the game – the fact that you have a court and there's another person on the other side. You're not alone.'

Although a few of the children had played badminton for fun in the yard or courtyard, none of the children had ever played badminton as a sport. Some, however, did have greater potential for learning to play the game well. Mark was a first-team footballer and former table tennis champion, whereas Erik described himself as 'a quiet indoor type of person' who has 'always been afraid of the ball in sports'. Frannie and Sara were good team handball players, whereas Aylia and Bitte had tried many sports without much success. While ability was not officially marked in this particular setting, children were self-conscious about displaying their ability, or lack of it, while playing. Children played 'real' games that produced winners and losers, but, in keeping with ideals of inclusive, non-competitive recreation, knowledge of who won and lost was not formally distributed. Nor were there prizes or official recognition of match winners at meets. Ranking with regard to athletic ability was thus never totally disregarded, but rather successfully diffused. To know who won or lost, children had to either pay attention to each other's games (which they rarely did at practice and only sometimes at meets) or ask each other about their results – a practice that did, of course, occur.

Eigil had been afraid that he would be the 'worst player' when he joined – 'I didn't think I would have a chance against them' – but soon found that other children played at different levels and that there were others 'worse' than he. Aylia thought it was tough to start because she was afraid of 'doing things wrong':

> It was a little hard in the beginning – trying not to do anything wrong, but always doing things wrong anyway. And when you have to serve, maybe you make a wrong serve and it goes crooked. In the beginning I often served crooked – and even when I didn't serve, it went crooked. Sometimes, they were way too high, and now they're all too low, I can't get them high enough (Aylia).

Bitte was rather nervous about her first recreational meet because, as she says with a laugh: 'I'm not very good.' Zoë, who joined later than the others, also mentioned that she had been nervous, worried that all the others would be so much better: 'I thought that they all would be really good players and that I wouldn't be able to play at all, but there are a lot of beginners out here, so I thought it was a lot of fun' (Zoë).

The children knew that this was not a competitive association where they would be expected to play against other children in ranked tournaments. They could sign up for recreational meets if they liked, but, basically, they were just learning to play the game of badminton. As many put it: 'It's fun to learn something new.'

Balanced 'Play'

Katrina planned and ran practices but encouraged children to suggest warm-up activities they thought 'fun', such as ball tag, soccer or basketball. In general, practice sessions included both 'playful' and 'serious' activities. For example, Katrina alternated exercises to improve racket techniques with hectic round-robin games that kept children rushing from court to court. She turned volley exercises into 'fun' by asking the children to practise volleying while sitting down or lying on their stomachs across from each other in two long rows. Picking up on the playful tone of these exercises, children created variations on the theme, attempting to volley while lying flat on their backs or sitting with their backs to each other. Two boys even had a go at volleying while holding rackets between their legs and hopping to hit the birdie (shuttlecock).

As has been noted previously, the children represented a wide range of ability. Some could easily have played in bigger, more competitive clubs, while others would never have been able to keep up. Katrina chose to combine serious training with fun and games to accommodate both those who could not have handled 'serious' training, and those who might have dropped out had there not been some discipline and a sense of learning badminton. She believed she might have 'lost' half the children had she insisted on running a more strict programme, i.e. on framing badminton as a serious competitive sport. As was noted earlier, her choice of a balanced, middle-of-the-road approach that did not take explicit notice of differences in children's ability and experience is in keeping with the normative pedagogic ideas of keeping groups functioning together that are found in Danish comprehensive schools (Anderson 1996, 2000a). This suggests that the children were quite practised in the communicative art of defusing ability differences by balancing the 'serious' with the 'playful'. One example of this is the sit-down volleying exercise mentioned above. Given the playful task of volleying from a sitting position, children might choose to take the task seriously or to play with the task, as did several boys who proceeded to create variations on the theme. The pedagogically staged exercise precluded any serious display of 'real' badminton volleying that might serve to rank the children as badminton players. Still, children who took the task seriously might have displayed a superior ability to volley while sitting down. The play frame, however, accommodated another frame of 'play on play' that once again thwarted any explicit communication of ability to play the game of badminton as such.[9]

Besides accommodating a group with diverse ability levels, a 'playful' approach to the serious business of training a sport is commonly thought to motivate adults and children alike. Maintaining an element of 'fun and play' (*leg*) in training sessions is therefore a canonical, moral theme in Danish sport pedagogy at all levels of play. Taking oneself, one's training or the game too seriously is potentially isolating, and thus anti-social. 'Fun' should be a regular component of all training at all levels of play. An elite tennis player, who thoroughly enjoyed driving herself to the limit during training sessions, reported being prompted by colleagues and trainers alike: 'Remember, this should also be fun' (Charlotte Baarts, personal communication). Michael Laudrup, a famous Danish soccer player, is revered for his skill in maintaining an element of 'play' in his approach to both the ball and the game throughout his professional career in top European soccer (Anderson 2000b).

At the level of Wednesday afternoon badminton, some children invoked the moral theme of balancing 'serious' elements with 'playful' elements when commenting on those who played too earnestly or those who just 'mucked about'. Erik found it uncomfortable to play with other children who focused so hard on playing the game that they found his friendly chatter irritating: 'I like a good game – to play with some – where I can learn something. Some – where I can talk to them. Because some of them just take it way too seriously. It doesn't matter whether they are good or bad [players], they just snarl at you, if you talk' (Erik). Frannie, on the other hand, felt that 'play' and 'playing around' could be taken too far. For her, it was a matter of maintaining the right balance: 'It's okay to relax and have a good time at badminton, but I still think some [of them] could take it a little more serious and not muck around doing all sorts of stupid things that interrupt' (Frannie). Camilla was particularly indignant about those so concerned with winning that they made a point of calling public attention to their successes: 'They win and then, "Yeah man!" and "Yoo hoo! I won, I'm the champ here."'

As we saw earlier from the children's interviews, being 'good at something' was attractive, while being 'bad at' or 'worse than the others' was worrisome, awkward and embarrassing. The latter could, however, be articulated publicly without moral sanctions and often was; it was all right to talk about not being very good and about wanting to learn in order to become better. On the other hand, Katrina pointed out that wanting to be 'good at something' or wanting to 'be the best' was associated with shamelessness, and thus was best left unarticulated: 'In general, it's "shame on you!" – if you want to be the best and to say this out loud. You shouldn't mention that you want to be good. It's best to talk about the process and the group' (Katrina).

Inclusive Ambitions

As we have seen, Katrina planned and structured the 'serious fun' that encouraged children to keep coming. Keeping SBC's 'laid back' ambitions for a comfortable, inclusive social experience in mind, she tried to create an atmosphere that encouraged free and open interaction among all the children. She was aware that three of the boys isolated themselves from the others, and thought it her fault for approaching them wrongly from the start. She also knew that some children joined simply because they were 'glued to' certain other children, and not because they particularly wanted to learn to play badminton. With regard to children's balking at having to play with 'those they didn't know', Katrina rationalized that 'they're like children everywhere', it took them a while to get to know each other:

> They tend to stick to their own groups, their own classmates, the ones they know best. Some of them were very difficult to pry away from each other. They didn't want to play with that one and would only play with the one they usually played with. I told them they could play together at home or in school. If they wanted to be here, they would have to play with some of the others too. Otherwise, they wouldn't get to know any of the others (Katrina).

One inclusive ground rule was, thus, that all should play (badminton) with each other without loud public complaints such as: 'Do I have to play with Aylia again, I just played with her', or 'I don't want to play with David!' Katrina also hoped to teach them 'match manners', such as not to yell when others made mistakes.

As has been noted earlier, there has long been an uneasy relationship between 'serious competition' and 'children'. In the first half of the twentieth century, many Danish educators considered serious sporting competition to be detrimental to children's physical, intellectual and spiritual development. In the mid-1970s, educational critiques of competition in sport in general and children's sport in particular drew on psychological, pedagogical and sociocultural theories (Rønholt 1998). It was commonly argued that competition strictly delineated winners and losers, making it difficult to create and maintain inclusive, non-differentiated social groups. Over-explicit differentiation was considered antithetical to *trivsel* (well being leading to growth). Although pedagogical critiques of children's competitive sports had lost steam by the mid-1990s (Rønholt 1998: 246), Katrina felt that competition in individual sports was still problematic: 'It [competition] is coming back in, but in terms of badminton, kids are afraid of this sport because you clearly stick out. You cannot explain your losses through the others, or hide behind them a bit in the field. With badminton, you're on' (Katrina). 'Sticking out', or differentiating oneself too distinctly from the others in the group-at-hand, is generally thought to cause problems in social relationships (see Anderson 1996, 2000a). Children are socialized in school classes to 'not stick out too much', either above or below the line, so to speak, because too much difference may lead to loss of social access to others. In the interactional field of recreational sport, individual displays of ability or lack of it are thus full of tension.

As noted, Katrina deliberately kept this particular group of children from competitive tournaments, because only some, and not all, of the children would be able to compete with favourable results. As for 'serious' badminton, the season's first and only formal technique demonstration came about when several interested children urged Katrina to show them how execute a 'smash'. Katrina obliged them, creating the only practice session where all children sat quietly in two rows, paying close attention to her instruction. Such a scenario might be interpreted as inclusive, but it was clearly not a preferred scenario seen from Katrina's viewpoint, as children had specifically to encourage her to bring it about. From a pedagogical perspective, teaching children sport in this manner was too trainer-centred, too disciplined, too quiet and too all-in-a-row. The aesthetics of undifferentiated inclusivity called for movement and open-ended interaction across the group of children.

Provisional Summary

In these first sections, I have tried to give a sense of the association's and trainer's ambitions to bring forth an inclusive 'way of being together' and the children's concerns about fitting themselves into the differentiated interactional field of recreational badminton. Children were particularly concerned with questions of social access and displays of ability or the lack of it. Not knowing anyone and thus 'not having anyone to keep to', however, seemed a worse fate than 'not being very good at badminton'. Children spoke of both having fun and learning something new, and argued for a moral balance between 'too much mucking about' and 'taking the game too seriously'. The trainer worked to promote inclusiveness, using pedagogical strategies to work with this diverse set of ability levels and social backgrounds in such a way that 'none would be lost'. This meant balancing 'seriousness' and 'playful fun' while gradually encouraging children to interact with each other across strong 'symbolic fences'[10] of 'those we know' and 'those we don't know'. The association, SBC, had few competitive ambitions on behalf of the sport of badminton. It was concerned to promote inclusive sporting relations, tolerance for people of all abilities from all walks of life, *hygge* (social cosiness) and *socialt fællesskab*.

Environment of a Way of Acting

I have argued that this particular group approached badminton practice in a comfortable, socially inclusive manner, one that promoted having fun with one's friends while learning the basic techniques of the game of badminton. As is described above, badminton practices generally proceeded in a relaxed and non-competitive fashion. Unlike other sport settings, where children seemed to come and go at whim, most children stayed for the entire badminton season and jointly contributed to gifts for Katrina at the season's end. Badminton was clearly 'fun';

but a socially comfortable atmosphere does not necessarily preclude confrontation. There were, of course, conflicts in the form of heated bickering over scores and line calls, a few tears, hurt feelings, accusations, name-calling and non-relations between certain children. However, these actions never managed to upset the frame of badminton as being 'comfortable' and 'fun'. The instructor explained 'bad days' as days when 'the children seemed more tired than usual'.

I now want to explore certain recurrent interactional routines I observed during a badminton season. Badminton practices may be seen as a type of 'behaviour setting' (Barker and Wright 1951, cited in Kendon 1990) or as a recognizable, recurring type of 'social occasion' (Goffman 1953, 1963, cited in Kendon 1990). My assumption is that these practices are 'ordered affairs', not just in terms of the instructor's explicit activity planning, but also in terms of how child and adult actors simultaneously accomplish interaction by moving and positioning their bodies.[11] Interactional routines played out in badminton practices are also part of a larger 'environment of a way of acting', a concept Jackson (citing Wittgenstein) suggested using as a frame for exploring connections between actions and particular environments of practical activity (1989: 126–7).

In Denmark, where most parents work outside the home, a majority of children spend weekdays in various types of public day-care institutions: nurseries (for those aged 6 months to 3 years), kindergartens (ages 3–6), 'leisure-time homes'[12] and 'school leisure programmes' (ages 7–9) and 'after-school clubs' (ages 10–14). The institutional landscape, of course, also includes comprehensive schooling for children (aged 7–15). Because of widespread enrolment in public institutions, I suggest that most Danish children are veterans at moving beyond their homes into public institutional settings, where daily interaction is circumscribed by small groups of twenty to thirty children. These often-continuous groups of age-mates 'belong' to one or more adults authorized to organize and supervise their activities, form their behaviour and enlighten their bodies and minds. The maxim, 'we all have to be here' is commonly heard in these settings to remind participants to make 'room for everybody' understood to be part of the group at hand. 'Making room' entails stretching too narrow group norms and curtailing too expansive individual expressions. It also entails not withdrawing, but remaining more or less socially accessible to all members of the group.

In this light, badminton practices share many features with other public settings organized for children. There are, however, differences. First, in most sport settings, body display and physical ability are constantly foregrounded. Secondly, participation in sport associations is generally more open and discontinuous. While most Copenhagen children tend to stay in the same day-care 'garden', 'home' or 'club' over a period of years, they may choose different recreational activities each year, or 'go to' more than one activity per year. Children are, as such, not enrolled in sport associations as they are in schools and day-care, nor are they members that meet as a group on a daily basis, as in 'leisure-time clubs'. In Vesterbro, where most children walk, bike, or take a bus or city-train to sports, there is leeway to manage their own attendance. Children may choose to stay home to play with a friend, or stay in the 'leisure-time club' if something exciting is happening or if they do not 'feel like badminton'. Group membership in recreational sports is thus a less continuous affair than is participation in other settings, as it is possible for children to come and go more easily.

In SBC badminton, the trainer and children recruited an age-mate cohort, related through classmate connections,[13] coming from five schools and two urban neighbourhoods. Children joining SBC badminton were expected to interact inclusively with a relatively small, relationally clustered group of public age-mates. One may assume that children bring with them experiences and notions of proper age-mate behaviour, of the range of behaviour expected and accepted by other children and adults in public institutional settings (James, Jenks and Prout 1998: 174–8). Thus, I contend that 'badminton practice' is a familiar 'behaviour setting' for these children, despite the fact that they are all quite new to the game and to each other as a practising group. If what is going on at SBC's badminton practice may be understood as 'including everybody', 'having fun', 'learning something new', and 'being with one's friends', it is reasonable to assume that the forms of sociation children and adults accomplish through interactional routines here are homologous to forms of sociation in other institutional settings in which children take part.

Bodying Forth the World

Michael Jackson writes that 'persons actively body forth the world' (1989: 136). My understanding of what children 'knew' about the social routines of interacting as a group of children at badminton practice is mediated by the patterns of body use manifest in their actions. I do not mean to imply that children, as performative informants (Fabian 1990), merely followed 'pre-existing scripts' laid down by mechanical rules or innate programming, but rather to imply that patterns are a 'consequence of the way bodies are informed by habits instilled within a shared environment' (Jackson 1989: 128). Thus, children drew on common cultural repertoires and familiar routines from other domains when bodying forth a present 'world' for each other at badminton practice.

The interaction routines children produced at badminton practice were also a consequence of the work of relating attended to by all participants in the room. In negotiating how to move through this interactional space, children were guided by the body orientations, movements and trajectories of other children. Kendon asserts that interaction is an ongoing, emerging process requiring:

an ability to recognize the nature of a given interaction system and to receive and interpret information from others in light of this, and to produce acts of maneuver, orientation and utterance that will at once further our private purposes and serve so as not to disrupt, distract or otherwise render the situation socially impossible (Kendon 1990: 1).

People constantly negotiate a 'working consensus' of what is going on, working both to attain and maintain a consensus that does not break down (Goffman 1959). According to McDermott and Tylbor:

such a consensus represents an achievement, a cumulative product of the instructions people in the scene make available to each other; and because no consensus ever unfolds simply by predetermined means, because social scenes are always precarious, always dependent on ongoing instructions, the achievement of a consensus requires collusion (1995: 218).

The authors use the notion of collusion to understand 'how members of any social order must constantly help each other to posit a particular state of affairs, even when such a state would be in no way at hand without everyone so proceeding' (1995: 219). This perspective adds a sense of what must be obscured, non-attended or un-recognized for interactional alignment to occur, and thus more directly addresses the power relations of any social scene.

In negotiating interaction, people draw heavily on indexical information embedded in the body movements of co-participants. Jackson writes that body practices, not 'preceded by any verbal definition of intention', remain ambiguous and open to interpretation both to the performers and the ethnographer (Jackson 1989: 133). Non-verbal communication embedded in body movements, trajectories, orientations and positions is likewise open to interpretation and thus monitored closely for instructions on how to proceed. According to Kendon, patterns of body use, attended to in coordinating interaction, do not need and rarely receive verbal commentary (1990:1). I would add that collusional senses of what is going on in emerging situations are also rarely explicated.

Corporeal Fields of Interaction

Carrying out fieldwork in gyms full of noise and constant motion left me with many visual data and few immediately comprehensible verbal data. In observing badminton practices, I tried to grasp the overall interaction patterns of all the children taken together, in order to understand the elements and forms of sociation they were creating. The notion of 'corporeal field', introduced by Hanks (1990), may be useful in understanding the bounded though broad level of interaction

I have chosen for my analysis. Hanks proposed the concept of corporeal field to extend Merleau-Ponty's *schema corporeal* beyond the individual body subject, so as to bring 'corporeality to the next level of social space occupied by co-participating parties'. He argued that 'we do not communicate as neatly bounded subjects but rather as parts of interactive frameworks, temporary occupants of relationally defined roles' (1990: 84). Thus Hanks introduced 'corporeal field' to address the 'boundaries of corporeality, the limits on who can occupy what positions of social formations, the varieties of reciprocities (and their breakdowns)' (1990: 85).

Studies of face-to-face human interaction have focused on interaction sequences that are short, 'complete', routine and relatively simple in structure, to help ease both collection and examination. Examples of these are greeting events and social formations, both of which are important in the management of social relationships, widespread and thus broadly comparative (Kendon 1990: 8). Even with short sequences, trying to understand how multiple communicational cues and indexes of speech, silence, gesture, mimicry, body orientation, spatial organization, movements and turn-taking sequences become cooperatively-produced orderly affairs is a complex endeavour.

While in awe of the extreme complexity of very brief interactional episodes, I have nevertheless rather boldly chosen to concentrate on interactions *writ large,* to facilitate an analysis of the entire 'room' of interaction, the very 'room' I assume 'every body has to be in', in keeping with local maxims. To accomplish this, I focused on how children move their bodies through the corporeal field spatially bounded by the four walls of the gym and temporally bounded by the hour and a half that practices lasted. The interactional genres discussed below are extracted from movement patterns produced repeatedly in weekly practices. I call them 'genres' to distinguish them as units of analysis. Although they are not delineated as genres at practices in any way, I am convinced my informants would recognize them as patterns were they explicitly pointed out. Making these practices explicit, however, clearly cuts across the grain of the non-attention that is generally accorded them. By distinguishing these practices as genres, I am making an analytical move that bounds them more neatly than emerging action warrants and makes them more explicit than relational strategies generally allow.

The Room

The gym used for badminton practice was a new, very large and well-equipped gym marked by architectural ideas of material simplicity and natural light. A row of full-length windows along one side filtered the glow of long winter sunsets. The opposite side sported a bleacher-like arrangement resembling an oversized wooden staircase reaching the length of the gym. These wide stair-like ' bleachers' provided a place to sling gym bags and jackets and comfortable niches for chatting, changing, lolling about or sliding down the banister-like sides.

In general, children colonized the gym (Olwig 2000) quite naturally during practice, checking it out and filling it out, making it their place for the interim. For example, children knew where to find the badminton nets and how to set them up, how to raise the basketball nets left down by previous users and how to run the music system. They placed themselves in and occupied the gym with the casual authority of 'rightful owners'. They divided the bleachers, and to some extent the floor, into social zones; some parked their gear in the uppermost corner, while others stashed their things more centrally, closer to the main floor where Katrina kept her own gear, including extra badminton rackets and birdies.

Activity Sequences and Tempo

Each practice started with an opening circle, used to greet everyone and pass information. It was followed by a warm-up game chosen from among the children's suggestions. Some, though not all, children took these games seriously, and thus rules were often overruled and supplanted by *ad hoc* power plays. Certain of the boys, however, tended to take warm-up football rather seriously. Football is Denmark's national sport, and a major arena for male identity negotiation, which means that many boys have difficulty playing football 'just for fun'. Their too-serious approach was, however, aborted by Katrina, who returned them to 'play mode' by stopping the game and asking them to find partners and play football two by two, holding hands. Warm-up games were generally followed by simple technique exercises. These could be played out in a serious mode on a court with one particular, usually self-selected, partner, or, in a more playful mode, without a court and with many partners. After this, the children were given the opportunity to play 'real' games. Sometimes they played with self-selected partners, sometimes with appointed partners and sometimes with partners whose names were pulled out of a hat. Rounds of play were sometimes set up as 'mini-tournaments', where winners moved up the courts and losers down the courts to face new partners. Children also practised playing both singles and doubles. A practice ended with a final circle gathering, during which Katrina passed out information and led stretching exercises.

The general tempo of badminton practices was slow. Despite this, the action never seemed plodding nor did it ever break down. One activity flowed into the next at a calm, slow-moving pace with little sense of urgency, of wasting time or of not having time enough. This composed tempo may have played a role in the production of the interaction I am about to describe.

Interaction Genres

The three interaction genres highlighted in the following are abstracted from
patterns of body movement performed by the group of children attending badminton. These patterns are of interest, first and foremost, for their ambiguous,
indexical nature. As far as I know, neither the instructor nor the children verbalized
or commented explicitly on these patterns of interaction during practice. The
relative silence surrounding them nevertheless gave me the impression that
they were acceptable, normative features of interaction in this particular sphere.
Secondly, these patterns of body use are of interest because they appear to address
the concerns children expressed of 'not being as good as the others' or ' being all
alone'. I argue that these genres both point out and blur the contours of the
relational tensions embedded in displaying ability and finding a partner.

Slack Badminton

The children had many ways of playing the game of badminton, depending on
their ability level and interest in the game. Indeed, certain children, with certain
partners, played the game very seriously, concentrating on the game from start to
end. Nevertheless, in the course of the season, children co-produced an acceptable
style of badminton, which appeared to keep the game itself at an ironic arm's
length. Games played in this particular slack mode incorporated a wide variety of
movement displays of a different quality than those displayed in a serious game.
Children would twang and beat their rackets like rock stars or set their rackets in
pendulum swing only to lose grip, letting them fly into the next court. Children
would display dance moves, such as little hops, pelvic thrusts, and hip wiggles.
Children would reach out lackadaisically with their rackets, shrugging and raising
their eyebrows in mock surprise when they missed the birdie by a mile. Children
draped themselves over the nets, while waiting for the next serve or the next
partner. Some maintained rather heated discussions about something that had
happened in school while vigorously volleying. Falling on the floor was a common
move – particularly among boys – often performed after missing a shot. Girls
tended to roll their shoulders forward, dangle their arms and roll their eyes heaven-
ward when they missed. Arguments about rules and scores could also be played
out with the same ironic distance, as though arguing were more ritual than real
disagreement.

As has been mentioned earlier, these children spanned a full range of athletic
potential and ability. Serious badminton, where the game remained in focus, could,
however, only be played with certain partners. Slack badminton, on the other hand,
appeared to be a more conventional, inclusive mode of play, effectively defusing

ability differences by undermining serious or earnest play. In general, children played badminton with slack, dangling limbs, non-tensed muscles and unfocused attention on the game as game. Their movements were sporadic, and up and down in place; they kept their weight on their heels and were rarely 'ready for action'. This is not to say that children did not shift frames and play with concentration and intensity at times, but only to point out that the working consensus appeared to generate a certain labile, ironic take on the frame of 'playing badminton' (Bateson 1972).

While this performative genre is often conventionally understood as 'children being children', or 'just horsing around', I suggest an alternative interpretation. As an interactive genre, slack badminton may be interpreted as a forceful way of performing inclusive non-differentiation among age-mates. In an interactional field where physical ability is at stake, slack badminton seriously undermines any one child's bid to display greater ability by attempting to play badminton in earnest.

Joining and Withdrawing

Over the course of practice sessions, children moved themselves, individually or in groups, in and out of the marked collective activity. There was a latent potential that some group or one individual would not join a certain activity sequence, would join after it had started, or withdraw before it came to an end. Katrina did not explicitly sanction or pay this behaviour much official attention, nor did children remark on it. Joining and withdrawing appeared to be played out and bracketed as 'children needing and thus taking a break' or as 'children having a chat with a friend'.

Examples of this genre are numerous. Children handed out candy, causing classmates to flock around. They ate ice cream bars, cooling each other's foreheads with the cold bars and attracting others who begged a bite. One put on roller skates and skated around the outside of the gym. Others slid down the bleacher banisters or catnapped on the bleachers every now and then. Children sat on the bleachers watching and commenting on others' play, chatting with Katrina or reading. Children rode around on the badminton net wagon. A group of boys removed themselves to the top of the bleachers to relax and talk. One girl took time out to tend to the needs of two younger siblings (aged 2½ and 4) she had brought along. Children sat in the final circle without participating in stretching exercises. Others participated in stretching exercises from the lower or upper levels of the bleachers.

Most of these 'withdrawals' took place in and around the general flow of interaction, and perhaps for this reason did not draw directive comments. Katrina was, however, quite aware that some children were 'glued' to each other; if one withdrew, she expected certain others to withdraw as well. In cases of children becoming 'unglued', Katrina might intervene to bring a 'withdrawn' child back into his or her customary constellation of relations.

The interaction genre of coming and going, of joining and withdrawing never directly sabotaged activities; but it did keep their boundaries porous. Withdrawing and rejoining was part of the flow of moving to and fro between activities, games, partners and friends, between display of ability and display of relation. I argue that this genre, like the one above, was effective in positing badminton as non-serious, non-urgent business. It was also useful in realigning or taking a brief break from 'friend' and 'classmate' relations. It also allowed some who had trouble finding partners, or didn't want to play with the partners available, to take 'natural breaks' in the bleachers and elsewhere.

Inclusive Exclusion

The final interactional genre highlights the difficulties of finding a partner when there are not enough possible relations from which to choose. My child informants reported that in spheres of public activity, children tend to associate exclusively with those whom they already know. This practice effectively isolates any child who comes in 'directly', meaning 'alone', without 'knowing anybody'. Their thesis was born out at badminton practice. Most children stayed close to the friends and classmates who had recruited them, not seeking contact with children in other constellations. The strongest boundary of non-relation was between Christianshavn and Vesterbro children. This might be explained by neighbourhood territoriality, or by distancing due to differences in social background (Gullestad 1992), although social differences were not readily apparent; however, that non-contact was more a function of the number of classmates the Christianshavn children had mustered. This 'critical mass' afforded them many potential partners within their own ranks. My assumption is supported by the fact that children with the least number of 'own', and thus potential contacts, were those left hanging as 'lone bodies' without relational mates. The two younger brothers were particularly loosely related, as they were connected to others only through sibling relations in a setting where classmate relations were most salient. Common age being a strong unifier, the two 10-year-olds sometimes 'found' each other across the relational boundaries that separated them; but just as often, they remained apart, each seeking contact within their elder sibling's relational spheres.

Non-related and loosely related children became visible whenever the children chose partners, but also when the instructor attempted to match children for games. 'Lone bodies' were, for example, very visible in 'partner football'. Some children who moved toward desirable partners found these non-attending the intentions of their approach or sometimes directly moving away. Other children detached themselves from possible partners, because their usual mate was either absent or currently occupied by another close relation. Thus, children looking for partners or rejecting partners played as 'lone bodies', while other players held hands with their usual mates. Loosely related children were also quite visible in games of tag. They were often able to stand quite alone and still in the midst of a rather wild game, because no other children chose to chase them.

Contact across group boundaries did, of course, occur sporadically and without conflict. However, cross-group contact occurred almost exclusively within the bounds of formalized activities, and rarely in more informal forms of interaction.

The production of 'lone bodies' was a rather quiet affair. Though clearly noticed, and commented on, as the interviews show, practices leading to non-partnering were rarely addressed by other children or Katrina in immediate situations. Interaction producing 'lone bodies' appeared, thus, quite natural and to a certain extent unavoidable. Katrina, who was aware that some children lacked partners more often than others, rationalized the phenomenon in terms of some children being more 'difficult to match with others'.

This interactional genre marked and re-marked social boundaries between 'those we know' and 'those we do not know'. 'Knowing somebody' meant having a 'natural mate', an accessible 'body' to stand and sit beside, play badminton with, talk and fool with, share food with, come and go home with. 'Not knowing somebody' led to what might be seen as a classic avoidance relation, practised either as complete avoidance or formalized, distanced contact.

Concerted Activity

My focus on a corporeal field of interaction, bounded by the walls of a gym and encompassing the general movements of the children present, allowed me to distinguished three interaction genres: (1) slack badminton; (2) joining and with-drawing from the activities at hand; and (3) exclusive alignment in an overall inclusive field of play. Moving across the gym toward 'ones they knew', children cut swaths of non-attention and non-relation to other children, who likewise were working on attending more in certain directions than others. Children were practis-ing modes of remaining exclusively related while moving in close proximity with others. At the same time, children bodied forth an implicit 'conversation' on relations between 'better' and 'worse' badminton players.

Thinking in terms of *choreography* helped me to see the movement patterns; but as the term implies prearranged movements, it does not grasp the contingent nature of interaction. Jackson reminds us that patterns of body practices are regular only as a 'consequence of ways people's bodies are informed by habits instilled within a shared environment and articulated in movements . . .' (1989: 128). He suggests with Bourdieu that these movements are *collectively orchestrated*, albeit without the organizing help of a conductor (ibid.). As was argued earlier, I believe these interaction genres played out at badminton are, in part, a consequence of a larger 'environment of a way of acting' which includes a variety of public instit-utional settings organized for children. However, to explain their saliency in this particular setting, I must refer to the specific ambitions, fears and tensions played out within the sport setting at hand. Here, the concept of *concerted activity* is useful, as it suggests that all participants are working together to 'formulate' the interactional order organizing their movements, positions and orientations, which signal contexts for each other (McDermott, Gospodineff and Aron 1978). Together, the children and their trainer accomplished the interactional genres of slack badminton, joining and withdrawing, and inclusive exclusion. I contend that these practices are effective means of (1) down-playing ability and keeping earnest players at bay; (2) maintaining an understanding that withdrawal is a natural break, a matter of individual choice and not social exclusion; and (3) maintaining non-attention to 'lone' positions produced by both formal and informal partnering among socially accessible partners. The notion of *collusion*, of playing into each other's strategic understandings of the situation (McDermott and Tylbor 1995), helps us understand how these facts are kept implicitly rather than explicitly recognized as practices of power relations. Although these interaction genres are salient and recognizable, they are never absolute. They are characterized by obscured, ambiguous boundaries open to interpretation from situation to situation.

'Going to' badminton practice week after week from September to April, the children and their trainer achieved a 'room for everybody' with some success. Through specific interactional routines cognized as 'normal, child-like behaviour', they bodied forth a form of sociation that downplayed and defused exclusive differences thrown up by athletic ability and strangers generally held to threaten comfortable social inclusion. Recreational ideologies and inclusive pedagogies emphasizing *socialt fœllesskab* over competitive results clearly head up these particular interactional practices. However, the ambiguous activity of bodying forth inclusive universality succeeds only when co-players are both knowledgeable and cooperative performers. Getting the right ambiguous balance by co-constructing when, where and how to move in relation to whom is not a cultural performance for novices. I suggest that this form of sociation is a proto-typical 'way of being of and for each other' in age-mate cohorts of officially undifferentiated children in a Danish context.

Transformations

To conclude, association sports for children in Denmark have gained legitimacy for their purported transformative powers. Politicians and academic researchers suggest that Danish association sports sustain a healthy civil society and promote community integration. Educators and laypersons tout associations as sites of socialization where children learn to be democratic members of a social *fællesskab*. Indeed, in Danish sport discourse endpoints of community and social *fællesskab* appears to be inevitable and beyond discussion. I have suggested that unexamined presumptions that associational sociality (automatically) transforms individual players into a *socialt fællesskab* appear analogous to Simmel's theoretical assumption that 'forms of sociation' lead to individuals growing together into a 'unity'. I argued that neither theoretical stance deals with issues of embodied interaction sustained in sport activities and in the close physical proximity of face-to-face sociation.

The analysis of children's recreational badminton presented here was based on the assumption that social transformations are embedded in concrete, embodied interactional genres. A focus on the corporeality of interaction routines highlighted performative elements of sociation in recreational sports, which, I contend, have a bearing on the type of transformation possible in such contexts. My analysis suggests that 'unity' or *fællesskab* growing in this context centres around concerted efforts to 'body forth a room for everybody' by taking issues of 'not knowing anybody' and 'not sticking out as best or worst' quite seriously. Furthermore, the analysis suggests that transformations toward *fællesskab* and 'social integration' rest on the contingent and collusional art of converting potentially exclusive boundaries of ability and friends into an inclusive 'room for all' while implicitly sustaining social distinctions of importance and ignoring the production of 'lone bodies' and 'slack badminton'.

Notes

1. Badminton is considered a common Danish sport, although it was originally an English import along with football (soccer), tennis and cricket. Danish badminton players have traditionally been among the top competitors at international tournaments. Badminton also has status as a recreational sport, one that most all Danes have played at some time in their lives.
2. Unlike other activities that usually meet only once or twice a week, 'leisure-time clubs' attendance is on an everyday basis and club activities are generalized, with little official focus on gaining new proficiencies.
3. There are two national sport organizations in Denmark, DGI and DIF (The National Olympic Committee and Sports Confederation of Denmark). DGI profiles itself as the proper site of recreational sports, promoting social fellowship in voluntary associations through sporting activities. DIF organizes both recreational and elite sports leagues and tournaments. Most local sport associations are members of both organizations.

4. The new 'sport and culture' complex has two gyms, one egg-shaped movement and theatre room, a bowling alley, a shooting gallery, a super-ellipse swimming pool, a restaurant and a three-star hotel.
5. Copenhagen municipal recreation authorities (The People's Enlightenment Secretariat) require membership in sport associations in order to access public sport facilities for free.
6. I did fieldwork in gymnastics, basketball, kickboxing and badminton associations along with a *capoeira* school and an Open Gym project.
7. This is a point made by Frykman in an article discussing the relationship between the rise of gymnastics in Sweden in the 1930s and 'becoming a perfect Swede'. Frykman argues that by opening an arena for 'ordinary bodies' of both sexes, gymnastics associations established new channels of body display, communication and mimesis and produced 'a painstakingly visible statement about the variation of bodies that were to be accepted as the national' (1993: 266).
8. See Dyck for an interesting discussion of how parents profile themselves as 'good parents' by 'affording their sons and daughters access to activities commonly defined as being "good for children"' (2000: 152). Whereas this practice is also common in Denmark, my focus here is on how the government and certain sport organizations and associations profile themselves as 'good providers' of forms of sociation that are 'good for children'.
9. Working in school and sport association settings, I observed a wide variety of examples of how children are allowed, and even expected, to play with or ironically parody the proper order of given tasks. Whether set the task of making pom poms in sewing class, singing in music class, playing games in PE class (Anderson 1996, 2000a), practising saltos or putting equipment away after gymnastics (Anderson 2001), children and adults appeared to work together to maintain a fine balance between 'seriously' getting the job done and 'playfully' undermining the significance of better or worse performances.
10. For a discussion of social accessibility and inaccessibility in Norwegian urban neighbourhoods, see Gullestad 1992.
11. For detailed ethnographic examples of how actors accomplish interaction, see Kendon (1990) and Varenne and McDermott (1999).
12. 'Leisure-time homes' (*fritidshjem*) provide government subsidized day-care for the youngest school children, aged 6–9. Children enrolled in a *fritidhjem* are under constant supervision and not allowed to leave the premises without an adult. *Fritidshjem* are open both before and after school to accommodate working parents. At the age of 10 children change over to 'leisure-time clubs' (*fritidsklubber*), where they may come and go on their own.
13. These are often closely interwoven, owing to the school practice of continuous class groups.

References

Anderson, S. (1996), *Chronic Proximity and the Management of Difference: A Study of the Danish School Practice of Klasse*, Specialerække nr. 69, Institute of Anthropology, University of Copenhagen.

—— (2000a), *I en klasse for sig*, Copenhagen: Gyldendal.

—— (2000b), 'Enquete: Dansk fodbold – at spille med', *Tidsskriftet Antropologi*, 42: 99–100.

—— 2001, 'Practicing Children: Consuming and Being Consumed by Sports', *Journal of Sport and Social Issues*, 25(3): 229–50.

Bateson, G. (1972), 'A Theory of Play and Fantasy', in *Steps to an Ecology of Mind*, New York: Ballantine Books.

Bøje, C. and S. Riiskjær (1991), *Fritidens Orden og Uorden*, Idrætsforsk, Gerlev: Bavnebanke.

Dyck, N. (2000), 'Parents, Kids and Coaches: Constructing Sport and Childhood in Canada', in N. Dyck (ed.), *Games, Sports and Cultures*, Oxford/New York: Berg.

Fabian, J. (1990), *Power and Performance: Ethnographic Explorations through Proverbial Wisdom and Theater in Shaba, Zaire,* Madison, WI: University of Wisconsin Press

Frykman, J. (1993), 'Becoming the Perfect Swede: Modernity, Body Politics, and National Processes in 20th Century Sweden', *Ethnos,* 3–4: 259–74.

Goffman, E. (1959), *The Presentation of Self in Everyday Life*, London: Penguin.

Gullestad, M. (1992), 'Symbolic Fences', in *The Art of Social Relations. Essays on Culture, Social Action and Everyday Life in Modern Norway*, Oslo: Scandinavian University Press.

Hanks, W. F. (1990), *Referential Practice: Language and Lived Space among the Maya*, Chicago: University of Chicago Press.

Hansen, J. F. (1980 [1970]), *We are a Little Land: Cultural Assumptions in Danish Everyday Life*, New York: Arno Press.

Holstein, B. (1997), 'Motionsvaner blandt børn og unge', in *Idræt i København går nye Veje*, Copenhagen: Danmarks Højskole for Legemsøvelser.

Ibsen, B. (1995), 'Det offentlige og idrætten', in E. Trangbæk (ed.), *Dansk Idrætsliv. Velfærd og Fritid 1940–1996*, Copenhagen: Gyldendal.

—— and L. Ottesen (1996), 'Denmark', in P. de Knop, L. Engström, B. Skirstad and M. Weiss (eds), *Worldwide Trends in Youth Sport*, Champaign, IL: Human Kinetics.

Jackson, M. (1989), *Paths Toward a Clearing: Radical Empiricism and Ethnographic Inquiry*, Bloomington, IN: Indiana University Press.

James, A., Jenks, C. and Prout, A. (1998), *Theorizing Childhood*, London: Polity.

Jørgensen, P. (1998) '"Ikke at more, men at opdrage" ca. 1898–1940', in I. Berg Sørensen and P. Jørgensen (eds), *'Een Time dagligen'. Skoleidræt gennem 200 år,* Odense: Odense Universitetsforlag.

Kendon, A. (1990), *Conducting Interaction: Patterns of Behaviour in Focused Encounters,* Cambridge: Cambridge University Press.

Københavns Idrætsanlæg (1997), *Idrættens vilkår I København. Oplæg til idrætspolitisk Konference,* Copenhagen, April.

Korsgaard, O. (1997a), *Kampen om kroppen,* Copenhagen: Gyldendal.

—— (1997b) *Kampen om lyset,* Copenhagen: Gyldendal.

Larsen, K. (2000), *Befolkningens Idrætsdeltagelse,* Gerlev, DK: Idrætsforsk Skrifter nr. 7.

McDermott, R. and H. Tylbor (1995), 'On the Necessity of Collusion in Conversation', in D. Tedlock and B. Mannheim (eds), *The Dialogic Emergence of Culture,* Chicago: University of Illinois Press.

McDermott, R., Gospodinoff, K. and Aron, J. (1978), 'Criteria for an Ethnographically Adequate Description of Concerted Activities and their Contexts', *Semiotica* 24 (3–4): 245–75.

Monaghan, J. (1995), *The Covenants with Earth and Rain: Exchange, Sacrifice, and Revelation in Mixtec Sociality,* Norman, OK: University of Oklahoma Press.

Mortensen, M. (1999), 'Sport Clubs as Social Communities', Paper given at the 'Fourth Congress of the History of Sport in Europe' held 2–5 December, Florence, Italy.

Olwig, K. F. (2000), 'Børn i lokalsamfund – børns lokalsamfund', *Barn* 3–4: 5–22.

Rønholt, H. (1998), 'Fra sundhedsopdragelse til udvikling og læring, ca. 1975–1998', in I. Berg Sørensen and P. Jørgensen (eds), *'Een Time dagligen'. Skoleidræt gennem 200 år,* Odense: Odense Universitetsforlag.

Salamon, K. L. G. (1994), 'Denmark – A socio-cultural outline', unpublished background paper for the OECD, STI division, Paris.

Schwartz, J. M. (1985), *Reluctant Hosts: Denmark's Reception of Guest Workers,* Copenhagen: Akademisk Forlag.

Simmel, G (1950 [1910]), 'Sociability', in K. H. Wolff (trans. and ed.), *The Sociology of Georg Simmel,* Glencoe, IL: The Free Press.

—— (1971 [1908]), 'The Problem of Sociology', in D. N. Levine (ed.), *Georg Simmel. On Individuality and Social Forms,* Chicago: University of Chicago Press.

Trangbæk, E. (1995a), 'Idrætsdebat og -kritik', in E. Trangbæk (ed.), *Dansk Idrætsliv. Det moderne idræts gennembrud 1860–1940,* Copenhagen: Gyldendal.

—— (1995b) 'Fra folkeforlystelse til folkebevægelse', in E. Trangbæk (ed.), *Dansk Idrætsliv. Velfærd og Fritid 1940–1996,* Copenhagen: Gyldendal.

Varenne, H. and R. McDermott (1999), *Successful Failure. The School America Builds,* Boulder, CO: Westview.

–3–

Embodying Success: Identity and Performance in Children's Sport[1]
Noel Dyck

Introduction

Children's sport: what could be simpler, safer and of less consequence to anyone but the participants themselves? On the face of it, children's play seems prosaic and juvenile stuff that hardly warrants much in the way of adult concern, let alone ethnographic analysis. Indeed, in Canada a nostalgic and oft-invoked national representation of both sport and childhood is that of 'pond' or river' hockey. In this scenario children are envisioned as clearing snow from naturally occurring ice surfaces and entering into spontaneous and free-flowing games that incorporate any number of players and feature whimsical and inventive forms of play. Scores, if kept at all, tend toward ties, for the initiation and continuation of this type of fluid, informal contest depends solely upon the inclination of players to brave the cold and to keep the 'game on'. In this romanticized rendering of 'old-time' hockey as the quintessential Canadian pastime, skaters glide freely, enthusiastically and creatively into a zone of playful exuberance and delight that stands well apart from and in marked contrast to the workaday world of adults and the tutelary realm of the schoolroom. 'Pond' hockey cannot be readily envisaged without at least an implicit sketching in of attendant qualities of freedom, fun and innocence.[2] Thus, adults *qua* adults rarely figure in public imaginings of this confluence of sport, childhood and nature that resurfaces rhetorically and intermittently from one sport setting to another.[3]

Yet beneath the canopy of these romanticized ideals of sport and childhood exists a vast complex of formally structured community sport activities, organizations and leagues[4] that are unambiguously shaped and operated *by* adults *for* children and youth in Canada. In contrast to 'pond hockey', these community sport organizations are substantially defined and driven in terms of the dutiful commitment and meritorious tasks performed by parents and other adult participants. They do this so that children may enjoy the divers benefits of playing carefully structured sport on properly lined playing fields or in climate-controlled indoor ice rinks. The enthusiastic enactment of adults' work alongside children's play tweaks an ethnographer's curiosity as to whether there may not be something more unfolding within this field than either simple, idyllic leisure or unassuming, selfless parenting.

My re-acquaintance (as an adult) with children's sport came during a season when I and other team parents watched our six- and seven-year-old daughters engage with a scaled-down version of the 'world game', or 'soccer', as it is known in North America. In the course of a string of mostly cold and rainy Sunday afternoon games a parental 'team' of sorts began to coalesce on the sidelines. Our reasons for being there varied. A few fathers and mothers who identified themselves as 'athletes in their younger days' explained that they wished to give their children a chance to see whether they liked playing sports. One mother, who had cajoled her daughter into signing up for soccer, fervently hoped that lots of running around might have a salutary impact upon her daughter's slightly tubby appearance. Several other parents freely acknowledged that they had little or no background in sport, but that their daughters had wanted to be with friends who had enrolled in soccer. But one couple, whose daughter quickly proved to be a consistent goal-scorer, introduced a qualitatively different tenor into the ongoing parental discourse. They spoke of the prospects of highly accomplished youth players receiving athletic scholarships that would take them to top American universities and pay for their entire college education. When I first heard this possibility raised, I smiled and turned back to watch the action on the field. Nevertheless, ten years later their daughter did, indeed, win a 'full-ride' athletic scholarship (for soccer) that took her to a large American university.

This girl's participation in community sport was informed from the outset by adult purposes attached to her play. But in this she was scarcely alone, for in Canada community sports for children and youth have evolved to bear a substantial, though mixed, cargo of parental hopes and adult expectations. Children's sports not only provide athletic and leisure opportunities for boys and girls but also sustain communities of sporting and parental practice that revolve around the objectification and direction of children's bodies for distinctly adult purposes.

In this chapter I examine some of the premises and practices of adult-organized community sport for children and youth that surreptitiously but systematically violate the cherished ideals of 'pond' hockey. How and why does this paradoxical betrayal of ideals recur year after year? Moreover, what does it tell us about the ways in which childhood and relations between children and parents are envisioned in Canada and articulated through sport performance? What is sport as a form of embodied practice and performance supposed to be capable of accomplishing and for whom? What are the presumed and practical social and cultural capacities of sport that render it a favoured means for seeking to transform children into 'successful' adults? In sum, how are the identities of children and adults hewn and interconnected through children's sports?

What Sport Offers

Flying over or driving through Canadian cities and towns reveals the consp-icuousness of sport in the geographical layout, architecture and public priorities of these communities. Ice rinks, playing fields, swimming pools, tennis and basketball courts, lacrosse boxes and baseball diamonds bespeak the level of support committed to sport in Canada. What sport is said to offer Canadians, and particularly children and youth, is rehearsed frequently by the news media. For instance, a widely publicized national survey conducted by the federal government reported its findings that children who participate in organized activities outside school, such as sports, 'tend to have higher self-esteem, interact better with friends and perform somewhat better in school'.[5] Conversely, the report noted that among young people aged twelve to fifteen, those who rarely or never participate in organized sports were also more likely to smoke. In a similar vein, a Vancouver newspaper article (entitled 'Let's give our kids a sporting chance') introduced a weeklong series of articles on the *need* for children's sport thus:

Kids are getting bigger, slower and lazier and it's not just their bodies that are out of tune.
It's their minds as well.
Studies show that kids who are out of shape are less likely to socialize, will get lower marks in school and eventually will become a greater burden on the health-care and court systems.
It's not hard to figure out that with television, video games, the internet and so many other options to keep kids on the couch, getting out and having some 'fresh air' – be it a game of tag at a playground or an organized sport – has fallen off the charts.[6]

The beneficial outcomes attributed to children's participation in sport are extensive and extraordinary. In addition to offering physical exercise, sport is identified by many sport organizers and parents as being especially well suited to equip children with self-esteem and confidence.[7] The lessons of teamwork and sportsmanship that are supposed to be imparted through participation in organized sport are touted as being invaluable for nurturing a sense of responsibility and sociality in children. Organized sports are also regularly championed as effective means for keeping children 'off the streets' and out of the trouble that is feared will ensue in the absence of adult supervision. Not least, the competition that is con-structed as a central facet of sport is looked to by many adults as an essential means for preparing children to meet the challenges that are thought to await them in their future occupational and professional lives. The values of diligence and achieve-ment that are believed to be engendered through the pursuit of athletic excellence

have remarkable currency amongst middle-class mothers and fathers who increasingly have good reason to be apprehensive concerning the likelihood of their sons
and daughters reproducing their parents' class status. Finally, of course, children's
sports are heralded as intrinsically enjoyable activities that offer children fun.

Together these ascribed capacities contribute to a commonly encountered thesis
that 'sport is good for kids', because it offers to prepare them to be 'successful'
both as children and, in due course, as adults. Quotidian renderings of this sentiment may vary in composition or emphasis, but the essence of the claim is widely
familiar to Canadian parents. An implicit corollary of this stance is that 'good' and
caring parents will take the measures required to enable their children to participate
in organized sport.

Making sport accessible to Canadian children entails a variety of costs. The
playing-fields, gymnasia, ice rinks and swimming pools provided and/or maintained by municipal governments and school boards account for millions of dollars
annually. The local sport organizations that make use of these facilities also collect
membership fees as well as voluntary contributions from businesses and individuals to underwrite their substantial operational and equipment costs. The vast
majority of the coaches and officials of these organizations are volunteers who
freely contribute their time, to which it may be difficult to assign a monetary value,
but which would be impossible to replace were it withdrawn. Child and youth
athletes, along with their parents, are also obliged to pay membership fees and
purchase personal sports equipment and apparel, which, depending upon the sport,
may run to more or less considerable amounts. The ability of families to meet these
financial requirements introduces an inescapable class factor into the access
afforded to children's sport. Yet the amounts of time that parents are also obliged
to invest into providing transportation to practices and competitions, attending
games and tournaments themselves and participating in endless fund-raising
projects make the decision to enrol one's son or daughter in organized sport no
small commitment.

The efforts made by parents to enable their children to participate in organized
sport point to the manner in which this sphere has been incorporated to a greater
or lesser extent within the child-rearing strategies of many Canadian families.
Playing-fields and other venues of community sport have in certain respects been
designated as extensions of domestic space. Adults are supposed to ensure the
physical safety and security of child and youth athletes in these settings. Observant
parents monitor any approaches toward their children by unknown adults or those
who cannot be readily accounted for. But in addition to constituting reasonably
'safe' places where children are meant to encounter 'fun', the venues of children's
sport are also decidedly purposeful spaces within which significant matters related
to child development are expected to transpire. Within these environs operate
notions of socialization that tend to view children as vulnerable and incomplete

persons who need to be moulded, directed and completed by parents and other tutors (James 1998; James and Prout 1990). Thus the training that children receive in organized sport is designed not merely to equip them with particular physical skills and, hopefully, pleasurable experiences of playing games, but also to attend to the appropriate development of their future selves. The disciplined management of children's bodies through community sports is aided and abetted by parents who have an eye not only on the future prospects of their sons and daughters but also upon current assessments of their own performance as parents and, in some cases, as sport officials.

Alongside the Fields of Play

When parents enrol children in community sport and take them to the ice rink, soccer field or swimming pool, they must further decide whether to accompany their sons and daughters into these settings and, if so, how they will organize their own deportment and involvement once there. Parents who consistently drop their children off at games and competitions and then return to pick them up at the conclusion of these events may be said to be in breach of 'normal' expectations of paternal and maternal interest and engagement in their children's sports. It is widely held that, even though children might not express the sentiment explicitly, nonetheless, 'deep down' they desire their parents to witness and support their athletic performances. Indeed, some parents even come to observe training and practice sessions on a regular basis. Accordingly, in the course of an entire season spent transporting children to practices and attending scheduled games and competitions, most parents of child athletes on a given team or club will not only meet fairly regularly but may spend many, many hours in one another's presence. Scattered discursive partnerships that venture beyond pondering the vagaries of the weather may give rise to a roughly inclusive parental 'forum' or 'team', whose members not only exchange comments on the fortunes of the players on the field and cheer on their efforts, but may also be mobilized for fund-raising events or meetings convened by the coach. From these forms of involvement develop loosely structured, temporally limited, and situationally specific but, nonetheless, keenly engaged parental communities of discourse and practice. Although parents on the sidelines may have little or nothing in common with one another except that they have a son or daughter on the team or in the club, this in itself is more than sufficient to fuel continuing, complicated and frequently controversial interaction and interchanges beside the fields of play.

A predictable consequence of the considerable levels of discretionary financing and adult time channelled into this sector is the manner in which parents, coaches and other sport officials endeavour to fashion the management of particular teams or leagues in order to realize their preferred visions of how child and youth sport should be organized. The conventional representation of adult views of children's sport tends to locate the principles of participation and inclusion on one side and the pursuit of competitive excellence on the other. These distinctions are supposed to correspond with the common division of most child and youth team sports into 'recreational' teams and leagues, on the one hand, and 'elite' teams and leagues, on the other. In most team sports in Canada children under the age of ten tend to be placed exclusively in recreational leagues or competitions. Shortly thereafter elite teams and leagues are formed to accommodate more able athletes, who, it is said, would lose interest in sport and miss the opportunity to develop their talents to the fullest extent were they required to continue playing with children of lesser ability. While recreational teams and leagues continue to operate parallel to their elite counterparts, far greater access to sport facilities and infinitely more in the way of resources and attention are granted to the latter.

The competitive tryouts for positions on a select team, the greater amount of time spent in practices and travelling to games outside the immediate locality and the unequal amounts of playing time allocated to players in elite sports are justified as being necessary to create athletic excellence. These routines serve to generate competition between not only teammates, but also parents who wish to secure favourable treatment of their sons or daughters. While recreational sport is supposed to be primarily about participation and 'fun', it is frequently difficult to distinguish between the ways in which the two levels of sport are played. In short, recreational sport too can be pursued in highly competitive and ambitious ways. Much, though not all, of the ambience of a team or league tends to be set by the coach or officials placed in charge of it.

Parents who enrol sons and daughters in community sports encounter existing organizational structures, procedures and personnel that will prove to offer varying levels of satisfaction over a longer term. In due course they may express concerns and offer suggestions for effecting improvements, although they may not be thanked for doing so. Coaches or executive members who threaten to resign their posts can usually trigger acquiescence on the part of most parents. Unless fathers or mothers are prepared to assist with coaching or to stand for election to an executive position in a community sport organization and, thereby, to take on the substantial responsibilities that these entail, they are obliged either to accept existing arrangements or to remove themselves and their children. This structural disposition has the effect of privileging activist parents and adults who are prepared to invest themselves significantly into pursuing what amount to sport coaching and/or management 'careers' in this largely voluntary sector. Whether involvement of this sort is undertaken simply for 'the good of the community' or in support of one's child's inclusion and advancement on a team or to enable a father or mother to emulate the career of a professional sport coach or manager is open to speculation on the part of other parents. The ubiquitous maxim that 'sport is good for kids' furnishes coaches, managers and parental activists with an additional axiomatic, all-purpose explanation and rationale for advocating their preferred arrangements in any given situation: namely, that after all 'it *is* for the kids!' The 'it' invoked in this oft-encountered phrase refers to the general existence and presumed beneficence of community sports for children. But to recite this claim is to imply that the particular course of action one happens to be promoting at the moment is driven by principled and self-sacrificing, rather than personal and self-interested, motives.

At the centre of coaching lies the training of child and youth athletes in the different body skills and techniques required to perform the physical moves and actions featured in any given sport. Coaches also instruct young athletes concerning the performative objectives, playing styles or tactics of the game in question. The venues and rules of different sports are frequently simplified to enable novices to take part in games with only a very basic understanding of the practices of the sport and a minimal repertoire of physical techniques. For instance, soccer as played by six- and seven-year-old girls is contested on a small field with only six players a side and without concern for the 'offside' rule. Coaches at this level are initially pleased when individual players remain focused upon the game long enough to ensure that the ball is kicked 'out of harm's way' (around their team's goal) into the opposition's half of the field. To have a player or two who will fairly regularly and forcefully seek to kick the ball into the opponent's net is most encouraging. Whether a player scores a goal with an unsophisticated 'toe' kick or correctly with the instep of the foot is of little consequence in her first year of play in organized soccer. Indeed, at the end of the game most beginning players would have to check with the coach to determine whether they won or lost the game, if that is even a concern for them.

But in subsequent years athletes are subjected to coaching regimes that manifest more demanding expectations. In addition to acquiring general capacities such as balance, coordination and speed of movement, soccer players, for instance, will be expected to learn different ways of controlling a bouncing ball, passing the ball accurately to teammates and shooting on goal with sufficient power and accuracy to ensure that the ball eludes the grasp of the goalkeeper. The development of a child's general physical capacities reflects a range of factors, including inherited body type and rate of physical maturation, as well as the overall extent of his or her involvement in physical activities of all kinds. While the acquisition of sport-specific skills and body techniques may commence and continue in informal backyard scrimmages with siblings, parents or friends, it becomes the object of formally disciplined practice on the training- and playing-fields of organized sports. Hence, child and youth athletes become familiar with different versions of general 'warm up', 'cool down' and stretching drills conducted in conjunction with training sessions and competitions. They will also share the experience of being repeatedly subjected to physically demanding training exercises that are supposed to hone particular skills or playing tactics. The extent to which any given regime of physical training succeeds not only in transferring and developing specific embodied skills but also in retaining the interest and enthusiasm of child and youth athletes is a matter of some concern for coaches and attentive parents.

Depending upon the sport in question, the levels of technical sophistication that separate parents from the coaches of their sons' and daughters' teams and clubs may be more or less pronounced. There is, for example, a far broader and deeper understanding of ice hockey in Canada than of gymnastics. Thus, a coach who cannot skate reasonably well (or at all) and who 'never played the game' would be unlikely to serve in this capacity at anything but the novice level, and would be expected to cede the position should a better-qualified candidate be presented. Yet, whatever the sport experience and technical expertise held by coaches and other officials, they are all expected to demonstrate an acceptable standard of control in organizing children at practices and competitions. In addition to overseeing the training of children's bodies, coaches and sport officials are charged with maintaining levels of social discipline associated with adult-organized, formal activities such as schooling. Being 'friendly with the kids' is one thing; but allowing them to 'fool around' when they should be 'playing seriously' is quite another. Children who take part in community sports are expected to work at improving their skills and determination to succeed. Conversely, coaches and parents are expected to do what is required to facilitate these processes of self-improvement.

The playing-fields and gymnasia of community sports are thus also intentionally disciplined spaces, for this is seen as being an essential condition for nurturing the character-building properties and diverse forms of achievement sought from children's sport. When in the midst of a soccer practice an indifferently executed passing drill is suddenly halted by the coach, who abruptly sends some or all of the players to 'run a lap' or two around the field before they recommence the drill, what is being exercised is not only the children's legs and lungs, but also the coach's ability to retain control over the situation. But this discipline extends not merely to child and youth athletes but also to their parents and families. Parents who schedule family vacations during crucial periods of a sport season and who take their sons and daughters with them can expect to incur the displeasure of some coaches, and possibly even to provoke a downgrading of their child's position or status on the team. Similarly, fathers and mothers may discover that much-anticipated weekends can be pre-empted with little or no warning by fundraising events, team practices or exhibition games called at virtually the last minute by a coach or manager. Experienced officials might well take steps to mitigate the negative reaction that predictably ensues from such arbitrary moves by ensuring that whenever possible such events are announced somewhat in advance. At the same time, they also know that a coach who attempts to accommodate all the individual schedules and preferences of the parents on the team is surely courting not only frustration but also escalating 'interference' by fathers and mothers in various aspects of the organization of the team. To guard against this, a coach must establish a firm identity as a 'no-nonsense' individual who is most definitely in charge of the situation. At the same time, child and youth athletes along with parents are no less preoccupied with their own respective concerns about what their involvement in community sport says about them.

Embodying Identities

The venues of children's sport share a set of contextual properties. These are supposed to be places of 'fun' that are, however, to be made safe and secure by adult supervision. Cast as purposeful spaces where children are expected to address and resolve through 'play' fundamental processes of socialization, here their bodies are systematically subjected to regimes of adult discipline. Child and youth athletes' embodied performances within these settings are visible and amenable to scrutiny by coaches and parental onlookers. These performances may be read and evaluated in terms of any combination of criteria, ranging from technical proficiency and competitive zeal to, on occasion, even aesthetic appeal and entertainment value. But venues of community sport are also places where a child's character is believed to be revealed to discerning adult eyes. Indeed, the extent to which any given athlete or, for that matter, parent or coach may be deemed to be 'successful' in and through their respective engagement in community sport remains a continuing concern within this spatially and temporally limited, yet deeply intimate, realm. Thus the venues of children's sport are, among other things, sites for the construction, circulation and consumption of highly situated but personally consequential values, meanings, selves and identities. That these selves and identities are directly or indirectly anchored by embodied performances on the fields of play renders them liable to unpredictability and risk, as well as to attempts to manage these factors and the social relationships within which they are embedded.

Children who venture into community sports to be with friends, at the behest of their parents, or simply as a result of an enthusiasm for games enter into what are initially somewhat crowded and confusing settings. The risks that await them take different forms: 'I won't know anyone there', 'Nobody will be my friend', 'I don't like to run so much', 'It will hurt if the ball hits me', and so on. But child athletes also confront the abiding challenges of physical and social performance and the possibility that they may be found wanting by coaches, parents or teammates in one or another sensitive respect. The transparency of their embodied performances and the recounting, evaluation and instruction from adults that so often go along with it are quickly grasped by novice athletes. Over the longer term the lessons of overhearing teammates and other athletes being labelled as 'outstanding', 'pretty good', 'not very good' or downright 'bad' athletes are not lost on children. Being told by your father or mother that you are playing 'very well' gradually becomes less convincing and reassuring than hearing this directly from your coach or from teammates. Assessments of 'success' and 'failure' are rarely left simply to the athlete himself or herself to determine. Moreover, sport performances can wax and wane as children grow into different shapes and sizes at varying rates. Early 'phenoms' can just as easily drift out of the spotlight and into mediocrity in later seasons.

The juncture between recreational and elite levels of sport also brings the possibility that one may be separated from erstwhile friends and teammates. The thrill of being selected for a prestigious 'gold', 'inter-city', 'metro', 'double letters' or 'triple letters' team can be contrasted with the devastation of being 'cut' from such a team and consigned to a lower level of competition. In individual sports such as track and field or swimming the lack of medals or ribbons won in competitions and the embarrassing state of an athlete's 'personal best' in any given event may reveal one to be simply a 'try-hard'. Coaches and parents may be inclined to encourage not especially talented girls and boys, who, nonetheless, register heroic efforts to improve their performance and who never give up. But even before children turn into youth, the attractions of relatively clear-cut athletic 'success' begin to win out over garden-variety 'moral' victories. Child and youth athletes may be inclined to express their views to coaches and parents in terms of a particular practice, arrangement or outcome as being or not being 'fun', but this concept is far more opaque and problematic than it might at first appear. Since declarations of the presence or absence of 'fun'; are the primary and sometimes the only evaluative vocality readily permitted children by adults in community sports, there is reason to exercise caution when appraising adults' reports of what is and isn't 'fun' for kids.

The assistance that children's sports offer mothers and fathers in fulfilling parental responsibilities do not, however, come without certain risks. Above and beyond the time and money that community sports expropriate from family schedules and budgets is the manner in which these activities potentially open intimate domestic relations and concerns to sustained view by outsiders. Indeed, the mundane matter of where parents who come to watch a son or daughter take part in, for instance, a soccer game will choose to locate themselves along the sidelines of the field is anything but simple.

Anonymity is not easily preserved at the venues of child and youth sport, for there is an assumption that any adult watching a match will be likely to have a connection to one or another of the players on the field or some other understandable reason for being there. Furthermore, the notions of domesticity and sociality associated with children's sport make it quite acceptable for nearby adults to speak to one another and to enquire into the reasons for their presence. The initiation of such conversations and the identification of which child is the son or daughter of which woman or man paves the way for further discussion, either then and/or in days and weeks to come, with now partially known 'others'. The identity of a man or woman or that of an apparent couple who opt to stand well apart from other parents can, nonetheless, be worked out by sustained observation of which child arrives at or departs from the field with which adult(s) or by consulting with other equally observant parents. Over the course of a season the jumbled, jigsaw puzzle pieces of 'who is who' both on and around the field are not only fitted together in preliminary form, but become the medium for increasingly particularized levels of discussion. To situate oneself near one or another gathering of onlookers is to expose oneself to friendly interrogation and inclusion in serial chats about the nature of kids, the progress of games and the travails of parenthood. Standing steadfastly and habitually apart from other parents even after one or another of them has wandered over and tried to strike up a conversation may save one from having to make dutiful small talk with strangers. By no means, however, will this prevent one from being assigned an identity and incorporated *in absentia* in parental discussions that proceed elsewhere along the sidelines.

The focal events at community sport competitions are embodied performances by child athletes. Goals scored or saved, tackles made or missed, times recorded, and leads held or lost all unfold under the watchful gaze of coaches, parents and other child and youth competitors. The keeping of scores, the posting of results, the celebrating of victories, the awarding of ribbons, medals and other prizes are all based upon the scrutinized physical performances of child athletes. Parents who may initially not be well versed in the rules and standards of a given sport cannot help but overhear longer and shorter verdicts and explanations concerning the relative achievements or shortcomings of a team or club and of its individual athletes both 'on the day' and over a season. The ethic of achievement associated with sport renders it a vehicle for pursuing self-improvement in forms that range from the beneficial building of character to the attainment of competitive excellence or, ideally, both. Competitive accomplishment is, of course, demonstrated by sporting victories and is typically promoted in terms of the injunction that every athlete should dedicate him- or herself to 'be the best that you can be'. Yet the same dictum can also be harnessed to less tangible products of sport participation, such as the perceived enhancement of an athlete's self-esteem and self-discipline. The tendency to conjoin competitive results with an athlete's presumed character creates situations where comprehensive assessments of children's embodied performances on the field of play may be taken as providing highly telling readings of their nature and comparative worth as individuals (Lithman 2000). Ironically, the animated and moving bodies of boys and girls are placed before audiences of adults who sit or stand virtually motionless, yet in judgement of child performers both as athletes and as persons.

Since children and youth, by definition, are viewed not as mature and finished persons but rather as 'works in progress', their perceived strengths and weaknesses may be attributed in larger or smaller part to parental influence or negligence. Canadians are broadly familiar with and scornful of the stereotype of the unabashedly self-serving sport parent who obviously or vicariously 'lives through their kid' and inappropriately takes credit for the sporting exploits of a son or daughter. While no one ever confesses to being this sort of parent, mothers and fathers might on occasion acknowledge to some of those around them that they are 'pleased with' or 'proud of' a child's performance. Although mothers or fathers may be quite willing to parody their own physical capacities and athletic prowess, this is most effectively done when it contrasts sharply with the demonstrated abilities of a son or daughter. But when competitive sport produces, not reasonably regular and unproblematic success, but obvious and repeated failure, the search for explanation may venture toward the matter of character or, more precisely, the lack of it. Why one player seems to 'give up' in adverse or pressured sporting situations while others are observed not to do so can give rise to quietly expressed but probing questions about the way in which a child is being raised or even whether 'there may be problems' within his or her family.

It is scarcely surprising, then, that venues of community sport host ostensibly casual but nonetheless persistent demonstrations of conspicuously conscientious parenting. Achieving an acceptable balance as a father or mother who evinces a sustained and supportive interest in one's child's sport involvement as well as that of other children and of the team or club as a whole requires a deft touch. Nevertheless, the conversational links forged between some parents along the sidelines of community sports events can also provide fairly secure settings within which to explore, model and mutually reaffirm one another's renderings of 'good parenting'. In practice, the onus for attending to and demonstrating such virtues falls perhaps somewhat more heavily upon a mother or father whose child is only an average or marginal athlete than upon a parent whose son or daughter manages to achieve recognition as a 'great kid' primarily by virtue of on-field exploits.

A parental identity may be declared indirectly, as in the case of one mother who explained that she brought her daughter and son to track and field 'because this sport attracts the sort of kids who will do well in the rest of their lives, so my kids might as well get to know them now'. A more direct and seamless form of identification between parent and child was adopted by one father who when asked why his daughter was not competing in her usually favoured track events explained that, '*we* have a sore knee today, so *we* are trying out some field events instead'.

An accomplished athlete who is said to be a 'good kid' may be rhetorically separated from eccentric deportment on the part of his or her parents. By the same token, a parent who has been successful in establishing the credibility and durability of his or her efforts as a father or mother may be partially or even substantially absolved of responsibility for the unseemly behaviour of a son or daughter. This is aptly illustrated by an incident that occurred during a soccer match played by two elite girls' teams, the Stars and the Kickers:[8]

> Karen, a strong but sometimes temperamental player for the Stars, was moved to the goalkeeper's position after the Kickers took an early two-goal lead. When the Kickers scored a third goal, Karen could be heard by everyone around the field loudly proclaiming that 'I don't want to be in goal any more', an assertion that she repeated intermittently but vociferously until half-time. At that point the coach of the Stars opted to grant Karen her wish and handed another player the goalkeeper's jersey and gloves. During the second half a debatable call by the referee was disputed by Keith, the father of a Kickers player, who called out in exasperation, 'You've got to be kidding!' This prompted Karen, playing then in midfield for the Stars, to proclaim to the Kickers' parents on the sideline that 'We want to be able to play without any comments from the sidelines.' Margaret (Keith's wife) quickly replied, 'And we want to be able to watch the game without any comments from the players.' At this point Karen ended the interchange by yelling out to Margaret 'You are such a bitch.'

This incident was taken by the Kickers parents as more or less speaking for itself. Significantly, no questions were raised about whose daughter Karen was, for the Stars and Kickers had been keen rivals for more than five years, and the children and parents of each team were known to one another. Nor was the reputation of Karen's dad, Ernie, as a sometimes 'loud' observer of his daughter's matches raised. Indeed, two years earlier Ernie had approached the coach of the Kickers in the parking lot after a game and asked whether Karen (who had temporarily quit the Stars' team after a disagreement with the coach) might be able to join the Kickers. The coach of the Kickers explained to Ernie that he couldn't take on another player in mid-season. What he didn't tell Ernie was that he had previously spoken with Carole, the then coach of the Stars, who had explained that 'Karen is a real horror show for a coach to deal with.' When Karen had decided to leave the Stars, she had telephoned Carole and 'swore and yelled at me for about twenty minutes'. At the same time, however, Carole maintained that Ernie was 'really not a bad parent to have around, even though he sometimes sounds like a bit of a rough customer'. Carole referred to Ernie as a 'black ace'[9] and praised his ability to deal with sensitive situations involving other parents. 'The problem in this case', Carole insisted, 'is not the dad but the kid.'

Conclusions

Organizing child and youth sports in the manner adopted in Canada serves to produce varying types of experiences for different athletes and their parents.

Players who demonstrate superior athletic ability at an early age and/or whose parents are determined to do whatever it takes to see their son or daughter play on an elite team are more likely to remain involved in youth sports throughout their teenage years. Since considerable peer prestige accrues to celebrated athletes, the competition for status and recognition spills over into 'off-ice' or 'off-field' settings. Parents of demonstrably successful athletes – including those forecast to become professional athletes and/or to receive athletic scholarships – can and often do take credit for their own 'modest' efforts to 'support their children's efforts'. Children whose parents are not anticipating that their son or daughter could or should win an athletic scholarship are likely to have somewhat shorter and less celebrated – although not necessarily less enjoyable – careers in child and youth sports. Ostensibly, this ought to leave them free to play just for the fun of it and to leave the pressures of competitive sport to elite athletes. Yet even recreational players' participation in community sports is shaped in countless ways by the ambitions and arrangements characteristic of elite sports. Thus, in the case of the girl who won the soccer scholarship, every one of her teammates during the 10-year period of her child and youth sport career had to contend with the ramifications of her parents' unflagging determination to ensure that every team that she played on was organized to enhance and showcase their daughter's athletic prowess and superiority.

The management and direction of children's sport by adults may be rationalized in terms of a range of ostensibly worthy purposes, but its impact is to eviscerate any possibility of the freedom and independence offered by 'pond' hockey. In effect, adult-organized sports for children constitute a form of double colonization. First, adults have injected themselves so completely into controlling children's sports that it has become impossible for these activities to continue without their involvement. In the absence of mothers, fathers, coaches and other youth sport officials, who would provide transportation to and from practices and games? Who would arrange the use of sport facilities and purchase uniforms? And who would draw up comprehensive schedules of games or competitions for an entire season? Indeed, it is far easier to procure new players than it is to replace a disgruntled coach.

The second form of colonization concerns the manner in which the realm of children's play and leisure has been transformed from a source of pleasure in and of itself into an instrumental means for delivering an edge for parents who are concerned with augmenting the future educational and career-building prospects of their children. The impact of this development has been to extend the tutelary regime of the schoolroom into what are supposed to be the leisure-time and play activities of children and youth. Within this schema, the perceived trouble with 'pond' hockey is that it would squander valuable time and resources that might be more profitably applied to improving the athletic performances and life prospects of children through participation in 'real' sport. Curiously, far beyond the inner city, where 'hoop dreams' may be understood to offer disadvantaged children perhaps their only slim chance of securing some hope of social mobility, countless members of the suburban middle classes have fastened upon children's athletic performances as a convenient mechanism by which parental concerns about enabling the social reproduction of class status may be assuaged. A vital difference between children's sport in the inner city and in the suburbs, however, involves the manner in which community sports that feature high levels of parental involvement provide middle-class parents with a tailor-made medium with which to express their own competitive fitness and proficiency as parents.

It should scarcely be surprising that there is a significant and steady decline in the proportion of Canadian boys and girls who remain active in organized sport once they reach their teenage years. Organized sport can become hard work for children and youth, who may opt to escape to the comparative freedom afforded by a television set. Yet the vast apparatus of organized community sport endures and continues to regenerate the patterns and the products discussed above. Ironically, nostalgic reveries of 'pond' hockey seem to function primarily to induce parents to enlist their sons and daughters into highly organized regimes of child and youth sport that systematically preclude the spontaneity, innocence and carefree fun celebrated in this cherished Canadian myth. In shifting our attention from 'pond' hockey to the adult-financed and supervised indoor ice rink we move from the realm of whimsy to one where complex relationships of class, power and patron-and-client relationships between adults as well as between adults and children come to the fore. This is a venue where child and youth athletes are coached to perform competitively, where parents display their parenting skills, and where adult coaches and sport officials may pursue their own dreams of living and acting much like highly publicized professional sport coaches and officials.

Paradoxically, in spite of the demonstrable instrumentality of children's sports, these highly organized activities still manage to provide discernible measures of enjoyment and pleasurable memories for child and youth athletes as well as for parents, coaches and sport officials. The capacity of sport not only to facilitate these and other outcomes but also to provide a distinctive perspective from which to examine intricate yet powerful social and cultural processes would seem to suggest that ethnographers of contemporary life cannot afford to overlook the lessons afforded by child's play.

The premise that childhood can be conceptually revealed and suitably contained within the tenets of conventional socialization theory has recently been subjected to sustained and penetrating critique within the anthropology of childhood as well as in other social science literature dealing with children (Caputo 1995; James 1998; James and Prout 1990; Stephens 1995). The notion of children as unfinished, dependent and not yet fully social beings incapable of knowing or acting in their own interests has been challenged vigorously by approaches that treat children as active agents. As in the case of the analytical enfranchisement proffered the working classes by Marxian theorists, children too are now viewed by social constructionists as being capable from birth of exercising various forms of agency and of contributing to the shaping of their lives and worlds, although not always with the outcomes that they might prefer. This has presented a significant challenge to the intellectual hegemony long held by developmental psychology in the field of childhood studies.

But mounting a persuasive critique of socialization theory has not thus far served to bring into question, let alone to alter, the complex and overlapping practices and institutional arrangements that have evolved under the rubric of this conventional way of understanding and managing childhood in Western society. Within educational institutions and other public and private spheres concerned with children and youth the assumptions of developmental psychology are still very much accepted at face value and continue to be implemented without much, if any, evidence of reflexivity. What is more, the rugged durability of the institutional arrangements underwritten by socialization theory has not even been adequately acknowledged within the ranks of its opponents. In consequence, it is necessary to focus ethnographic attention upon the ways in which conventional socialization theory continues to furnish the pre-eminent operating models of childhood and appropriate adult–child relationships. The continuing acceptance and unquestioning operationalization of these models reaches from the household to the consumer economy and up to the level of state policy and oversight of domestic life. As this chapter has demonstrated, the assumptions about children that have long governed the schoolroom have been comprehensively extended on to the playgrounds and sporting fields of Canadian communities.

How does the widely held image of children's carefree play on frozen ponds lead us to the utter seriousness of endeavour and intensity of organization featured in community sports for children? Clearly, the ideals of 'pond' hockey are violated not because parents simply wish to accompany their sons and daughters into this zone of pleasure to share their enjoyment. Instead, this occurs because adults feel compelled to take charge of this field of embodied activity and identity play precisely because of its social and cultural potency. Organized sport offers a means for fulfilling the extensive responsibilities assigned to parents by socialization theory. In effect, childhood is deemed to be too important to be left to children. But to reveal this is to point to the deep insecurities of parents concerning not only the future class prospects of their sons and daughters but also of the relative success of their own individual lives as adults and efforts as parents. These are heavy preoccupations to place upon the playful bodies of child and youth athletes. Children's play has, in the process, been transformed into embodied performance that speaks first and foremost to the concerns of adults as parents, coaches and citizens.

In general terms, children's sport performances need to be seen as comprising rather more than just the moving bodies of young athletes and the rules of a given game or event. Embodied performances also revolve centrally around elements situated beyond the bounds of the playing-field (or stage). Audiences, not least, are essential to performance. They serve not only as witnesses or fans but also as benefactors, facilitators and arbiters of performance. In the case of child and youth sports, adults select the form and purposes of these activities and determine which modes of participation by children will be celebrated and which will simply not be allowed. In short, the parents stationed on the sidelines of the venues of children's sport are no less engaged in shaping the actions of players on the field of competition than are the coaches who undertake to train and discipline the bodies of child and youth athletes. To concentrate solely on the action 'on-field' is to ignore the deeper dynamics of the settings within which these performances are produced and consumed.

To be analytically worthwhile the conceptual enlargement of venues of embodied performance – including the fields of children's sport – must venture beyond mere acknowledgment of the presence of an audience. Audiences tend to be viewed as separate and removed from the performances conducted before them, be these sporting, artistic or musical in nature. Surely the distinction between frontstage and backstage (Goffman 1959) was never intended to provide an impermeable and monolithic boundary between performers and their audiences. To cast audiences in the severely constrained role of merely receiving and interpreting performances is to preclude examination of the complex ways in which their members may be inconspicuously, much of the time unselfconsciously, but nonetheless centrally implicated in shaping that which they might otherwise appear to be merely appreciating from a distance. Ethnographers of performance would be well advised to entertain the possibility of more active, complicated and integral roles for audiences, lest we fall captive to forms of performative artifice that are at least as subtle and significant as those displayed by the featured performers.

Notes

1. I wish to thank Vered Amit for her critical and constructive reading of an earlier version of this chapter.
2. In this, as in a number of other respects, 'pond' hockey (or 'shiny', as it is sometimes also known) has much in common with the forms of unorganized football played on *potreros* in Buenos Aires (Archetti 1997: 35) and the *peladas* (Leite Lopes 1997: 85) of Brazil. All three types of venue stand apart from the organized spaces and activities of everyday life.

3. Although players of the ages of four to ninety-four might conceivably engage in pond hockey, age and status demarcations between children and adults are not recognized. Within the bounds of this game, a player is a player.
4. Community sport organizations are typically affiliated with provincial and national sport organizations and structures.
5. 'National Longitudinal Survey of Children and Youth: Participation in activities, 1998/99', *The Daily*, 30 May 2001 (Ottawa: Statistics Canada).
6. Vancouver *Province*, 21 October 2001, p. A.13. Additional articles that were part of this series appeared on 22–25 October, 2001.
7. See Dyck (2000) for an account of the role of self-esteem in children's sports in Canada.
8. The names of the teams as well as the individuals mentioned subsequently have been changed to preserve confidentiality.
9. This was not in any way a reference to race, but rather a backhanded compliment to Ernie.

References

Archetti, E. P. (1997), '"And give joy to my heart": Ideology and emotions in the Argentinian cult of Maradona', in G. Armstrong and R. Giulianotti (eds), *Entering the Field: New Perspectives on World Football*, pp. 31–51. Oxford/New York: Berg.

Caputo, Virginia (1995), 'Anthropology's Silent "Others": A Consideration of Some Conceptual and Methodological Issues for the Study of Youth and Children's Cultures', in V. Amit-Talai and H. Wulff (eds), *Youth Cultures: A Cross-Cultural Perspective*, pp. 19–42. London/New York: Routledge.

Dyck, Noel (2000), 'Parents, Kids and Coaches: Constructing Sport and Childhood in Canada', in N. Dyck (ed.), *Games, Sports and Cultures*, pp. 137–61. Oxford/New York: Berg.

Goffman, Erving (1959), *The Presentation of Self in Everyday Life*. Garden City, NY: Doubleday Anchor Books.

James, Allison (1998), 'Imaging Children "At Home", "In the Family", and "At School": Movement Between the Spatial and Temporary Markers of Childhood Identity in Britain', in N. Rapport and A. Dawson (eds) *Migrants of Identity: Perceptions of Home in a World of Movement*, pp. 139–60. Oxford/New York: Berg.

James, Allison and Allan Prout (eds) (1990) *Constructing and Reconstructing Childhood: Contemporary Issues in the Sociological Study of Childhood*, Basingstoke/New York: Falmer Press.

Leite Lopes, Jose Sergio (1997), 'Successes and Contradictions in "Multiracial" Brazilian Football', in G. Armstrong and R. Giulianotti (eds), *Entering the*

Field: New Perspectives on World Football, pp. 53–86. Oxford/New York: Berg.

Lithman, Yngve Georg (2000), 'Reflections on the Social and Cultural Dimensions of Children's Elite Sport in Sweden', in N. Dyck (ed.), *Games, Sports and Cultures*, pp. 163–81. Oxford/New York: Berg.

Stephens, Sharon (ed.) (1995), *Children and the Politics of Culture*, Princeton, NJ: Princeton University Press.

−4−

Embodied Play and Gender Identities in Competitive Handball for Children in Norway[1]

Harald Beyer Broch

Introduction

Many students of sport claim that it has never been proved that participation in sport activities has a lasting impact on athletes' behaviour outside the arenas of play (Bakker *et al.* 1990; Olsen 1994). However, competitive sports take up too much time, during several years in the lives of too many children, to allow this question to be excluded from further scrutiny by social scientists (see also Fasting 1987).

This chapter is based on ethnographic investigations of varying intensity conducted during approximately ten years of observation of handball-playing girls and boys from nine to eighteen years of age. These observations have been carried out from various positions and levels of involvement in children's handball sports. I have been involved as a parent of a handball-playing daughter and son, as an assistant trainer, as a team manager (*lagleder*) and as a board member of a handball club. Information for this essay has been taken from unobtrusive observations of a variety of handball activities and contexts along with directed conversations held with children and adults, primarily in informal settings. Finally, four formal interviews, focused on gender and personality issues, were carried out with coaches and parents of child handball players.

Feedback processes that work in several directions are always operating between sports and society at large. While gender roles and gender expectations may have lost some of their traditional rigidity, many sport arenas have become interactional stages where new roles are tested out. In this context, it is interesting to note that the women's handball team was the first Norwegian national team (male or female) to achieve major success. The women's team is the only one that has ever won both a World and a European championship. This team has also captured two silver medals at Olympic games. The point to be stressed is not the success of Norwegian women's handball *per se*, but rather that the fame and popularity of the team are far above those of the women who play in the almost equally accomplished national football team.

Girls and women who play handball are usually featured as models for sporty and healthy Norwegian female youth. This image is not similarly attached to girls who play football in this country. The reason for this cannot be explained by a single factor, and is not the topic for this chapter, but may indeed be related to the social environment or venue within which handball is played. A factor of some relevance is the different shape of football and handball arenas. Football is played outdoors on large fields where the spectators are positioned relatively far away from the athletes. Handball is played on an indoor court 20 metres wide and 40 metres long (see Figure 4.1). Each team consists of six field players and a goalkeeper. The players have somewhat different roles. Two players are positioned in the middle: the centre back and the line player. The centre back usually directs the team's attack on the opponents' defence and feeds passes to teammates, ideally creating chances for them to score goals. A goal is scored when a player manages to throw the ball into the net, in spite of the defenders' and (finally) the goal-keeper's efforts to stop it. The line player has the difficult job of 'creating space' inside the opposing team's defensive area. Most of his/her job is done around the six-metre line, and the line player should always be alert to receive the ball between opposing defenders. A team also has two side-backs and two wings. During handball matches the spectators are seated near enough to the court

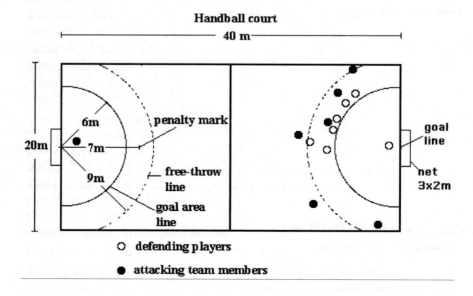

Handball court

Figure 4.1 Handball court and player positions

to watch both the body language and the facial expressions of the contenders. Because the game of handball is played in a more compact space than football, most of the handball players on both teams can be watched by the spectators simultaneously. The players are very aware that they are under close spectator surveillance during most of the match. This visual access to individual players has been utilized in televised matches and has probably contributed to their popularity. Because of this unusually close visual access many spectators quickly come to feel they know their handball idols. Also the media coverage given to women's handball, arguably at the 'expense' of the men's game, is an example of what some men claim to be unfair treatment that influences patterns of recruitment to the sport.

It is, however, interesting to note that explanations given for women athletes' international success are similar in Norway and in China. Explanatory factors mentioned in both countries include, for instance, low levels of international competition, relatively high levels of support from state authorities, and the positive effect of women's generally favourable position within their national cultures (Brownell 2000: 56). (These are, of course, similarities in terms of official governmental rhetoric that do not necessarily indicate that the social position of women in China at the grass roots is at a similar level to that of women in Norway.)

In this presentation I focus on how gender ideology and gender stereotypes influence children's handball in Norway. This is done by examining boys' and girls' behaviour during training and competitions, the social milieu that surrounds them and, in particular, the role of their trainers or coaches. Consideration of these materials suggests that competitive sport, team interaction and more relevant contexts, such as management of sports identities at school and in children's homes, do indeed colour the behaviour of many young handball-playing girls and boys. The acquisition and rehearsal of techniques of the body that are fundamental to handball interconnects the performing, the experiencing and the reflecting upon one's place and position in the game. What the individual performers also experience is self-consciousness. Thus the children's learned physical movements, perceptions of their bodies and bodily expressions, together with other identity markers, constitute important components of their embodied identities.

Contrary to what is often suggested, many boys playing handball are just as vain as girls may be. Members of both genders are concerned with body image, and tie their identity within the team and outside the sports arena to such factors as looks (hairstyle, dress and team uniform, weight and height), personality, aggressiveness and various skill indicators. In her book, *Brilliant in Playing Handball* (*God i håndball*), Susan Goksør Bjerkrheim, a star player from the Norwegian woman's national team, promotes the official handball association's view that this sport is for everyone. In handball, everyone has the ability to excel: it does not matter whether you are short or tall, stout or thin (1999: 24). We shall see that this is not how all of the girls and boys playing the game perceive the situation.

The particular forms and expressions taken by many of the issues presented below are age-dependent, and change with the growing maturation that occurs between childhood and adolescence. Here I concentrate on children between approximately thirteen and sixteen years of age. This is a developmental period that may be of particular interest, because it is generally seen as being characterized by identity insecurity and experimentation. Owing to limited space, this chapter only considers brief examples illustrating matters of identity management and presentation as they are revealed through the children's discourses on dress, body and athletic talent. Related discourses among young handball-players, along with communications between them and their coaches, are also highlighted. By paying close attention to the actual ways in which children engage in sport, this analysis presents them not simply as players of an athletic game but as social persons whose engagement in sport is complex and variable.

Thus the supposedly innocent nature of children's sport may be less unproblematic than many parents and other observers wish to believe. Participation in sports is a serious business for many young participants. Sport is not only leisurely fun, but also involves competition, demonstration of skills, popularity, gender and personal identity-related issues.

Before I proceed, it is necessary to note my awareness of a methodological problem. Thorne (1993) and Chodorow (1995), amongst others, have pointed out the need for exercising caution when we generalize about gender. They both emphasize that differences in gender identity vary enormously within as well as between gender groups. Indeed, some individuals do cross back and forth across the cultural divide between gender groups. In a careful analysis of individual children and their reactions, the significance of idiosyncratic tastes and whims also becomes apparent. This further complicates efforts towards generalization. Still, the fact that individuals differ in their motivations, values and identity presentation and goals is recognized by leading sports ideologists and theoreticians such as the Norwegian football guru and coach Nils Arne Eggen, who has inspired and influenced Norwegian team handball. Eggen claims that, from the first time children get in contact with a ball and team sport, they should be encouraged to develop their individual skills, but always in ways that will benefit their team. Team sports are about individuals doing things together and working towards a common goal. The point is to bring out the best (including skills like speed, technical brilliance, endurance and temperament) in each player. They are all different individuals and need to be recognized as such (Eggen 1999). Thus it should be to borne in mind that in the following examples, where coaches or single players are focused upon, they are presented as *types* often encountered in children's sports. It is not possible to make generalizations from each and every one of the examples, but we must nonetheless consider how to deal with the variation that is endemic to most team sports for children.

The Coach's Role in the Team Building Processes

Children's sports activities in Norway are generally club-organized. The clubs are primarily run through the voluntary efforts of parents, who spend much of their spare time organizing club activities such as money-generating efforts, supplying necessary equipment, planning tours and tournament activities, coaching and providing team management, amongst other things. It is generally a problem to recruit enough skilled persons to carry out all the various tasks facing clubs. Most people involved in children's sports are well aware of the importance of finding good coaches, but the finances to hire competent persons are generally lacking in all but a very few professional clubs. In Norway, as in Canada, open criticism by any number of parents or children of what they might regard as mismanagement in a club or team could pose a serious risk. Offended coaches, umpires or other officials might simply decline to continue to volunteer their time and efforts to the club or team (Dyck 2000:154). This means that persons involved in children's sports are seldom criticized and rarely 'sacked'.

The coaches' influence on the children they train may have a very strong impact on team-building, social relationships, skill achievement, collective and individual team motivation and identity formation among the players. What is less obvious is that coaches may also have some impact on how players visualize and concept-ualize their gender and gender roles. This is so because coaches approach their work with children armed with their own ideas about how gender, personality and talent influence the development of handball skills. Most coaches have little experience of working with children other than their own sons and daughters. Some have experience as players in the sport they are coaching or have part-icipated as players in other sports. This is usually viewed as a valuable background. Adult-organized sports for young children are a relatively new phenomenon in Norway. Because few coaches began their own sport careers in organized children's activities, many of them lack insight into the most basic principles of child psychology and pedagogy. And this may not perhaps be too important when we consider the youngest recruits to handball. Girls and boys of eight to eleven years old are usually allowed to have fun. It is generally understood that these children are participating in sports to have a good time. Ideally, at least, coaches do not press children as young as these to perform and do not have grand ambitions for their teams.

In this chapter, however, we are focusing on somewhat older children: boys and girls from approximately thirteen to sixteen years of age. Why do coaches so often have a particularly strong impact on children in this age group? This is so because many of the children, when they like their coach, tend to look up to her or him. Children are inclined to listen to their coaches not only as experts on handball, but also as experts on everything that goes into the sport and teamwork. Most children not only look up to their coaches, but also compete with each other to be noticed, to harvest recognition not only as members of the team, but also as individuals. They strive to have their value confirmed, not only as players on the current team or as potential future stars, but also as individuals. How much influence a coach will have on different players of these ages also depends upon relations within the child's family. Some, but not all, children may discuss problems or alternative views with a mother, father or elder sibling. Some, but not all, find the desired recognition as a unique individual at home. Some children have parents or siblings who have faith in their ambitions, whereas others do not have a significant 'other', except the coach, whom might care about sports and sport involvement. Many parents have had the experience of having their views on what they regard as important values being contradicted or supported by handball coaches. Thus family friction may erupt when an admired young coach teaches boys both by his own behaviour and by verbal statements that the chewing of tobacco is all right or, at least, is far better than smoking tobacco. But just as frequently parents may have reason to thank a coach for help in supporting, for instance, a family goal of providing a nutritious and varied daily diet. Many coaches make repeated efforts to explain to their players that athletic performance is positively influenced by eating healthy vegetables and fruits and by staying away from too much junk food, alcohol and cigarettes.

People who appreciate, believe in and support team sports often argue that these activities generate positive experiences, attitudes and values. For instance, they stress that in sports children are together and have fun, learn to respect each other, develop many good friendly relationships, acquire body control and skills and learn to cooperate to achieve common goals (see also Dyck 2000). Much of this may be true when everything works out ideally. However, everything does not always work out as is hoped. In fact, in most instances teams do not reach all their goals, and most players end their involvement in sports when they are between fourteen and eighteen years old. Some children who already are confronted with problems at school or in their homes or who find it difficult to form friendships are confronted with additional setbacks in the sport arena.

Age and gender are also important when we look at the role and behaviour of children's coaches. There may, for instance, be inappropriate signals transmitted concerning the presumed gender distribution of handball and leadership skills when the majority of coaches of girls' and women's teams are men. This could be interpreted as indicating that men are better qualified than women when it comes to possessing, and also teaching, handball technique and strategies and, further, that men are the best team-builders.

Interestingly, the majority of coaches of both genders that I have talked to and observed in their work with the children share some widely distributed stereotypes about gender behaviour. For instance, they seem to agree that with girls even the young ones (ten to fourteen years) are significantly physically weaker than their male age-mates. Girls of these ages are also regarded as being less aggressive than boys are, and are supposed to be generally afraid of physical contact during play. Girls are also widely presumed to be less ambitious, to lack motivation to reach high levels of skill and to be less oriented to results than boys are said to be. It is supposed to be typical of girls to claim that 'I can't do that' when coaches teach new techniques. These gender stereotypes are not confirmed by my own observations of children's handball practices and competitions (Broch 1994, 1995). Girls, like boys, want to win matches. They sulk when they lose, try to stir each other to better performances and get angry when technical errors are made. Perhaps the most widely shared opinion in this context – and I am now referring to nearly all relevant ages when handball is under discussion – is this: girls go to the gym or the practice arena to be trained, whereas boys go there to practice (or to train). To make the meaning of this saying explicit, it connotes that girls are passive (receivers) whereas boys are active (doers). Eggen admittedly does not write about handball, but about Rosenborg, the most successful football team in Norway. What he tells us is noteworthy. He explains how he copes with professional male football players who come to a training session and say: 'I can't do that', and what he does when players are misled into believing that they are to be trained by him (Eggen 1999). Eggen doesn't tell them that their reactions are feminine. He asks his players to attend to their attitudes to the sport and their possibilities of improving their games in a team context.

Although gender stereotypes at times are reaffirmed, and even learned by a few children who did not believe in them before, and even though many coaches design their handball instruction in accordance with these stereotypes, that was not my sole purpose in raising the issue in the present context. I am not claiming that girls are always better off under the command of women coaches. Neither am I suggesting that boys fare best under the supervision of men when it comes to learning sports.

Many examples show that children and their coaches need not share a common gender in order to achieve excellent rapport and outstanding results in handball. However, because boys and girls tend to relate differently towards men and women coaches, certain combinations of ages and gender bring out similar responses time and again. Boys generally look upon young male coaches as idols they want to make friends with. When they begin to mature, boys (from fifteen years upwards) place more emphasis than before on how they assess the skills of their coaches. At this age they start to become more critical. This can be very difficult for the youngest coaches (approximately from eighteen to twenty-four years old) to handle. Many take on the role of being a popular, admired, and 'cool' friend of the boys on the team. When this position is threatened by questions the players ask about technical details, team dispositions or tactical matters, young coaches often respond with authoritarian measures. A rhetorical strategy that consists of declaring 'trust my judgements and dispositions' or 'I do what is the best for the team' or 'no discussion needed' will often sever most 'technical' handball communication between coach and players. Older coaches usually do not encounter the same problem. Their rapport with the team members is less likely to be based on off-court relations than may be the case with their younger colleagues. When I have observed teams of boys in this age group coached by adult women, it always seemed to work well. These women knew the game of handball very well; they had natural authority and earned the reputation of being just. Yet I have never observed or heard about girls in their late teens or women in their early twenties coaching boys older than twelve to thirteen years old. Most coaches of both boys' and girls' teams are men between twenty and forty-five years old. It is my impression that the girls prefer men as coaches; but when women have settled with a team they have been just as well liked as their male counterparts. Teams do equally well under the leadership of women and men.

Girls, like boys, seek to be on friendly terms with their coaches. There is, however, a significant difference between boys and girls when it comes to how they relate to their youngest male coaches. The boys hope for recognition, to be seen and to receive some expression of friendship. With the girls another dimension must be added. Girls from the age of thirteen years and upwards show a marked tendency to flirt with and 'fall in love with' young male coaches. This often leads to situations where most of the girls on a team compete for the attention of their coach. Some girls 'fall in love' from a distance. This may pose a severe hindrance to athletic achievement, and for some may turn the training sessions into real ordeals. Energy is directed away from teamwork and handball training. Girls are watching each other to see who does what to get the coach's attention. Occasionally girls pretend they are hurt or slightly injured in an effort to be tended by the coach. Others are devastated because they feel left out, unseen and ignored by team members and coach alike. Some express feelings of inferiority, start to dislike their looks and body, and can be observed sitting quietly by themselves on the peripheries of the locker room. Many girls of this age are not particularly nurturing with team-mates, but instead define them as competitors. Thus there is usually little support or encouragement from them when social blows fall on girls low in the team hierarchy. If this feeling of gloomy loneliness lasts through some months then all motivation to continue with handball usually evaporates.

Some young male coaches visibly enjoy the position they develop within girls' teams. Not all are aware of the impact they may have, but some like to stay 'cool' and popular, surrounded by some ten to fifteen adolescent girls. It is these coaches whom one may often observe outside an arena during tournament events, involved in a friendly chat, smoking away with some of their thirteen- to fourteen-year-old players. Most coaches respect the official attitude on abstaining from the use of tobacco expressed by the handball association. It is recommended that when coaches or parents feel an urge for nicotine that they should locate a place to smoke well out of the sight of young players. Coaches are often reminded that they are important role models for many girls and boys on their teams.

Young coaches are sometimes unaware of the emotional turmoil they create among their team members. Arguably, they should be observant enough to detect what is happening around them. But it always seems to take time for new coaches to learn. One young coach, approximately eighteen years old, was very popular with the thirteen-year-old girls on his team. He had the ability to motivate them before matches, and they often won – not because they were especially skilled in handball techniques, but because they were fighting hard, utilizing aggression in a handball-productive way. During a tournament these girls won several matches. However, they were far from content. Many of them looked miserable. After each victory the coach ran towards two of the girls and gave them huge hugs in appreciation for their contribution to the victory. Other teammates were onlookers; some watched with tears in their eyes, and one or two cried afterwards in the dressing-room. Most of the girls had hoped that they too would be rewarded with that famous hug. It turned out that this coach also had the habit of distributing special bear-hugs during training sessions. When the coach was told about the reactions created among the girls whenever he distributed his rewards, he said that he had never realized. He dropped the habit, and extended his popularity for the rest of his coaching tenure with the team.

It is not difficult to understand the impact that coaches may have on young players. It should also be reasonable for us to accept that the age and gender of coaches may influence how communication may develop between them and the children to whom they teach handball. During a board meeting in a handball club one of the participants said, partly as a joke, 'we should never allow a married man the responsibility of coaching young girls before we know how he treats and talks about his wife'.

The influence of coaches can be further illustrated by what a woman handball idol remembers from her first years as a child player. At that time (in the 1970s), all the girls on her team wore their hair long. Then one day the coach discovered that one of the girls had cut her hair quite short: 'Oh there you have really got a handball hairdo', he proclaimed. The result was that before the next training session all the other girls had also cut their hair short (Bjerkrheim 1999: 70–1). This they did, of course, to get attention and recognition from the adored coach. That the coach is often a very important person in child athletes' lives is confirmed in other studies. For instance, among young elite gymnasts the coach may even suggest 'proper' leisure activities, diet and hairstyles (Weiss 2000: 195).

Embodied Play

During the late 1990s a wave of social scientists regained an interest in the human body and bodywork. Embodiment became a serious buzzword and a marker of an updated and modern approach to the study of cognition. Outside academia few people had probably been totally convinced about Descartes' separation between thought/soul and body/substance. This dichotomous distinction may have served lay people well in particular contexts in Europe, but nothing even approaching a general cross-cultural validity can be established for it. How we experience our bodies, as a form of self-representation, and how bodies are manifestations of others are culturally defined and learned. Anthropologists influenced by Foucault have examined the ways in which culture is 'inscribed' on the body. These processes contain various tangible manipulations, such as tattooing, scarification and the use of make-up, but also include often unconscious assumptions about body structure and function, gender differences and the relationship of physical factors to emotional expression (Bock 1999: 246).

Bodies are part of our own identities and influence our self-awareness (Ingham 1996) and the identity of all others because of processes of comparison (Lupton 1996, 1999). We interpret the bodies of others as expressions about who they are and what qualities they may have and what they can do. Various cultures and societies, historical time-periods and social subgroups, such as the practitioners of particular sports, develop definable body ideals. In modern terms, the body signals much information concerning the personality of its owner. In Norwegian youth culture a slim body signals general control over most desires, and in particular over that of food intake. Slim bodies are generally regarded as being aesthetically pleasing, whereas obese bodies are ugly and negative (Duesund 1995; Grogan 1999). The modern Euro-American obsession with body shapes also reaches children playing handball. When even young boys and girls use body shapes to evaluate teammates, they draw the same conclusion as many English children do. Fat or obese children are ugly, stupid, dumb and unpopular; but the slim ones are nice, pretty/handsome and popular (James 1993).

How does this fit with the statement that in handball all body types, short or tall, bulky or slim may fit into the sport? The statement has some merit if we consider the first encounter children may have with the sport. Still, the obese, the skinny and the red-haired child all often start out with a handicap when team roles are created. These roles, or rather the pecking order, are usually based on criteria of popularity made up by the children themselves. In this social world a popular boy or girl will, in most instances, also be regarded as a good, talented player by teammates. It takes time to learn, or perhaps rather to accept, that even an unpopular (that means ugly) teammate can be a good player. Most coaches encounter this problem among their youngest players, and it appears that girls are somewhat meaner or express less emphatic sympathy with teammates than do most boys of the same age.

It is not uncommon that coaches of twelve- to fourteen-year-old girls should find considerable difficulty in convincing some of them that they really are skilled players and should try more shots during matches. An example illustrates the problem. A team of twelve- and thirteen-year-old girls was participating in a handball tournament. In one of the matches that the girls won, the usually modest and shy Anna suddenly scored four goals. The coach was thrilled, and called out loud when she scored for the second time: 'There, you see, it isn't all that difficult. I've told you before that you have an excellent jump shot. Get going Anna, this is really good.' Anna of course, was very happy. After the match, when the girls came out from the locker room, it was obvious that Anna had been crying. She was no longer the happy girl of half an hour ago. I was told that right after the match, one of the girls had started to scold Anna. She asked why on earth she had tried so hard to score goals so many times during that match. Why did she not pass on the ball to Eva (the star of the team) or to herself. Had she (Anna) not realized that they too had been in a scoring position? The girl had been very angry when she spoke, and then she closed in for the final kill: 'You should have seen yourself when you performed those jump shots. You just looked stupid, like the fat, ugly toad you are.' Most of the other girls laughed at this. For the rest of the tournament and thereafter Anna resumed her invisible position on the floor. She did not try more shots, but passed the ball on to the team stars. When she had to decide whose advice it was best for her to follow, that of the coach or the team stars, she made the choice she was offered by the girls. It was her considered best choice to comply with the demand of her teammates. It was among them she looked for best friends. She met with them every day during classes at school. So the coach came second to the girls in this broader context.

The boys' teams, like the girls', are far from free of internal conflicts, but these often take a somewhat different form. The boys also demand that some stay out of the spotlight, and they too have their team stars who are allowed to fail where others are not. Also, boys criticize each other loudly. However, it seems that boys of this age are more loyal to authorities than the girls are. When the coach tells a player that he should do this or that, the boy may be just as likely as a girl would be to say that he does not have that skill. But when a boy does as he is told he will seldom be ridiculed or scolded for that by his teammates. Now and then boys, like girls, become angry at teammates during play; but it is my impression that boys are usually quicker to overlook disagreements than girl players are. Regardless of gender, the best teams are those that function well socially. These are teams where few players are competing with each other for attention or praise, where the children feel they are justly treated, where they have a coach they respect and who will also manage to make it fun to exercise.

All children have to find their place and position on the team. From early on, the coaches choose what they believe are the right persons for the different positions on the court. Ideally the centre (mid) back should be quick in his/her movements and able to make fast decisions, or be an expert in 'reading the play', as it is expressed in handball jargon. The line player should ideally be physically strong and courageous. The side backs are ideally among the tallest players on the team. In children's handball the wings are often short and physically among the least mature members of their teams. Ideally they should be fast runners and have good body movement control. In children's handball the best players and team stars are usually placed in the positions of mid and side backs.

A coach places individual team members where she or he thinks they help their team most or, alternatively, where they will do the least damage. Most children understand this strategy. They too evaluate the performances of each other. All look for talent. Having talent means for the children that they have what it takes to be a good handball player, if they are willing to put the needed effort into the task. To have this talent is to have social merit. If you have talent, then you get recognition for it from the coach, the team members and the handball audience. Talent, as the children understand this, is expressed in some quite tangible ways. Recognizable talent may take the form of 'having guts' or showing controlled aggression. It also materializes as having speed or being able to run short distances very fast, to move quickly sideways in defence and to make speedy feinting movements to trick opponents. Talent is also manifested in observable body shapes. Tall girls and boys are regarded as being full of talent that only has to be cultivated. Bodily strength or muscular bodies carried by fearless children who do not appear to be bothered if they are hurt a little are another sign of talent in this contact sport. In spite of the valiant efforts of most coaches in telling the children that they are all equally important to the team and its results, children usually organize their teams in contradiction of that ideology. Boys and girls older than thirteen readily observe that small and not particularly speedy team members are usually positioned as wings. Generally speaking, you find the tallest and the best players in the middle. If one considers who is seated on the bench (on the sideline) and plays less than the rest, then it is clear that skinny and short children are over-represented. Thus the children pick up messages about themselves that they and others use as components for identity construction. What has been said about children's elite ice hockey players in Sweden also illuminates Norwegian handball: 'The individual is seen in terms of his or her immediately available presentations and prestations. The value as expressed in a coach's selection of skaters during a hockey powerplay . . . or of some players having to sit . . . is immediately demonstrated' (Lithman 2000: 173).

Children this age also read the magazine published by the Norwegian Handball Association. There they also find information on the definition of talent; for instance, the coaches for the national junior teams write that they are searching for boys and girls with extreme attributes. Young people who are exceptionally tall and have long hands and fingers are regarded as being 'interesting' in the present and future handball context. My argument here is that many children, in spite of what they regard as inconsequential comments to the contrary, learn that they are less than talented. They may be too short, too weak or too slow for a secure position on their present team, and their future as handball-players is not going to take them anywhere. For instance, time and again coaches urge their young players to come to obligatory training sessions. They say that girls or boys who exercise regularly will be preferred over those who skip some of these sessions when it comes to games. However, when it comes to matches most coaches tend to forget their own rules and let their favourites play even when they have been absent from many of the preparation exercises. Good coaches discuss motivation and help to define goals for *all* team members. They inaugurate team solidarity and a 'we can do it together' feeling (Railo 1996). However, at times the experience of playing handball can be very frustrating to young players of both genders.[2]

Fifteen-year-old Ola, for example, was told by his coach that he was actually 'quite good', but that the coach did not know where to place him on the team because he was too short. Ola was very strong, and one of the most eager players at training sessions, but in matches he was only allowed to play for short periods. He did, however, find it rewarding to continue with handball, because he was often allowed to take the penalty shots for his team. With a change of coaches Ola lost that opportunity, and it was impossible for him to understand why this had happened. The new coach never told him why he was no longer granted his old privilege, but repeated the old message that the boy was too short. Once, when one of the team stars was ill, Ola was allowed to play a whole match and scored several goals. After that match the coach expressed surprise and said, 'I did not know you were that fast and had such a good shot.' Ola answered, a little irritated, 'Well the problem is that I can't score any goals without being allowed to play.' The coach did not like the answer, and Ola did not get more time on the floor during subsequent matches. Ola started to wonder whether he should quit handball.

Sixteen-year-old Karen misunderstood her coach. One day when the team was practising, the male coach asked all the girls about their ambitions. Karen was the only one who said she hoped one day to make the national team, or at least to play in the elite series. When the coach heard that, he laughed: 'Karen, you are far too ambitious, you are too weak and do not have the guts.' During subsequent training sessions, whenever Karen made an error this coach reminded her about her ambitions. Karen did not quit at that time, but continued just to prove her coach wrong and to take him down a peg through her hoped-for future success.

You Are So Vain – On Body, Looks and Handball Uniforms

Both boys and girls are concerned about their looks; but this vanity is expressed differently by girls and boys when they play handball. The youngest girls have a tendency to wear knee and elbow protection on the court, even when this is not much needed. They do so because they copy adult handball stars. Also the protective garment 'signals' that they are *real* handball-players, who play a tough game. They feel that they look great in this gear. For some reason small boys do not take this need for protection to the same extent that the girls do. Boys are of course not afraid of some minor bruises and rough play. Such ideas are cultural gender markers played out among the ten- to thirteen-year-old boy players, and are positively confirmed by coaches. Yet when children this age are observed on court, most of the boys are not that tough. Some of them make sure they stay away from body contact with opposing team members; some whimper off the court when they have made an error, blaming the misery on what is, for others, an undetectable injury. Conversely, there are girls who have a rough style of play. They are often praised by coaches and spectators for their willingness to 'fight' to defend their own goal. To fight in this context means that they will use all their physical strength to stop opponents and that they will test the limits that referees allow for rough play in the game. When occasionally, for instance, fourteen-year-old boys and girls play practice matches against each other, the girls may well and often do win. On one occasion when a girls' team won such a match the boys complained that the girls were far too tough when it came to body-contact situations, and claimed that their aggressive physical style was the reason for their victory (Broch 1995).

In spite of these differences, boys and girls alike express pride when they can show off black and blue marks and bruises after handball combat. Many also say that they wish for a small injury as a proof and a marker of their merit. All agree that handball is a contact sport, and state that they are proud of taking part in combat on the floor.

Boys and girls are equally concerned about their team uniforms, and have ideas about how they could be improved. When they reach the ages of fourteen and above, they may propose a special playing uniform for their particular team. Their wish is, however, never granted. They compare their own uniforms with those of other teams and rank them. But logos and the like for handball uniforms are matters left strictly to adults. Some sixteen-year-old boys were fantasizing about logos that they would introduce for their team. They wanted to copy the practice of the National Hockey League and the American Basketball League. For its part, the Norwegian Handball Association works to make child and youth handball more popular and trendy. When one of the board members was confronted with the idea of introducing fancy logos, he turned it down as being childish and without interest for the adult sport organizers.

The uniforms, of course, make the children look much alike. Most players appreciate this, but at the same time they strive for markers of individuality within the available possibilities. Thus some let their shorts hang down, others prefer to play with their shirts loose, others try to order very wide or extra large sizes, and still others ask for regular sizes. All handball shirts have a number on the back, and these numbers are significant to many boys and girls, especially when they are sixteen or seventeen and older. There are (personal) lucky numbers, and some numbers have special significance (to some) because they are worn by an older idol. These idols may be handball players, but need not necessarily be so. They can also be famous ice hockey, basketball or football players. This preference for certain numbers may also result in temporary grudges. First, there are often not enough of the popular numbers to go around, and second, few Norwegian handball clubs allow numbers above nineteen. Thus there is often a competition within the team for the most popular numbers, and here too the 'star players' usually get it their way.

At the highest level adult (men's and women's) handball matches attract some 2,000 match spectators, and top matches from both the women's and men's leagues are televised extensively. When it comes to children's handball, this is also staged indoors. The size of the floor is the same as in adult matches. The arenas are usually modest – quite similar in layout to many high-school basketball arenas in the United States; but the size of the court equals two basketball courts. The audience is placed near the floor and has a good view of all players, and of their facial expressions, dress and behaviour. The audience that watches children's handball is recruited from the local milieu near each handball club, and consists primarily of relatives, boyfriends and girlfriends of the players, other similarly aged children and handball players from other local teams. Thus the audience is primarily made up of people the young handball players know reasonably well, to some of whom the players wish to present themselves in a favourable way.

Girls and boys mature at different ages, and this is reflected in their handball activities. Thirteen- and fourteen-year-old girls are noticeably more concerned about the audience when they play than boys usually are. Specifically, the girls seem more concerned about how they appear, and especially aware of the gaze they receive from somewhat older boys in the crowd. Typically, girls who are approaching puberty prefer shirts that hide their budding or not yet emerging breasts along with shorts that cover an emerging female body shape. In this age most of them are shy about their body and do not feel wholly comfortable within its frame. A few years later, when they are about fifteen or more years of age, they return to uniforms that emphasize their beauty. It is easy to say that this has little to do with handball; but on the court no one can escape the real and imagined gaze of others. To feel comfortable on the handball court one also has to come to terms with one's appearance. Many of this age have been heard to exclaim that if the club wants them to wear tights or what they call 'bicycle-shorts' they will quit handball altogether. Most, but not all, girls say they feel uncomfortable, almost nude, in tights, because their groin, belly, hips and behind are revealed for all spectators to examine.

Some years ago four fifteen-year-old girls discussed the members of a team that had just beaten them. This after-match conversation was focused on the looks of the girls from the other team. They had all used make-up during the match and were, it was argued, 'so vain'. These girls were surely a bunch of stupid persons, it was agreed, but admittedly good enough players. Half a year later, 'our' girls followed suit! They too wanted to look good on the court and to be as pretty as any opposing players.

Male players of the ages of fifteen to sixteen are also prone to grabbing hold of the vanity wagon. Prior to that age it is often difficult to get all the team members into the shower; many prefer to use the shower at home. At the age of sixteen that is no longer an issue. Now they begin to spend more time in the locker room after the matches, and deodorants are applied generously before they come out. Also, before matches many of the boys comb their hair to look good. Some boys use hairdos to obtain personal attention from onlookers. This serves as an emblem of personal identity and style. The boys, just like the girls, make many remarks about their teammates' appearances. The boys too know that what matters is not only what you do and how you perform during the match, but that how you look also makes a difference.

In this context I argue that both girls and boys use handball activities and the handball arena to experiment with gender identities. They also seek out new ways to negotiate gender ambivalence. Because handball was originally a male-dominated sport, it is possible to argue that modern handball represents another arena where women have transgressed traditional definitions of gender behaviour. Women's handball has gradually evolved into a rough, aggressive sport that includes considerable physical body contact. According to Laberge and Albert (2000), there is a general difference in the stereotypical connotations attached to men's transgression into typically women's sports (rhythmic gymnastics, aerobic dance, and synchronized swimming) and to women's entering men's sports (ice hockey, football, boxing). 'Men's transgressions would signify an erosion of male superiority, whereas women's transgressions would signify transcending women's weakness' (2000: 214). Some of the solutions for identity management employed by the girls considered in this chapter seem to transgress widely shared definitions of masculinity and femininity. If it is the case that girls who are taught to play with a high level of assertiveness, independence, and directed aggression (usually regarded as typically male attributes) will do best in competitive contact sports (see Cox 1998: 256–7) such as handball, they will, indeed, challenge some gender stereotypes. Because of the popular impact of women's team handball and the favourable image and reputation that these sportswomen enjoy in Norway, handball-playing girls encounter significant positive feedback in response to their work as gender entrepreneurs. In television, radio and newspaper coverage of handball, they are portrayed as prototypical strong, healthy and ambitious Norwegian sportswomen. Such connotations carry over also to younger players, and afford them positive esteem among schoolmates and among groups of same-age peers, including those not involved in sports.

In this chapter particular individuals and episodes have been presented in an effort to identify typical, observable social processes as they are played out in children's sport. It is argued that handball-playing girls and boys also learn about gender behaviour and express significant collective and personal reactions through identity management in their interaction with teammates, coaches and onlookers.

To the extent that gender identity is an issue for handball-playing boys and girls, an interesting gender difference emerges. It could be that generally girls' gender identity is less threatened by failure in the sport than would be the case for some boys. It is argued in this paper that in handball girls get recognition for their success *as girls* within the sport. However, even those girls who quit handball because, perhaps, they find it too rough may still score positively on a scale of femininity, although that constitutes an alternative scale. Boys' gender roles are more directly tested during handball training and matches. For a boy to quit for the expressed reason that the sport is too rough would not receive broad approval, and hence he would probably identify other reasons for quitting. More research is, however, needed to verify these assumptions.

It is suggested that in handball girls can be seen as gender entrepreneurs. This implies that the girls utilize some personal potential as well as both personal and collective attributes in their expression of femaleness. Supported by the popularity of adult women players in the sport, even young girls can experiment with new combinations of gender activities to (re)construct their femaleness. They show a tolerant audience new yet suitable styles of female behaviour. In this way they contribute to a widening of legitimate space for women's activities, adding complexity to gender roles and demonstrating novel combinations of female space and opportunity. Thus it has become legitimate for girls to remain tomboys long after puberty. The tomboy image can even be prestigious in one's twenties and thirties. To be a physically strong handball-player, known for an aggressive playing style on the court, does not rule out the wearing of a ladylike gown and make-up in the evenings. At the elite level, Marit Breivik, head coach of the national women's team for many years, has deliberately fought widespread ideas about women in sport. She has emphasized that even the toughest girls on her team should appear as the women that they are, well dressed and appropriately good-looking outside the sport arena. Also Breivik insists that her national team-members have to visit operas and attend classical music concerts in addition to rock/pop concerts and cinemas when they are gathered for important tournaments. She insists that mind and body are integrated parts of a whole, and that sports idols should have many interests in social life outside the playing court.

The handball arena assuredly mirrors the larger society of which it is but a small part; and yet it may also serve as another stage where gender roles are confirmed, modified, reconstructed and tested. This alone should suffice to validate the need for more ethnographic work on the socio-culturally dynamic aspects of children's sports.

Notes

1. I am grateful to the editors of this volume, Noel Dyck and Eduardo P. Archetti, for a number of helpful comments and suggestions. Thanks also go to Anne-Katrine Brun Norbye, who contributed valuable critique during the final stages of my work with this chapter.
2. See Fasting (1987) for a general discussion of both positive and negative experiences and consequences of children's sport.

References

Bakker, F.C., Whiting H.T.A., and van der Brug, H. (1990), *Sport Psychology. Concepts and Applications*. New York: John Wiley & Sons.

Bjerkrheim, S. G. (1999), *God i håndball*, Oslo: Gyldendal Tiden.

Bock, P. K. (1999), *Rethinking Psychological Anthropology. Continuity and Change in the Study of Human Action*, 2nd edn, Prospect Heights, IL: Waveland Press.

Broch, H. B. (1994), On the Influence of Children's Competitive Sports (European Handball) in the Formation of Gender-identity and Roles, *Arbeids notat* 3, Papers from a seminar: *Social Construction of Gender in Children's Worlds*, pp. 42–52. Oslo: University of Oslo, Senter for Kvinneforskning.

—— (1995), Håndball er ingen frøkensport. Antropologiske perspektiv på håndball for gutter og jenter, *Barn*, 2:21–38.

Brownell, S. (2000), Why Should an Anthropologist Study Sports in China? in N. Dyck (ed.), *Games Sports and Cultures*, Oxford: Berg.

Chodorow, N. (1995), Gender as a Personal and Cultural Construction, *Signs*, 20:516–44.

Cox, R. H. (1998), *Sport Psychology. Concepts and Applications*, Boston: WCB/McGraw-Hill.

Duesund, L. (1995), *Kropp, kunnskap og selvoppfatning*, Oslo: Universitetsforlaget.

Dyck, N. (2000), 'Parents, Kids and Coaches: Constructing Sport and Childhood in Canada', in N. Dyck (ed.), *Games, Sports and Culture*, Oxford: Berg.

Eggen, N. A. (1999), *Godfoten. Samhandling – veien til suksess*, Oslo: Aschehoug.

Fasting, K. (1987), Barneidrettens positive og negative konsekvenser for utvikling av psykisk og sosial helse, *Rapport*, 11: 52–72 (Trondheim: NAVF's Senter for barneforskning).

Grogan, S. (1999), *Body Image: Understanding Body Dissatisfaction in Men, Women and Children*, London: Routledge.

Ingham, J. M. (1996), *Psychological Anthropology Reconsidered*. Cambridge: Cambridge University Press.

James, A. (1993), *Childhood Identities. Self and Social Relationships in the Experience of the Child*. Cambridge: Cambridge University Press.

Laberge, S. and M. Albert (2000), Conceptions of Masculinity and Gender Transgressions in Sport Among Adolescent Boys, in J. McKay, A. M. Messner and D. Sabo (eds), *Masculinities, Gender Relations, and Sports*, London: Sage.

Lithman, Yngve Georg (2000), 'Reflections on the Social and Cultural Dimensions of Children's Elite Sport in Sweden', in Noel Dyck (ed.), *Games, Sports and Cultures*, pp. 163–81. Oxford/New York: Berg.

Lupton, D. (1996), *Food, the Body and the Self*. London: Sage.

—— (1999), *Risk*. London: Routledge.

Olsen, K. (1994), Idrett, kropp og grenser, *Norsk antropologisk titdsskrift*, 5:1–14.

Railo, W. (1996), *Den nye Bedst når det gælder*, Copenhagen: Nyt Nordisk Forlag Arnold Busck.

Thorne, B. (1993), *Gender Play. Girls and Boys in School*, Buckingham: Open University Press.

Weiss, M. S. (2000), Culture, Context and Content Analysis: An Exploration of Elite Women Gymnasts in the High School World, in N. Dyck (ed.), *Games, Sports and Cultures,* pp. 183–98. Oxford/New York: Berg.

Part III
Reshaping Adult Identities

5

Long-Distance Football Support and Liminal Identities Among Norwegian Fans
Hans Hognestad

Introduction

As a social and cultural phenomenon analysed in terms of the number of players, media coverage and crowd attendance, it is possible to argue that football has been the most popular sport in Norway ever since the inter-war years (Goksøyr and Hognestad 1999). Yet as a sport modern football has maintained its position as a British invention, and the links to Britain have been strong in the development of the game in Norway throughout the twentieth century. Skiing holds a more central position as a key national symbol and carrier of national virtues linked to both natural geographical conditions and the sociopolitical structure upon which Norwegian society has been developed (ibid). Put stereotypically, a wintry land-scape in the mountains could be singled out as the ideal time and space for sports, rather than a green pitch within a stadium in the city (Hognestad 2001). These preconditions are essential for understanding football support in Norway. In this chapter I have not limited my understanding of 'Norwegian identities' to focusing merely on questions about Norwegian national identity. Nevertheless, dominant national narratives may structure and influence the contestation of identities around football, seen here as a 'liminal' phenomenon. As a hugely popular phenomenon in Norway, football becomes interesting as a possible generator of identities that are liberated from the role of carrying its key national symbols. One hypothesis that might be related to this is whether this position leaves more space for liminal experimentation and options for playing with 'imagined' identities.

A key issue here, drawing on my own research, will be how the widespread support for English clubs in Norway, in which the term 'imagined communities' appears to be a precise one, might also provide liminal worlds that stretch beyond dominant Norwegian national imageries and narratives. The concept of 'imagined communities' has been widely used in academe ever since it was developed by Benedict Anderson (1983), who related it to his accounts of the origins of nationalism. Anderson showed how a national community must be constructed as imagined in order to thrive and to compensate for the absence of a physically shared sociocultural environment amongst its citizens. I argue that, since the communities created around specific local football teams are more real than imagined (cf. Hognestad 1995), long-distance support creates a context in which the sense of belonging to a football club located in another nation leaves more space for imagining identities. In a Norwegian context, football support, as a carnivalesque, liminal cultural form, might be a particularly illuminating case that raises questions about the ways in which the autonomy of supporter groups is constrained by national imageries. This is what the Norwegian anthropologist Tord Larsen once labelled 'anti-ritual' (Larsen 1984). I will comment on Larsen's portrayal of 'national imageries' in greater detail later in the chapter. Significantly, the apparent admiration of English football has not led to a simple adoption of local English football cultural practices. I argue that the passion for English football in Norway should be viewed in relation to Norwegian discourses on sport and as a possible 'individual escape' from more general hegemonic national narratives.

Football Support as Carnival Liminality

In academic discourses on football support it is commonplace to view events and procedures evolving around games as a ritual. For a supporter, games are played with a certain frequency; people might meet in a regular pub to watch games on TV or share a drink before going to watch a game at a ground nearby. The ritual aspects are further manifested through continuous and active support of the team during games. This support is expressed in various ways through symbolic constructions or, sometimes, through violent confrontations with rival fans within a limited time–space frame. If we regard a game of football as a potential ritual, this might include travelling to games and socializing and drinking with other fans before and after a game. This would hold whether we are talking of the local fans of a local club or long-distance fans gathering to watch a game on satellite TV in pubs that specialize in showing football.[1] Through football's male homogeneity it is possible to sense a resonance with Victor Turner's accounts of ritual and liminal phenomena as marked by comradeship between individuals of equal status (Turner 1969: 96). Hence, as a ritual, football contains elements resembling his accounts of *anti-structure* (ibid), indicating a set of norms and moralities that do not necessarily conform to those of the structured everyday life. This also affects the kinds of masculinities that might be expressed and experienced in football (cf. Archetti 1999; Cornwall and Lindisfarne 1994).[2]

Culturally specific versions of football rituals taking place in a complex society are in many ways self-contained, with their own moralities, commitments and loyalties. Viewed from a supporter's perspective, the football-space may be seen

as constitutive of *a different reality*. As a liminal ritual it is conducive to experimentation with verbal expressions and behaviour. In this way the football-space
can partly be regarded as a 'decoupled' space, where the element of play provides
a basis for events unfolding around a match. Entering the ritualized frame around
a football match is, for a supporter, often experienced as passing a threshold, a
limen, where the codes embedded in the immediacy and authenticity of active
support tend to transcend other concerns (Hognestad 1997). Owing to a focus on
expressive and indeed excessively expressive practices, the term 'liminal ritual'
denotes the more collective aspects of supporter practices. A football game can be
a ritual in the manner in which affirmations of identities and of belonging to certain
clubs are confirmed; yet as a liminal world football can also be viewed as a space
in which actuality gives way to possibility and positivity gives way to negativity
(Turner 1992). In brief, it is more inquisitive than affirmative; and, worldwide,
football supporters have been famous for their mockery, sarcasm, parodies and
deriding of authority, resembling Bakhtin's famous depiction of the carnivalesque
(Bakhtin 1968). As a game football has always provided a clear-cut 'us against
them' drama, in which the logical preconditions for conflict, rivalry and a confrontation between potentially opposing identities are fairly obvious (cf. Armstrong and
Giulianotti 1997, 1999). The expression of rivalries in world football is regularly
fuelled by local antagonisms and contrasting social identities. Characterized by an
often-playful negativity from the stands, opposing sides are generally constructed
in terms of a stereotypical otherness during matches (Armstrong 1998; Archetti
1992; Hognestad 1997). Applied to such a local context and viewed from the
supporters' own perspective, 'imagined community' might invoke the wrong
connotations, as the bodily participation of the supporters and their sense of
communitas (Turner 1992) is experienced as real, immediate and authentic more
than as merely imagined (Hognestad 1997).

Despite the massive media coverage and current public interest in football in
Norway, the game still operates on the margins of central national narratives if we
relate the role of football in Norway to traditionally dominant national sports
narratives. Skiing is basically what makes Norway mythologically different as a
nation. It is not uncommon to view skiing as a Norwegian invention, while football
has never been 'our game' in the way British and Latin countries have adopted
football as a national sport. Football and support in Norway are influenced by
international football cultural practices and evolve as more fragmentary and
limited liminal worlds because the participant supporters are unable or unwilling
to integrate some of the central national narratives in their practices. This point is
particularly manifest in comments from long-distance fans who claim that the
presence of Norwegian footballers in their English teams does not affect the ways
they follow and support the teams. As one Manchester United fan noted:

I don't care if the player comes from Kristiansund[3] or Kuala Lumpur so long as the player has proved his quality to perform in the red shirt. I find it ridiculous how Norwegian papers only seem to focus on Norwegian players and their clubs in the coverage of English football. Real supporters support the club. The national origins of the players are of no relevance (Micro, age 25).

During the 1990s there was a great influx of Norwegian footballers to the English leagues, and there are currently 24 Norwegian professionals in England (1 January 2002). My own findings suggest that football support in Norway has a potential 'opportunistic' or esoteric edge in relation to what is considered 'national'. In a sense, as I will get back to later, it allows Norwegian supporters a chance to escape from authorized mythologies of Norwegianness. Connected to questions of what Giddens labels 'late modernity', this might be linked to a general decreasing significance of more unifying traditional identities, which also include social and cultural conditions often associated with modernity, such as class and national identity (Giddens 1991). However, in the world of club football the traditions of the football club, the town or the region stand out as important building-blocks in the symbolic construction of identities. My findings indicate that contemporary football provides a space in which the meanings of 'partisan fanhood' are more focused on local than on national conditions and realities, whether 'the local' means the physically immediate surroundings or the location of a club located elsewhere or in a different country. This is in accordance with what happen in many other footballing nations of the world. National team football is played with a lower frequency and generates substantial interest and passion in connection with the odd big games or international tournaments every second year. The everyday football is played out in the more esoteric universes of clubs on a frequent, week-to-week basis.

The sense of rivalry and hostility witnessed in many football leagues has also been expressed in violent ways for as long as the modern game has existed, and the issue of hooliganism has probably been the most widely researched aspect of football support in different parts of the world. A more limited number of researchers, however, have been aware of the fact that 'the psychosocial buzz of the carnival is . . . not entirely divorced from the liminality of hooligan confrontations' (Giulianotti 1999: 61). This should be tied to what Giulianotti refers to as the 'bodily *jouissance* of carnival', which 'is deeply associated with the possibility of social breakdown' (ibid.). Why then does the history of football support in Norway seem to be more ridden with polite applause than ballistic confrontations?

'Ola Nordmann Is Not a Homo Ludens'

Several foreign researchers and observers have previously suggested that Norway as a society is closer to what we might associate with a traditional society than a modern one (cf. Barnes 1954). Historically, the Continental system of feudalism, implying a very hierarchical social structure, was never adopted in Norway. The building-blocks for a modern Norwegian socialism and welfare ideology in the twentieth century were more influenced by the premodern egalitarian social structure of Norwegian local communities than the hierarchical class struggle witnessed in Britain and continental Europe (cf. Klausen 1999). Kramer (1984) argues that, as a consequence of this historical process bent on promoting equality, difference in general is treated awkwardly even in a more contemporary Norwegian setting. The privileged position of rural areas and ways of life over urban ones has historically been central to nation-building processes in Norway since long before independence in 1905 (cf. Sørensen 1998). In the modern history of the nation, rural community life has maintained its position as a vehicle for national virtues in Norwegian public discourses.

In the postwar-era urbanization and 'the escape from rural regions' has been strongly regarded as an undesirable development by leading politicians, both on the right and the left wing. Throughout this period various Norwegian governments have tried hard to sustain isolated rural communities by funding local industry and improving public infrastructures. The fragmentation associated with modern urban lifestyles is still flatly denied, and hence 'the strategies which maintain a rural ideal in an urban context are moving the rural community into the city' (Larsen 1984: 38). The Norwegian anthropologist Tord Larsen argues that the dominant position of sociopolitical ideals that were historically developed in large part out of more transparent and culturally homogeneous communities has generated a conformist society that gives little legitimacy to 'alternative' cultural expressions or, as we might add, to 'liminal worlds'. A major point in his argument is related to a strategy of 'taming' competing realities into a primary discourse that he labels 'the main reality' (Larsen 1984). Understanding sociocultural expressions in terms of their own premises becomes awkward with such a 'strategy'.

Larsen cites an incident from a 1 May riot[4] in Oslo in the early 1980s and how this was presented in the media. The windows of a shop were smashed in the main shopping street of the capital. In order to 'understand' this incident, some newspaper reporters interpreted these incidents not as ritual games in their own right, but as a sign of social frustration. Hence the smashing of shop windows was translated into more goal-oriented and instrumental interpretations, such as symbolic applications to the job centre or the public housing scheme. Put it in a different way: 'you drink because you can't handle the mortgage, not because you enjoy the drink'. In his arguably paranoid and rather one-dimensional depiction of Norwegian society and Norwegian national identities, Larsen argues that peripheral realities and provinces of meaning become 'responsible' to a primary reality, which is the ending-point and source of legitimacy for all causal explanations. A failure to succeed in such an operation leads to delegitimizing definitions of activities or expressions as either 'irresponsible' or 'sinful' or 'reactionary'.

Underneath such a normative pressure Larsen senses a fear that the journey might stand out as a goal in itself, that the point of the playing is the playing itself, detached from the chain of causality. This prompts him to label Norwegians as 'the masters of hermeneutical, interpretative suspiciousness' (1984: 22). Embraced by an ethos of an 'anti-ritual' character, it becomes impossible to be 'a drinking vicar' or a 'Christian communist' without causing a scandal. Not surprisingly, Larsen concludes that 'Ola Nordmann[5] is not a homo ludens' (1984: 21). A few of Larsen's examples are highly polemical and taken from experiences and observations from his life as a bewildered student in the 1960s and 1970s, examples that now appear somewhat dated in a contemporary context. Yet in his most recent book the Norwegian author Georg Johannessen also writes of current public discourses in Norwegian society as being guided by 'a claustrophobic consensus' in which all paths seem lead to a confirmation of the social democratic 'paradise' (Johannessen 2000). Is it, thus, a nation joined together in polite agreement (and repressed dissent) rather than fierce political conflict and expression of rivalries and opposing identities?

Sports in general have long played a fairly central role in the more general social democratic policies of equalization in Norway, especially since the Second World War. For various historical reasons described above, politeness is also a virtue in Norwegian sportsmanship. Historically, sports have provided a strong pedagogical instrument for promoting reconciliation and friendship, while the expression of passionate antagonisms has been disapproved of by various public bodies. There was a strong social incentive in the way that organized sports, heavily funded by the state in the postwar era, were valued for bridging the class divide and enhancing the national policies of social equalization (Goksøyr, Asdal and Andersen 1996).

In contrast to the emphases placed elsewhere on rivalry and conflict, Norwegian football has been more influenced by the ideals of a national sports movement committed to unification and consensus (cf. Goksøyr, Andersen and Asdal 1996). Positive support for teams has dominated supporter practices in the Norwegian league, rather than the dynamic negativity and the notorious hooligan practices witnessed in leagues elsewhere in the world (cf. Goksøyr and Hognestad 1999). The limited legitimacy of the participating, active spectator in Norway is indicated by the fact that in the Norwegian language there is no equivalent word for 'fan' or 'supporter', even though the more general term 'patriot' is sometimes applied. The most common word is the neutral term *tilhenger*, which literally means 'trailer', associated with a more passive spectator without autonomy. Traditionally, the morally correct and most legitimate participant in sports in Norway has been the athlete and not the spectator, whose 'participation' is ideally restricted to polite and positive applause (ibid.). It is within this context that the lack of adoption of British hooligan practices among Norwegian supporters must be understood. This relates both to fan culture surrounding Norwegian club football and the long-distance support of English teams.

However, the dawning of a few smaller groups of fans supporting Norwegian club teams in a more militant fashion has generated substantial public debate around the issues of sportsmanship and codes of conduct on the terraces. The autonomous, partisan supporter has generally been regarded with suspicion in public Norwegian sports contexts, especially if his behaviour entails exhibiting sarcasm or behaviour viewed as a threat to the normative and educational ambitions of the authoritative voices within Norwegian sports. This was ably demonstrated when an incident of verbal abuse at a premier league match between Tromsø and Rosenborg in 1994 hit the front page of a major tabloid newspaper (Goksøyr and Hognestad 1999). Discussion of topics relating to codes of conduct among players as well as supporters is a recurrent theme in the Norwegian media. In recent years a number of limited hooligan confrontations, especially involving fans of Brann and Vålerenga, have been reported, signalling a new trend. Yet support within Norwegian club football remains a relatively peaceful and marginal phenomenon in its overall impact upon how the game is structured in Norway.

Imagining Liminal Worlds from a Distance? Norwegian Support for English Football Clubs

It is interesting to learn that Norwegian football support is strongly linked to a British universe that sees many Norwegian fans supporting English clubs from a distance. One hypothesis that could be launched here is that such support is rooted in a quest for liminal experiences and identity, which are more awkwardly obtained within Norwegian societies. The historical background for this particular 'anglophilia' in Norway is complex. The interest in English football among the Norwegian public can be dated back to the introduction of the game in the 1880s. It was due in part to the number of English and Scottish coaches active in Norway in the early years and to a significant number of exhibition matches played there in the early twentieth century that involved English and Scottish clubs. Results and league tables from English football were printed in Norwegian sports magazines as early as in 1903, the year after The Norwegian Football Association was founded. Hence press coverage of English football started at about the same time as coverage of games between Norwegian teams or between Norwegian and foreign teams, many of which in the early years were recruited from the crews of British naval ships visiting Norwegian towns. As early as 1896 there is a tiny note in an issue of the periodical *Norsk Idrætsblad* about the apparently exotic realization that: '40.000 spectators attended a football match between Liverpool and Everton recently'.[6] The number of spectators and the sheer human density with which football in Britain evolved seemed to contribute to the construction of a magical and exotic phenomenon in the Norwegian press from a very early stage. The first reports of football matches involving English or Scottish teams were marked by pedagogical, instructive comments, accompanied with a servile attitude towards the British. This was often reflected both in the direct application of English football lingo,[7] rather than translating English terms into Norwegian, which did take place at a later stage, and in relevant reports and comments, which were often flavoured with overt signs of admiration of the British.

Professional teams from both England and Scotland played matches against Norwegian teams at an early stage. In fact the first three professional teams to visit Norway were all Scottish: Celtic (1911), and Rangers and Hearts (both in1912). Hearts visited Oslo in May 1912 and played two matches against a Kristiania[8] Select team and a Grenland[9] Select team. An enthused journalist of the periodical *Sport* wrote of the game between the Scots and Grenland Select:

A substantial number of interested football spectators met up at Frogner[10] yesterday to see the foreshadowed match between the Scottish professionals and the team from outside the capital that's name has the best ring to it. The weather was excellent and the pitch was in perfect condition. The same thrilling excitement overwhelmed us, on this occasion like so many times before in similar situations at our dear Frogner, when proper first class football has been approaching. The Grenland team . . . were brave, well proportioned fellows, and there was a tiny hope in my chest that progress in technical regard among the Norwegian boys should give hope before the summer's big event in Stockholm.[11] Unfortunately, from the first minute, the Scots' superiority was evident in the lack of technique and precision in the passing among the Norwegian boys.[12]

Coverage of Scottish football in the Norwegian press has always been rare, but by the 1920s news and brief reports from the larger English league had become a regular feature in the daily press. The Norwegian newspaper *Aftenposten* was a pioneer in this respect, even though their first reports of English football only covered London teams – no doubt a reflection of the fact that their correspondent was positioned there. In 1946 the Norwegian Parliament lifted the ban on betting, and soon after the state-run *Norsk Tipping* ('Norwegian Pools') was established. The first coupon in 1948 consisted purely of English matches, and English games have since the beginning generated greater betting turnovers than Norwegian games (Goksøyr and Hognestad 1999).

The popular status of English football in Norway was firmly established with the introduction of the live Saturday match on the Norwegian Broadcasting Channel (NRK) in 1969. *Tippekampen*, which became the vernacular term for the live English game, was shown during the long winter break in the domestic Norwegian league (ibid.). At a time of media monopoly, English football became accessible as the only alternative for those wishing to watch TV on a wintry Saturday afternoon. This is one factor that needs to be taken into account when explaining the fact that, while support for football is highly dominated by males, it is in class terms quite heterogeneous. In a survey conducted among Norwegian fans of English football teams in 2000[13] the respondents' occupations range from doctors and teachers to factory workers and students. In a society historically less marked by class divides than most European nations, working-class people did not stamp football with their own values in the same way as they did in Britain (cf. Hargreaves 1986).

One effect of the globalization and commercialization of English football is that long-distance fans with spending power from affluent societies such as Norway have during recent decades become more significant as customers of the football industry. The huge increase during the 1990s and into the new millennium of live English football televised by various commercially run TV-stations such as Sky Sports has given rise to a new and more interactive trend. This sees Norwegian supporters of the same English team gathering in specialized sports pubs to watch games in a closer simulation of the match-day experience of actually 'being there'. Moreover, many supporters extend these gatherings into travelling to watch games in England as well. Judging from the findings from our survey, every Norwegian fan travels on average approximately twice a year and spends up to £1,000 for each trip, all expenses included. Hence Norwegians travelling to watch football in England represent a substantial business.

During the 1970s and 1980s numerous Norwegian or Scandinavian-based supporters clubs[14] for English teams were established. In 1985 *Supporterunionen for britisk fotball* (The Supporters Union for British Football) was founded in Norway, comprising most of the supporter clubs for British teams. In 2001 the organization had a total membership of 55,000. While most of these are members of supporters clubs for the bigger teams, we have witnessed a new trend in the last decade or so in which supporters clubs for lower-division teams that have never appeared on Norwegian television have been established. This supports the assumption that television coverage is not the sole cause of the popularity of English football in Norway.

As part of fieldwork conducted among Norwegian supporters of English football teams I watched a televised league match between Macclesfield and

Darlington (in the English Third Division) in a pub in Oslo together with 12 Norwegian Macclesfield fans in September 2000. They were not joking about their support, and demonstrated a remarkable knowledge about players and club history, all the while complaining about the decisions of the manager, bad refereeing and players' performances on the pitch. 'Twynham; did he come from Darlington?' 'No, he played for Man. United and Hednesford.' 'What about Bulldog, who did he play for before?' 'When was Player X born?' 'We would much rather put on Whitehead than Glover.' 'Hedgemore [after scoring] is a great player. I voted for him as my player of the year last season.' Then there were more general questions concerning teams and players in the lower divisions: 'Who is that new 20-year-old at Millwall? What's his name again?' A 20-year old boy from Sandnes, a town located just south of Stavanger in the south-western part of Norway, explained that a computer game was the origin of his support for Macclesfield. Throughout the match the chairman of the supporters club demonstrates a bit of local knowledge about Macclesfield by telling me it used to be renowned for its silk industries – hence the football team's nickname, the 'Silkmen'. The chairman, a former teacher and now a sports journalist for a major Norwegian tabloid paper, claims he spends almost as much time working on their fanzine 'Silkmen News' as on his paid work. The fanzine was voted 'Fanzine of the Year' by the Supporters Union for British football last year for its profound articles and extensive news on Macclesfield FC.

Making Dreams Real; Explorations into the English Football Universe

Over the last decade many 'anglophile' Norwegian football fans have developed what amount to personal football geographies during their tours around England, visiting small towns and big cities and in some cases establishing locally based social networks around their support for several teams. In the process of doing this, the social and cultural aspects rather than the performances on the football pitch stand out as the most important elements. The joy of a 'match day' is insolubly linked to socializing, drinking and talking to locals and meeting English friends. These embodied explorations into the English football universe break down the more imagined relationship to the various clubs in England, often based on a duality between local Norwegian and English footballing worlds.

In March 2000 and January 2001 I followed some fans of the Norwegian team Brann Bergen, whose tour included visiting friends in Evesham, Rotherham and Middlesbrough and watching games in Chesterfield and Middlesbrough. Two brothers support Arsenal and Middlesbrough as their English teams, but occasionally wear the shirt of their Norwegian team, Brann, during footballing missions to England. Semiotically this signifies that their Norwegian club comes first, while generating puzzlement and curiosity among local English fans, inviting the question: 'Who are you'? This generates options for more community-based networking between Norwegian and English supporters. These explorations, often conducted into the depths of lower-division football in England, plunge the issue of support back from an issue of an imagined community into a reality in which socializing with their local English counterparts stands at the fore. This approach also explains an often-indifferent attitude towards Norwegian national team football. Bjarte (aged 37, a Brann and Middlesbrough fan) explains the privilege of 'the' club by stating that:

> I take little interest in the [Norwegian] national team. The real football, the week-in, week-out stuff is to be found on a club level. I would never buy a ticket to follow the national team. If you ask me to divide my loyalties I'd probably say that the support for Brann takes up 50%, Middlesbrough 49%, while 1% is left to watch the odd game with the national team on TV or reading about it in the papers.

Football as a door opener for new friendships and a widening of the access of their anglophile football geographies holds a clear privilege over the 'imagined community' constructed around the support for the national Norwegian team. This is quite parallel to what Gary Armstrong has found during his research in Malta, in which 'the tradition of Maltese support for English and Italian teams has become more important than support for the national team' (Armstrong and Mitchell 1999: 103). The significant difference between the Maltese and the Norwegian support for English teams consists in the former's genealogical link with England. Nearly all the Maltese fans are of English descent (ibid.).

Even at the club level, the English teams may be preferred to the local ones. A Manchester United fan compared his affection for United and his local club Viking Stavanger by stating that he was really more interested in Manchester United's reserve team than in Viking. In fact, when Viking won the Norwegian league championship in 1991, a picture of a fan celebrating in a Manchester United shirt was printed in a local paper the next day, underlining the impression of a highly schizophrenic community. In games between the national teams of Norway and England many Norwegians continued to support England well into the 1990s, a decade in which Norwegian football experienced considerable sporting success. When Norway beat England 2–1 in a World Cup qualifying match in Oslo in 1981 this came as a shock to the Norwegian public. A supporter and, more recently, a former director of a Norwegian Premier League club remembers the game like this:

> That was one of the strangest days of my life. To think that Norway should beat England was inconceivable at the time. It was something which we believed could never happen.

And I . . . didn't know know what to think or feel. When I walked up to Ullevaal Stadium that day I entered the end where the England fans were and . . . I mean what was Norway then? It was garbage, right? National team coaches saying things like 'Oh shit, we've got the Soviets in our group' or 'We've got England in our group . . . well, well, we'd better try to limit the defeats.' The national team was a joke. How could anyone support such lack of morale?

On a club level, Norwegian Brann and Liverpool fans went through a similar moral bewilderment when the two teams unexpectedly drew each other in the quarter finals of the European Cup Winners' Cup in March 1997 (see Goksøyr and Hognestad 1999). The admiration for English teams prevailed in Norwegian discourses on football throughout the twentieth century. A man aged around 50, currently working in a football pub in Oslo called Highbury, named after the London-based club Arsenal's home ground, remembers how his father, a sailor, talked about Arsenal as the ultimate contrast to the standards of Norwegian football in the late 1950s, especially as they were watching games with their local team, Frigg F. K. from Oslo:

. . . when the boys were in London, looking out for a football match – and this was in the 1930s – they went to Highbury, of course. Arsenal were the big team then. Therefore when we were at Bislet [a previous homeground for Frigg F.K.] he usually complained about the standards of Norwegian football, often punctuated with phrases like 'You should have watched Arsenal.' This was the sort of remark he used to feed me with from the age of seven.

It is within a climate of loathing one's own local teams for their general useless-ness on an international level that English football fuelled Norwegian imaginations and established a paradigmatic standard that local or national teams could not provide. It is within this context that the attraction of English football provides a possible creative space for hybridization (Archetti 1999), in which the geo-graphical distance itself generates options for a more liberated and imaginative playing with identities. Long-distance support in football may generate exper-iences that usually render the concrete realities that support for the club has grown out of less significant. A long-distance supporter develops a fairly abstract 'liminal space' in which news of and concern for the sporting performances of the club are actual enough. But these evolve parallel to a more imagined reality constructed around the club as a dream object, providing a space for playing in and with a different reality. The anthropologist Nigel Rapport says that 'Play amounts to a stepping out of "real life", temporarily but regularly, into a discrete domain with a distinctive disposition and meaningfulness – a meaningfulness often at odds with the order of the real world, . . . space is left for further "pure", "sacred play" periodically to reassert itself' (Rapport 1997: 109).

My findings suggest that for a Norwegian fan visiting the home ground of his beloved English club it is the dreamlike imagination of the club and an almost sacred depiction of the ground in which it plays that dominate. A Norwegian supporter of West Bromwich Albion (WBA), a club hailing from Birmingham, went on a footballing pilgrimage to England in October 1998, together with four friends who all support different teams. The trip was thus planned so that they all got to see each of 'their teams' once. The other teams in question were Fulham, Liverpool, Leeds and Ipswich Town. The West Bromwich supporter described his experiences from his first trip to 'The Hawthorns', the stadium of his club, located on the border between Sandwell Borough and Birmingham, like this:

> The morning came and we all boarded the train that was to take us to 'Football's Mecca': The Hawthorns. We got a taxi from the station to the ground. Suddenly the driver stopped the taxi so that I could see and touch the walls of the ground of my team, WBA. A dream came true. I got my camera out and eternalized a few moments, which I will carry with me all my life . . . before the match we went for a quick beer in the local pub until we actually entered the holiest site: The Hawthorns. Just entering the ground, enjoying the view and inhaling the atmosphere from the fans was an answer to a twenty-year-long dream. Wonderful!!!
> (Taken from *The Albion*,[15] no. 4–98. Original text in Norwegian, my translation.)

A point here related to the length of 'the dream' indicates an origin dating back to the late 1970s, when West Bromwich had a relatively successful team.[16] Today, however, the club is struggling to survive in the First Division, and there is every chance that 'neutrals' visiting their ground would not refer to it as 'a holy site'.

The current support for many teams can be at least partly explained with reference to a glorious, but highly temporary, period dating a few years back. This goes for the relatively large number of Norwegians still supporting teams like Derby, Stoke, Queen's Park Rangers and Leeds. However, success is not the only, and perhaps not even the most common, element in the origins of support. In the survey mentioned above one of the respondents, a Derby County fan and dentist living in Karasjok, the Lappish part of the very north of Norway, writes that when he was five and a half years old he told his parents that he wanted a blue bag. He continues: 'On the blue bag it read "Derby County Football Club". This was to exert a significant influence on my emotions and state of mind for the rest of my life.'

Among dedicated fans, English football provides options for carving out distinctions that are highly individualistic, almost private, for some fans, and hence comparable to Bourdieu's caricature of how members of the French bourgeoisie might dedicate themselves to a certain opera or composer (Bourdieu 1984: 18–19). When given the opportunity, long-distance fans travel and actively explore the physical and human surroundings of their beloved football club. Either way, for the dedicated long-distance supporter, the relationship to one specific club is generally experienced as lifelong and irreplaceable, by comparison with the norms and virtues existing in local club communities (cf. Hognestad 1997). Further, the physical presence of Norwegian fans at English football grounds has become so common that local English fans no longer treat them as 'exotic' others. Before a league match in London in October 2001 between Arsenal and Blackburn, Steve, a local Arsenal fan, noted that: 'We don't really look upon Norwegian fans, or Scandinavians for that matter, as outsiders to the game any more. It is so common to see them here we almost treat them as locals.'

However, most 'anglophile' football supporters in Norway were initiated into an imagined community from a distance, often out of a random incident or choice, in most cases relying heavily upon media coverage. Hence we might label Norwegian supporters of English clubs a kind of 'postmodern fan' to take account of the way their support is detached from their immediate local or national universe. Long-distance football support may in certain ways be related to general debates on diasporic identities; yet in this case there are usually none of the links with a lost country or considerations of genealogical decent that often form the basis for such an identity. Furthermore, these abstract and imaginative relationships to English football have been accompanied or perhaps extended into more concrete explorations and expeditions into the English football universe. In many ways this plunges the issue of a postmodern kind of supporter back to a reality in which localization and concrete encounters with the 'dream object' in question are the most important elements.

The concepts of imagined communities and liminal worlds have in this chapter not been viewed as mutually exclusive phenomena. Even though it could be argued that they move in slightly different theoretical directions, they are also highly complementary in aiding an understanding of how Norwegian identities are constructed within the context of football support. 'Imagined communities' appears to be a relevant concept for understanding Norwegians who support English football clubs. At the same time I have shown how Norwegian supporters relate to 'their' clubs in ways that are more focused on local than national contexts. Yet their concrete explorations of local English football create conditions for transforming the purely imagined into an embodied experience of a 'real' community.

Football never made Norway 'different'. Football is not 'our game' (Goksøyr 1994). This may in part explain why autonomous liminal worlds are, for Norwegians, more likely to evolve within football than, say, in the traditional winter sports, leaving more space for individual or collective experimentation and imaginings. Norwegians supporting an English club in a dedicated way can thus come to represent an example of a semi-public and sometimes almost private liminal space in which the imagined community is located outside the national universe altogether. Generally, in our age individuals have possibilities for building their identities across national boundaries (Giddens 1991). In a society that puts substantial pressure upon integration, the 'fragmentation' of liminal spaces may be regarded as threatening. The normative urge to integrate and rationalize the expressions and actions taking place in liminal spaces becomes hypothetically all the more urgent in such societies.

Notes

1. In recent years a large number of pubs specializing in showing live football matches on TV have been established in Norwegian as well as many other European communities. Fans meet up in pubs dressed in their respective club strips to watch games.
2. During my research among supporters of the Scottish football club Hearts I found that football provided an option for men to meet and socialize in a 'libero' version of manhood. This allowed them to act in ways that in other contexts would be regarded as 'feminine', such as expressing grief or 'delirious joy' (Hognestad 1995).
3. This is a reference to the Norwegian town that Ole Gunnar Solskjaer, one of the most prolific goalscorers at Manchester United, hails from.
4. In several European cities the night before the first of May, The International Worker's Day, has for various reasons been the occasion for riots or disturbances. In Oslo disturbances without obvious political links or aims occurred for a few years in the early 1980s, but the phenomenon had more or less died out by the mid-1980s.
5. A term frequently used to describe the stereotypical Norwegian male.
6. *Norsk Idrætsblad*, 5 Nov. 1896.
7. It was not uncommon to use terms such as 'football' (current Norwegian term: *fotball*), 'match' (Norw.: *kamp*) and 'points' (Norw.: *poeng*) in reports and comments from football matches in the early years.
8. 'Kristiania' was the name given to the reconstructed Norwegian capital by the ruling Danish King, Chrstian IV, after the great fire in 1624. Three hundred years later, in 1923 (some eighteen years after Norway gained independence from the Swedes) the citizens of the capital voted for the reintroduction of the old pre-1624 Nordic name 'Oslo'.
9. Grenland is an industrial district in the south-eastern part of Norway that had a pioneering role in the introduction of football to Norway, in large part owing to the influence of numerous British engineers employed by industrial companies in the district.
10. The name of the West End Township in which the oldest combined football ground (summer) and speed-skating oval (winter) is located in Oslo.
11. The Summer Olympics were held in Stockholm that summer. The Norwegian national side lost 7–0 to Denmark in the first game and was knocked out of the

tournament. In games between Heart of Midlothian and the select teams of Kristiania and Grenland, the Scottish side won 9–0 and 6–0 respectively – not unrepresentative scorelines for the early matches between Norwegian teams and British professional sides.

12. *Sport*, 16 May 1912.
13. One thousand questionnaires with 57 questions were sent out to members of Norwegian supporter clubs; 711 responded. The survey was conducted by Hans Hognestad and Svein Morten Gulbrandsen, a journalist and employee in the Norwegian Sports Player Organization (NISO).
14. The All-Scandinavian-based supporters clubs have an overwhelming number of Norwegian supporters.
15. A fanzine for West Bromwich Albion FC Supporters Club, Scandinavian Branch.
16. Despite gaining promotion to the top division again in 2002 for the first time since 1985, they are far from being considered a top club in England.

References

Anderson, Benedict (1983), *Imagined Communities: Reflections on the Origin and Spread of Nationalism*, London: Verso.

Archetti, E. P. (1992), 'Argentinian Football: A Ritual of Violence?', *The International Journal of the History of Sport*, vol. 9: 2.

—— (1999), *Masculinities: Football, Polo and the Tango in Argentina*, Oxford/New York: Berg.

Armstrong, Gary (1998), *Knowing the Score*, Oxford/New York: Berg.

Armstrong, G. and R. Giulianotti (eds) (1997), *Entering the Field – New Perspectives on World Football*, Oxford/New York: Berg.

—— and —— (1999), *Football Cultures and Identities*, London: Macmillan.

Armstrong, G. and J. P. Mitchell (1999), 'Making the Maltese Cross: Football on a Small Island', in G. Armstrong and R. Giulianotti (eds), *Football Cultures and Identities*, London: Macmillan.

Bakhtin, M. (1968), *Rabelais and His World*, Cambridge, MA: Massachusetts Institute of Technology Press.

Barnes, J. A. (1954), 'Class and Committees in a Norwegian Island Parish', *Human Relations*, vol. 7: 1.

Bourdieu, P. (1984), *Distinction: A Social Critique of the Judgement of Taste*, translated by Richard Nice, London: Routledge and Kegan Paul.

Cornwall, A. and N. Lindisfarne (1994), 'Dislocating Masculinity: Gender, Power and Anthropology', in A. Cornwall and N. Lindisfarne (eds), *Dislocating Masculinities: Comparative Ethnographies*, London: Routledge.

Giddens, A. (1991), *Modernity and Self-Identity; Self and Society in the Late Modern Age*, Cambridge: Polity Press.

Giulianotti, R. (1999), *Football: A Sociology of the Global Game*, Cambridge: Polity Press.

Goksøyr, M. (1994), 'Norway and the World Cup: Cultural Diffusion, Sportification and Sport as a Vehicle for Nationalism', in J. Sugden and A. Tomlinson (eds), *Hosts and Champions*, Aldershot: Arena.

Goksøyr, M. and H. Hognestad (1999), 'No Longer Worlds Apart? British Influences in Norwegian Football', in G. Armstrong and E. Giulianotti (eds), *Football Cultures and Identities*, London: Macmillan.

Goksøyr, M., Asdal, K. and Andersen, E. (1996), *Kropp, kultur og tippekamp – Stattens idrettskontor STUI og Idrettsavdelingen 1946–1996*, Oslo: Universitetsforlaget.

Hargreaves, J. (1986), *Sport, Power and Culture: A Social and Historical Analysis of Popular Sports in Britain*, Cambridge: Polity Press.

Hognestad, H. (1995), 'The Jambo Experience – Identity, Meaning and Social Practice Among Supporters of Heart of Midlothian Football Club', unpublished thesis, Institute of Social Anthropology, University of Oslo.

—— (1997), 'The Jambo Experience – An Anthropological Study of Hearts Fans', in G. Armstrong and R. Giulianottti (eds), *Entering the Field – New Perspectives on World Football*, Oxford/New York: Berg.

—— (2001), 'Viking and Farmer Armies: The Stavanger–Bryne Norwegian Football Rivalry', in G. Armstrong and R. Giulianotti (eds), *Fear and Loathing in World Football*, Oxford, Berg.

Johannesen, G. (2000), *Litteraturens norske nullpunkt – essay*, Oslo: Cappelen.

Klausen, A. M. (1999), 'Introduction', in A. M. Klausen (ed, *Olympic Games as Performance and Public Event: The Case of the XVII Winter Olympic Games in Norway*, pp. 1–8, Oxford/New York: Berghahn.

Kramer, J. (1984), 'Norsk identitet – et produkt av underutvikling og stammetilhørighet', in A. M. Klauasen (ed.), *Den norske væremåten*, Oslo: Cappelen.

Larsen, T. (1984), 'Bønder i byen – på jakt etter den norske konfigurasjonen', in A. M. Klausen (ed.), *Den norske væremåten*, Oslo: Cappelen.

Rapport, R. (1997), *Transcendent Individual – Towards a Literary and Liberal Anthropology*, London/New York: Routledge.

Sørensen, Ø. (ed.) (1998), *Jakten på det norske – perspektiver på utviklingen av en norsk nasjonal identitet på 1800-tallet*, Oslo: Ad Notam Gyldendal.

Turner, V. (1969), *The Ritual Process,* New York: Cornell University Press.

—— (1992), *Blazing the Trail: Way Marks in the Exploration of Symbols*, Tucson, AZ: University of Arizona Press.

6

'Ladies, Just Follow His Lead!' *Salsa*, Gender and Identity

Heike Wieschiolek

During the last decade much has been written about the lack of studies on dance in the past, the reasons for the earlier neglect of this subject in anthropology and its present popularity (Blacking 1985; Hanna 1987; Polhemus 1993; Reed 1998; Spencer 1985; Ward 1993; Washabaugh 1998; Wulff 2001). There have been various points of departure to describe the nature, meanings and features of dance. The most important of these, and the most motivating reason for more anthropological research into dance, has been the close connection between dance and society. I will elaborate on this argument, which I regard as crucial for understanding the relevance of the anthropology of dance, and then draw some conclusions about methods to be used for the study of dance. My empirical research into *salsa* dancing in the city of Hamburg, Germany, will be used to illustrate my considerations.[1]

The Epistemological Qualities of the Anthropology of Dance

To understand the nature of the connection between dance and society one has to be aware of the fact that dance, and even single movements, are always shaped by culture. As Ted Polhemus argues, 'culture in its broadest sense is embodied in the form of physical culture and this in turn is stylized and schematized in the form of dance' (Polhemus 1993: 4–11; Brownell 2000: 51). Posture, gestures, basic movements and physical tension vary in different societies, and are quite resistant to change (Birdwhistell 1970). Society creates dance, thus turning dance into 'the metaphysics of culture' (Polhemus 1993: 8). Therefore, dance is a tool 'most appropriate to the study of any specific situation or society' (Spencer 1985:38). As early as 1937 Curt Sachs wrote:

> If the dance, inherited from brutish ancestors, lives in all mankind as a necessary motor-rhythmic expression of excess energy and the joy of living, then it is only of slight importance for anthropologists and social historians. If it is established, however, that an inherited predisposition develops in many ways in the different groups of man and

its force of direction is related to other phenomena of civilization, the history of dance will then be of great importance for the study of mankind (Sachs 1937: 12).

The methodological consequence of this statement is that if one tries to understand a given form of dance, one has to know the cultural setting in which it is performed (cf. Polhemus 1993: 9; Spencer 1985: 38; Wulff 2001). Movements and postures in dance obtain their meaning from the context in which they are performed, and are only comprehensible within this context.

The study of forms and practices of dancing makes a deeper understanding of a given society possible because of the close connection between culture and dance. Developments in dance can be understood as reflections of trends in the economic and social sphere (cf. Klein 1992: 279). Many authors even argue that the non-verbal nature of dance as communication provides more and better information about a society than verbal media. Judith L. Hanna describes dance as being language-like (1988: 13–15) and claims that dance as 'a physical instrument or symbol for feeling and/or thought . . . is sometimes a more effective medium than verbal language in revealing needs and desires. . . . The dance medium often comes into play where there is a lack of verbal expression' (1987: 4). Thus, ideas or feelings that cannot (yet) be articulated in speech may be expressed collectively or individually through dance (Blacking 1985: 65; cf. Archetti 1999: 18; Polhemus 1993: 14).

Even though dance is closely related to culture, forms of dance can be transferred from one social and/or cultural context to another. At first glance this may seem to contradict my reasoning, as well as the views of many dance scholars who argue that specific forms of dance are connected to the cultural, social and historical constraints of their development and, consequently, are functional and comprehensible only in their specific contexts (e.g. Brake 1985; Frith 1988; Martin 1967). If a certain form of dance is nevertheless adopted in another cultural setting it will often be considered as a simple imitation. The interpretation of hiphop provides a good example for this kind of thinking: only hiphop performed by black male youths from American ghettos is considered to be authentic. Hiphop performed by middle-class Europeans, on the other hand, is considered to be artificial and without meaning. However, the fact that Western music and dance have long been influenced by African styles of music and dance, along with the current globalization of the music business – which brings new trends to each and every corner of the world, where they are taken up and transformed – reveals the shortcomings of this concept of authenticity. This phenomenon is too significant to be dismissed as mere imitation. It is more likely that elements of foreign cultures are adopted, dismantled, bricolaged, reinterpreted and integrated into the culture of the absorbing group. As Archetti (1999: 193) points out, Latin America sports originating in the UK (such as football) or the US (baseball) or dance styles (such as *samba, danzón* or *tango*) that have African and European as well as American roots were nevertheless incorporated into their respective Latin American national identities. These bodily practices of sport or dance serve the production of masculinities.

The idea of transferring a form of dance from one cultural or social context to another challenges scientific ways of thinking, as well as popular concepts. According to a widespread explanatory system,[2] the ability to dance is considered to be almost a matter of genes, which individuals from certain cultural groups possess and those from other groups lack. Particularly, members of non-industrial societies and of black communities are believed to be good dancers by birth. White Europeans and Americans, on the other hand, are expected to be poor dancers (with the exception of gay people). Ward (1993: 18) argues convincingly that it is the assumed 'essential non-rationality of dance' that produces the popular idea that 'as a non-verbal form of communication, dance is more important within pre-literate than other social structures'. As a consequence, in rational, industrial societies dance is regarded as a peripheral activity or is restricted to marginal groups or youths (who are constructed as living in a kind of transitional and marginal world). These popular ideas have influenced the response to Afro-American dance styles in Europe considerably.

Coming back to the connections between dance and culture, another remarkable aspect has to be mentioned: dance is not only shaped by society and its development, but may also influence society (Wulff 2001: 5). For dance can constitute a 'free' zone that is not an object of official and/or civic control like other public spheres. It can 'permit the articulation of languages and practices that can challenge an official and puritanical public domain' (Archetti 1999: 18). Thus Blacking argues that dance may change people's minds and consequently their conditions of life: 'Performances of dance and music frequently reflect and reinforce existing ideas and institutions, but they can also stimulate the imagination and help to bring coherence to the sensuous life, the "intelligence of feeling" . . . that in turn can affect motivation, commitment, and decision making in other spheres of social life' (1985: 65). And Blacking concludes: 'Just as some dance teachers insist that one moves as one thinks, so a change of movement may generate a change of mind' (1985: 69). This does not mean that experiences of dance alone can change political or social attitudes, but that dancing and the interpretation or reinterpretation of dance may challenge former experiences and expand the consciousness of dancers and spectators (ibid.).

The potential of the anthropology of dance may be exiting and promising, but we have to be cautious of functionalist interpretations of dance. In the past scholars too often described dance as a safety valve, as an organ of social control, a tool for education and the transmission of culture, or as a means of resistance, as escapism, etc. (cf. Spencer 1985). The most common interpretation of the function of dance in a Western context is the notion of dance as providing a meeting-place for potential marriage partners (cf. Ward 1993: 20ff.). These simplifying functionalist interpretations of dance point to the fact that the 'essential non-rationality of dance' (Ward 1993: 18) may be somewhat frightening to scholars, who feel the need for explaining the inexplicable. As Wittman (1987: 85, quoted by Ward 1993: 30) states:

> Dancing is intact and self-sufficient – and all the struggling to find proper meaning is only necessary because we have been so brainwashed by our social and sexual conditioning. I believe that these dances are not sacred in some symbolic way – they are not representational of some greater truth. They *are* that truth, pure and simple.

Some Methodological Considerations

The subject of dance raises some methodological difficulties for the researcher. I have already mentioned the necessity of considering the cultural, social, economic, and historical context of a dance event. Furthermore, the problem of the description of intricate physical movements and motions that are difficult to verbalize has to be addressed. The existing standardized notation systems for the transcription of movements (Labanotation, Benesh, Eskhol-Wachmann) are hard to learn, and particularly well suited for recording ballet and other Western dance forms. But their application to non-Western dances causes translation problems. However, even well-tried and recent techniques, such as photography, film, or video, may not be entirely suitable, because they always imply the danger of cultural selectivity (Wulff 2001: 5).

Considering the fact that movements and postures obtain their meaning from the context in which they are performed, and are only comprehensible within this context, the description of the visible features of dance and movement does not provide a sufficient basis for an anthropology of dance. Moreover, forms of dance can be transferred to other settings, which involves the interpretation of movements and the attachment of new meanings to them. We have to be aware that dance has no universal meaning, but rather a meaning that is created in a specific situation, time and place by the participant dancers and spectators.

Consequently, the most important information about the meaning of a dance is contained in the statements of actors, spectators and other participants in a dance event. Their perceptions and interpretations and their accounts of how dancing affects their lives are of particular importance.[3] The non-verbal nature of dance, however, raises some fundamental questions. Movement seems to resist translation into verbal language. The discourse of dance, like any non-verbal communication, involves the expression of the unspeakable, because verbal language has another quality, another grammar and logic than dance – dance and verbal language are two different 'modes of discourse' (Blacking 1985: 67). Thus, even talking with the participants in a dance event about their perceptions is no easy way out of this dilemma. Dancers often have problems explaining their dancing experiences, because dancing and talking about dance are two ways of expressing oneself, which are not easily reconcilable. They often hint at internal or external 'forces' that direct them, or talk about 'being danced'. However, the researcher should take care not to interpret these kinds of statements as proof of an altered state of mind. '[T]he experience of "being danced", far from being a passive reaction to external forces, is a consequence of actively sharing a non-verbal mode of discourse . . . whose logic and forms can be precisely expressed and understood, but not always clearly articulated in words' (Blacking 1985: 66–7).

It is thus particularly important to pay attention to the perceptions of dancers and spectators and to the ways their narratives are developed and shaped. It is important to pay attention to what they say about their experiences and inter- pretations as well as to the *way* they say it. The language they use, the metaphors they choose, the analogies they draw may reveal more than the content itself, and much more than a video tape or an analysis of their movements (cf. Blacking 1985: 65).

These methodological considerations were the starting-point for my case-study of *salsa* dancing in Hamburg. Apart from persevering, persistent and very active participant observation I listened to the narratives of dancers about what they were doing and experiencing, why they did it and how the global phenomenon of the *salsa* boom affected their lives.

The Global Salsa Boom

Even for people who are not particularly interested in dance, the triumphant rise of Latin music and dance all over the world must be striking. Wherever you are, you will hear some kind of Latin music: in discos, on the radio, in TV commercials, as background music in shops and bars, in concert venues or on the internet. Styles of Latin music range from the songs of top earners like Ricky Martin or Jennifer López to the Old Guard of Cuban *son* like Ibrahim Ferrer or Rubén Gonzáles to a multitude of *salsa*, *merengue* and *bachata* bands from the Caribbean, the US, Latin America, Africa or Europe.

I want to concentrate on one musical phenomenon, on *salsa*. To clarify relations between *salsa* and Latin music in general I have to elucidate briefly the history of *salsa*. *Salsa* music has been a hybrid from the very start. Thus, *salsa* was not really a musical style, as the famous *salsero* Willie Colón (1999: 7) explains: '*Salsa* is not a rhythm. It is a *concept*. An open, ever-evolving musical, cultural, socio-political CONCEPT.'

This concept developed during the 1960s and 1970s in 'El Barrio', New York's Latin American neighbourhoods. It was rooted in a variety of Caribbean musical styles like Cuban *son*, *guajira* and *guaracha* and Puerto Rican *plena* and *bomba*. These styles feature a variety of African (instruments such as the *conga*, *bongo*, *bata*; polyrhythms, extensive syncopation), European (guitar, bass, piano, violin, brass; European melodic and harmonic structures; French court dances) and Caribbean elements (*maracas*, *güiro*) (Alén Rodríguez 1992; Calvo Ospina 1997; Duany 1984; *The New Grove Dictionary* 2001: 175; Steward 1999). The numerous Caribbean musicians in New York mixed these musical traditions with already Americanized styles like *rumba*, *mambo*, *charanga* and *boogaloo* and with Afro-American jazz, rock and soul. The result was sometimes called *salsa*, a Spanish word that stands for 'sauce', i.e. a mixture of formerly different ingredients to a new and indiscriminate blend.

The transformation of this fuzzy musical trend to a music style, marketed under the trademark *salsa*, was a commercial achievement of the New York record label Fania (Duany 1984: 187; Pacini Hernández 1998: 102). Fania promoted Latin New York's take on Cuban dance music, played mostly by Puerto Rican and Cuban New York musicians,[4] and thus 'Fania's *salsa* set the standards for the rest of Latin America' (Steward 1999: 8).

In the 1970s Fania's musicians and their records defined a set of features that made *salsa* into a kind of distinctive and recognizable trademark in music, which could challenge other distinguished and well-known genres like rock 'n roll or soul. On the other hand, Willie Colón's claim of *salsa* as a concept was still valid; i.e. that *salsa* was still open for all kinds of new influences and was interpreted in various ways.

From the start, *salsa* underwent numerous changes, but constantly increased its dissemination. In its early development, *salsa* music and texts were rather rough and provocative. The lyrics were usually a mixture of Spanish and English words and related to the often rough and unpleasant life in New York's *Barrio*. In the 1970s and at the beginning of the 1980s the success of *salsa* went far beyond the *Latino* audience in New York. It spread to both Americas, and reached Europe as well. At the same time musicians from Panama, Venezuela and Colombia became popular and influenced the further elaboration of *salsa* music. Songwriters like the Panamanian Rubén Blades and Willie Colón introduced a kind of social realist story-poem to *salsa* lyrics. In the 1980s Latin music became trendy and *salsa* songs appeared in the charts, a *salsa* award was created in 1975 and got huge mass media coverage, and *salsa* stars were shown on the cover of *Life* magazine and acted in Hollywood films.

The next trend in *salsa* music was set in the late 1980s by commercial considerations: mainly Puerto Rican musicians started to produce *salsa* ballads, and later *salsa-erótica*. Now the lyrics dealt almost exclusively with love-affairs, lovesickness and the joys of love, and the music was much smoother, quite simple and no longer experimental: a kind of casual music for lovers (Alén Rodríguez 1998; Calvo Ospina 1997). At the same time, around 1988, over half a million Dominicans moved to New York, bringing with them their musical style, *merengue,* and changing the musical agenda of New York profoundly (Steward 1999: 68). But in the mid-nineties *salsa* came back in a new shape, with new stars like Gloria Estefan, India, Marc Anthony, Ricky Martin or Jennifer López, who mixed up *salsa* with Latin pop and rock, singing in Spanish, English or 'Spanglish', and had as much in common with rock stars as with *salseros.*

Today *salsa* has become internationalized to such an extent that it can no longer be associated with any one country or city. In Cuba, Miami, Colombia and West Africa new trends and styles developed in addition to the ones of the previous centres in New York and Puerto Rico. The boundaries between musical styles are even more blurred than in the early days of *salsa.* For the convenience of record shops and review pages all kinds of Latin dance music are included under the term *salsa*; not only its Cuban ancestors *son, guaracha, boogaloo,* and *mambo,* but Puerto Rican *plena* and *bomba,* and even the very different Dominican *merengues* and Colombian *cumbias* and *vallenatos,* as well. However, one can still recognize a genuine *salsa* song by certain features

1. Like every Afro-Cuban musical style, *salsa* adheres to a continuously repeated rhythmic motive of 1–2–3, 1–2, referred to as *clave* ('clef', 'key' or 'keystone'). This steady and unchangeable beat of the *clave* constitutes a relentless drive. The structure of the *clave* provides the grid or backdrop for the music, which is played in four–four time. However, the distinctive feel of *salsa* is not the four–four rhythm, but its foundation of interlocking rhythmic ostinati, so that for example the bass is always in the off-beat ('the anticipated bass': Manuel 1985) and the brass section is playing punchy brass choruses in the contra rhythm, whilst the melody goes with the rhythm. But every musician is constantly conscious of the *clave* (Cornelius 2001: 788; Quintero 1998; *The New Grove Dictionary* 2001: 4, 175).
2. The typical *salsa* rhythm section consists of piano, bass, *bongos, timbales* (kettledrums, originally brought to Cuba by Italian opera companies), *güiro* (Amerindian notched scraper), *maracas* (small round, dried gourds with handles, filled with seeds or pellets), *claves* (a pair of smooth wooden cylindrical blocks banged together), *congas* (long, cylindrical single-headed drums) and *cencerros* (cowbell). The last two instruments, *congas* and *cencerros,* always mark the fourth beat; other instruments follow their own patterns. The brass section may be made up of combinations of trumpets, trombones and saxophones. The ensemble may also employ flutes, violins, electric guitars and synthesizers, and it always includes vocals (Cornelius 2001: 788; Steward 1999: 13–17).

3. Songs most often have a two-part formal structure. Verses are sung by a lead vocalist, followed by a call-and-response section known as the *montuno*.
4. In contrast to Cuban music, there is a strong use of jazz harmonies and solo improvisations (particularly during the *montuno* section). The sound is clearly urban, i.e. rougher and more aggressive than the sound of Cuban or other Caribbean music.

By virtue of the above-mentioned features, *salsa* songs are easy to identify by persons looking for a chance to dance *salsa*. And one thing is for sure: you can dance to each and any *salsa* song!

The real boom of *salsa* music (after some less successful forerunners) reached Europe in the 1990s. It blended with the enthusiasm for Cuban music that arose after the partial abolition of the US blockade of Cuba that opened the island to mass tourism. The growing interest in Cuba was fostered by the success of the CD *Buena Vista Social Club* and the movie about the Cuban musicians. Simult-aneously with the music, *salsa* dancing spread over Europe; it started in London, proceeded to the continent and is now on its way to Eastern Europe. Wherever it arrives, *salsa* dancers are gathering around teachers or discos that specialize in *salsa* dancing.

The *salsa* phenomenon has several features that distinguish the *salsa* scene from other groups related to or defined by a specific dance. These differences make *salsa* particularly interesting for anthropological research:

1. In contrast to other scenes that are defined by a musical style and/or dance (rock 'n' roll, twist, beat, shake, stomp, soul, reggae, punk/pogo, heavy metal, techno, hip hop, trance) *salsa* is not danced by very young people or a marginalized group (this point will be elaborated in connection with the case study).
2. In contrast to all the popular social dance forms mentioned above, *salsa* is the first dance since rock 'n' roll (with the qualified exception of the disco dance of the 1970s, tango and swing) performed by couples and with body contact.
3. In contrast to most other popular dances, *salsa* is for various reasons rather hard to learn (see below), and many people have to take lessons in order to learn it.
4. In contrast to ballroom dances like the waltz, foxtrot and quickstep, *salsa* is not included in sports-like dance competitions, nor is it part of the standard pro-gramme of dancing schools. In contrast to Latin dances, which belong to the standard set of contest dances, it has until now not been subject to domest-ication and regulation. Instead a structure of its own came into being for instruction in *salsa*.[5]

There are several factors that make the acquisition of *salsa* difficult. These start with the musical scheme, which has inherited a polyrhythmic character from its

African roots (nevertheless, it follows a straight four–four time rhythm as well). Polyrhythmicity means that different instruments play different rhythms, so that the dancer has to train her/his ear to find out which beats are relevant for her/him. Moreover, the basic step of *salsa* defines only three steps for the four beats of a bar – thus one may make steps on beats 1, 2, and 3 and have a break on beat 4. The details of this arrangement may vary – in Cuba one puts the break on the second beat, in New York and Puerto Rico on the first – but anyway, unless they are trained in African or Latin-American dances, the fact that one has to omit a beat is quite unfamiliar to many European beginners.

Even more challenging are the *salsa* movements themselves, because they do not comply with most 'traditional' European standards of movement. In Europe, dancing, together with fencing, shooting and riding, was an essential part of the courtly education of noblemen until the eighteenth century (Eichberg 1986: 17; Klein 1992: 101). At European courts, and later in the dance schools of the rising bourgeoisie, the emphasis was put on shape and style, with a basic trend to con-figurations that structure space. Movements were systematically registered, organized, codified, and taught (Fritsch and Dietrich 1981: 74). The characteristic features of African dances, on the other hand, are isolated moves (different parts of the body are used separately and independently of each other) that correspond to the polyrhythms of African music. These are accompanied by kicks and shaking and jerking moves that are unfamiliar to Europeans (particularly the hip move-ments, which offend Christian moral conventions). Spatial patterns and fixed sequences of moves are rare in African dances – movements are most often strung together in a spontaneous way (Fritsch and Dietrich 1981: 75; Günther 1981: 14).[6]

Finally, the strict assignment of gender roles in *salsa* dancing – with divergent sets of movements for men and women, the man leading the woman, who has to accept and follow his lead – appears to pose another problem in some German contexts. Since rock 'n' roll, and, to some extent, disco dancing, the rigid definition of gender roles has become increasingly unpopular. Whether in beat, twist or pogo, men and women dance on their own, without physical contact. Often they do not even form couples, or they dance with partners of the same sex. This latter pattern of dancing with partners of the same sex was very popular with mods, skinheads, heavy metal and pogo dancers (Ward 1993: 23). Since the late 1960s most young people have refused to form male–female couples on the dance-floor and have rejected formal ballroom dancing education. This was regarded as a rebellion against traditional gender-role ascriptions (Klein 1992: 286) and the standard-ization of behaviour in a broader social context (Fritsch and Dietrich 1981: 75). Today, the *salsa* boom seems to have reversed the attitude towards dancing in couples.[7]

Thus, the *salsa* craze runs counter to the usual dichotomies of social dancing between standardized ballroom dances for couples and the more spontaneous 'street dances' of young people that are performed by individuals who do not follow prescribed steps or movements. By presenting the following case study I want to shed some light on the phenomenon of *salsa* and the possible meanings of *salsa* dancing in Germany.

The *Salsa* Scene in Hamburg

The place where I studied the global phenomenon of *salsa* dancing was the city of Hamburg in Germany – more precisely, the *salsa* discos and clubs of Hamburg. When I entered this field about three years ago, I had other things in mind than doing anthropological research. In the beginning I just wanted to dance. I already had some experience as a hobby dancer, and had tried several dance forms. However, I was looking for something else, something that was not restricted to the classroom like the other dances I had practised before. I was attracted to *salsa* because it took place in discos, where I could dance whenever I wanted to and as long as I wanted.

When I started to visit *salsa* discos I watched the advanced dancers with admiration and decided to follow their example. I was more and more drawn into the music and the dance. At peak times of my passion I was out dancing five nights a week, and I realized that other dancers shared or even surpassed my enthusiasm. There were cases of dancers who abandoned partners as a consequence of their passion for *salsa*, and many neglected former friends and hobbies because they spent most of their leisure time dancing. Simultaneously, I noticed that *salsa,* and Latin music in general, had become a worldwide fashion. I started to wonder what made *salsa* and Latin music so fascinating for so many people, and decided to have a closer look at the part of the phenomenon I knew best: the *salsa* dancers of Hamburg.

Furthermore, the extreme heterogeneity and flexibility of this group also attracted my attention. Men and women who gather in clubs and discos to dance *salsa* differ considerably in age, social background and ethnic identification. The only common ground seems to be their enthusiasm for *salsa* music and dance. Obviously, they do not fit into the category of young and socially marginalized dancers. According to a survey[8] that was conducted in three *salsa* places in Hamburg, *salsa* dancers range between 18 and 67 years of age – the largest group was 30 to 35 years old. The majority of dancers belonged to the middle class and were well educated. Occupations were rather heterogeneous, but a remarkable proportion (14 per cent) worked in the social and medical professions, and others in information technology or communications businesses. Many dancers held senior positions in their professions, and labourers or unemployed persons were rare. Thus these dancers did not represent a marginalized, but rather a core group of modern society.

Because of the heterogeneity of backgrounds I hesitate to call the *salsa* dancers a group; instead, I prefer to keep to the term that *salsa* dancers commonly use when they talk about themselves: 'the *salsa* scene'. This term includes everybody who shows up more or less regularly in places where *salsa* music is played. The overall number of people involved in *salsa* dancing is hard to fix, because the *salsa* scene is extremely mobile, flexible and fluctuating. *Salsa* nights are held every day of the week, but always in different places. There is not one *salsa* disco, but about a dozen discos, bars or restaurants that stage *salsa* nights. These are complemented by regular parties held in community centres and special events, such as *salsa* concerts, boat parties, or full moon parties. Moreover, these arrangements change quite often, and some discos close and others open or new events are introduced, especially in spring and summer. Thus there is constant talk about what is going on and where to go. Additionally, one can consult the trilingual periodical for Latin Americans in northern Germany, *El Nórdico*, which provides a wealth of information about *salsa* events. The internet plays an increasingly important role for the dissemination of information about places to go, *salsa* events and concerts, teachers, workshops and classes, books, videos and CDs, the history of various dance styles and contacts with potential dance partners.

As a consequence of the general boom of Latin music, *salsa* events are well attended most of the time. However, not all guests dance; quite a lot of them obviously prefer to watch the dancers and enjoy the atmosphere. I exclude this group of *salsa* spectators and 'wannabes', who prefer to just talk about dancing or classes rather than actually dancing. Limiting the scene to active dancers, I can only roughly guess that the *salsa* scene consists of about 500 dancers.[9] In the above-mentioned survey in *salsa* discothèques, 50 per cent of the respondents danced once or more than once a week. Seven per cent of them even danced three to five times a week. This group of frequent and very frequent dancers represents the core of the scene. They call themselves '*salsa* fanatics' or '*salsa* addicts'. They know each other and prove their membership of the core group by greeting each other with kisses on both cheeks – a kind of welcome that is not common in Hamburg outside the *salsa* scene.

Ethnically there is a division of the *salsa* scene into two main sub-scenes, which often intermingle but differ in some important aspects: one sub-scene consists of Latin Americans, the other of Germans. By concentrating on these subgroups I skip the sizeable number of persons of other nationalities, including dancers from Indonesia, Turkey, the Philippines, Portugal, Russia, Iran, Algeria, Cameroon, Kenya and other places. In the survey their percentage (21 per cent) even surpassed the share of Latin Americans (16 per cent). In general I tend to take the view that in their attitudes towards dancing they resemble Germans more than Latin American dancers.[10]

To come back to Latin Americans and Germans, these two sub-groups differ not only in language and ethnic affiliation but in their choice of favourite places and musical styles and the ways they dance as well. For Latin Americans, Latin music serves to establish and confirm their identity and the value of their culture in a foreign context. This aspect of music is particularly important for migrants (see for example Nettl 1978; Stokes 1994: 3, 103–4). The power of music and dance to confirm cultural identity is not necessarily limited to people who already identified with it in their country of origin. In the *salsa* places of Hamburg, you can find *Latinas* and *Latinos* who have never danced *salsa* before they came to Germany, because they came from countries like Chile, Uruguay, or Guatemala and regions like southern Peru where *salsa* is not so popular. Others belonged to social strata in their home countries in which *salsa* was not regarded as important. It was only when they came to Hamburg that *salsa* became an important element of their generalized cultural identity as Latin Americans.[11] Living outside Latin America, they feel as if they were living in a diaspora. This sentiment leads to the creation and maintenance of close connections to their respective homelands, the wish to return, or at least the myth of returning, to Latin America, and the consequent desire to maintain a diasporic collective identity reflected in cultural, linguistic and religious continuity. Willie Colón (1999: 6) explains: '[*Salsa*] is a cultural place where they [the *Latinos*] can belong, a socio-political movement, a platform to tell our stories and communicate across the broad expanses that we inhabit. It is a chronicle and a testimony that we were here on this planet, a showcase to display our talent to the world.'

For the majority of the German dancers, however, the cultural origin of their preferred musical style is of little significance. Thus they must have other motives than those of persons of Latin American origin to appreciate *salsa* – particularly because they spend a lot of time, energy and money on learning it. *Salsa* classes and workshops are the realm of the Germans. Latin Americans, on the other hand, never show up, and even mock the Germans for their excessive eagerness to learn *salsa*.

This controversy about how to learn to dance and acquire a reasonable degree of perfection is due to several cultural differences between Latin Americans and Germans. First of all, *Latinas* and *Latinos* often pride themselves on having 'the rhythm in their blood' – they know how to dance and do not have to learn it. Most Germans, however, feel a little uneasy when they are confronted with the unfamiliar rhythms and movements of *salsa* for the first time. Hence they believe that they need to be taught – preferably by a teacher with something that I would call 'ethnic competence'. This refers to the fact that most dancers prefer Spanish-speaking and coloured teachers, who, in their opinion, must be experts by birth.

Moreover, the need to be taught how to dance by a qualified teacher is deeply ingrained in European practices of dancing. In this tradition, dances are fixed sequences of movements that have to be performed in a certain way to be 'right'.

They are a means to discipline the body and to impose social control (Klein 1992: 99). Only folk dancing, and in recent times disco dancing, is acquired without formal instruction. However, many Germans regard *salsa* as too complex and difficult to learn without formal instruction. This attitude seems to be part of more general cultural models of learning that can be traced back to the beginnings of German industrialization in the middle of the nineteenth century. These models imply that one has to work hard to acquire proficiency, and that diligence is more valuable and honourable than talent. Consequently, formal education, certificates and titles are regarded as extremely important in German society. Not only in academic professions but also in skilled trade and in artistic careers the appropriate diplomas are considered almost indispensable. Whatever one starts to do, most Germans believe that one should learn it from the bottom up and from a qualified teacher (Kellermann 1985: 283–4; Schenda 1986: 88–108; Wieschiolek 1999: 112–17).

Thus Germans and Latin Americans learn *salsa* in different ways. This brings us to the characteristic organizational framework for the instruction of *salsa*. Because *salsa* is not one of the standard ballroom dances, dancing schools offer only extra short-term classes and teach only basic skills. The most common and easiest way to learn to dance *salsa* is to attend the classes that are held in discos in the early evening before the beginning of a *salsa* night. They are included in the admission fee for the disco, and thus these lessons hardly cause any additional expense in terms of money, energy or time.

The *salsa* classes held in discos attract many people who try their talent as *salseros*; but many of them vanish soon. Some are discouraged because they come to believe that they lack the talent or energy to overcome the initial difficulties they confront. Others, who are more dedicated and/or gifted students, soon turn to other classes, because the disco-lessons teach only basic skills. More demanding opportunities to learn *salsa* are classes offered by gymnastics clubs or workshops, which are held in various places by diverse teachers. It is quite common for teachers from Berlin, western Germany, London or New York to visit Hamburg just for a workshop. The common feature of all these forms of instruction is that you can take them up spontaneously, without booking, preparation or obligation. This appears to be an important detail for *salsa* dancers, as the experiences of organizers show: whenever they ask for pre-bookings of workshops (for instance when a teacher has high travel expenses) they customarily fail.

However, almost all Germans who learn how to dance *salsa* do so in workshops and classes. As I have argued above, it is not only the unfamiliar rhythm and movements that make it hard for Germans to get into *salsa* dancing. Many of them have great difficulties accepting the prescribed roles for men and women. As a New York dance teacher said: '*Salsa* is a macho dance, done to macho music, played by macho musicians' (quoted by Steward 1999: 12). Thus, in classes for beginners you can frequently watch men who make excuses because they consider it arrogant to lead a woman and to make her do certain things at a certain time – I have sometimes even heard questions like: 'Would you mind doing the turn now?' Many German women, on the other hand, stress their independence, which makes it very awkward and strange for them to accept another (male) person's lead. The instructors have to remind them over and over again: 'Ladies, just follow his lead!' Of course these attitudes – which are rooted in contemporary German culture and its norms about gender roles – may make dancing quite unpleasant for both partners.

Why do Germans stick to *salsa* in spite of all these difficulties and hardships, and why are they so fascinated by it? Following my methodological reflections, I will describe the way *salsa* dancers speak about their passion.

Why *Salsa*?

When I asked my interlocutors whether *salsa* had changed their life, to my surprise, all of them answered 'yes'. One woman explained to me:

> *Salsa* dancing was very important for me from the start; it was not like starting to play drums or the piano. It changed something about my emotional life and my attitude to life. I suddenly realized that I live in a different way, that many things have changed since I have started dancing so much. I have got much more energy – I was sometimes surprised how fit I felt at work, although I slept only a few hours – thus, *salsa* really gives me vitality and energy.

The positive effects of *salsa* on one's life were mentioned by all the dancers I talked to, but individuals stressed different aspects. They often used explanatory systems that are very similar to scientific theories about dance – when dancers talk about the release of stress or even aggression through dancing, their explanation corresponds to the idea of dance as a 'safety valve'. Others emphasized that dancing *salsa* helps them to relax and forget about the daily routine ('escapism'); and some used *salsa* as a sport to keep fit. Almost all the dancers mentioned the idea that they were energized by *salsa* dancing. However, none of these reasons explain why the person in question chose *salsa* and not some other sport or dance. Moreover, many of the dancers I met practise or have practised other sports as well, and many had danced in other dance styles before they started to dance *salsa*. Thus, the question remains: why *salsa*?

It was striking that in all interviews a certain characteristic of *salsa* was mentioned. In defining *salsa* music and dance, the most frequent associations referred to its vitality:

- 'joy', 'fun', 'joy of living';
- 'being in high spirits', 'having a good time'; and
- 'liveliness', 'vividness', 'passion'.

These associations constitute an interesting contrast to the words used to describe the world *outside* the *salsa* scene, the lives of persons who do *not* dance or self-images of the time *before* the current interlocutor started to dance:

- 'self-control', 'formality';
- 'stiff', 'dead';
- 'simple', 'square'; and
- 'boring', 'dull'.

The differing characterizations of *salsa* and the life outside the scene, the former characterized as being positive and the latter as negative, suggest that the *salsa* scene may meet needs that are not met or satisfied sufficiently in other spheres of modern German society. Some of these needs can be discerned from the dancers' associations: the experience of unrestrained fun and joy of living, which releases unexpected energies. I found it remarkable that many *salsa* dancers talked about dancing as a means of improving their self-esteem – some dancers even mentioned that their colleagues, friends and relatives are impressed by this 'exotic' hobby. Moreover, dancers occasionally bring friends or colleagues to show them 'the *salsa* scene'. Thus, *salsa* appears to be not only an important expression of identity for Latin Americans but for Germans as well. German *salsa* dancers construct a self-image of a vivid, joyful person, in contrast to what they regard as the boring, stiff and square German majority.[12]

Astonishingly, in spite of the transient character of the *salsa* scene, it seems to develop into a home for many of its members. This becomes strikingly evident in the days before Christmas, when singles urgently search for a *salsa* party where they can spend time – time that Germans are supposed to spend with their families. Moreover, it also became a habit of many *salseros* to celebrate their birthdays in *salsa* discos.

One very strong motive for dancing *salsa* was mentioned mainly by frequent dancers. They talked about an almost mystical experience that can be created by dancing with the right partner to the right music at the right time: the 'flow', a feeling of absolute harmony and correspondence, when every move and every combination turns out well. This experience cannot always be created; but, when it happens, it is felt to be really enchanting and satisfying. Even people who were not very good at dancing said that the movement was very pleasing and rewarding: 'I learned to move in a way I never saw before and to move muscles I didn't even know I had. This gives me the feeling of being able to master my body.'

These feelings are particularly significant in view of the reduction of physical exertion and the standardization of human movement in work, sports and even in dancing. *Salsa,* as a dance that schools of dancing rarely teach, has (until now) not been subject to this kind of domestication and codification. It, therefore, offers a larger variety of movements and physical sensations to dancers.

Finally, the divergent model of gender roles seems to be a relevant reason to choose *salsa* as a hobby. This alternative model is communicated by the return to dancing in couples as well as by the sensuality and eroticism that, in the opinions of my interlocutors, were striking features of *salsa* music. This applies particularly to the version of *salsa-erótica* that has been quite a success since the beginning of the 1990s. Moreover, many Germans associate a more traditional gender-role model, rather than the one promoted in German society, with Latin American culture. These ideas, in combination with the physical experience of leading and being led when dancing, challenge egalitarian gender-role models. Moreover, many women regard it as an advantage of the *salsa* scene that it allows for a dress code that is more sexy and flashy than the clothes they wear at other occasions. Thus being a member of the *salsa* scene is related to ideas of challenging the prevailing ideology of gender equality that is considered as a socially desirable norm by most members of the middle classes.

Although gender roles are less equal and symmetrical in the *salsa* scene than in other spheres of life, communication between men and women seems to be easier and less complicated. However, in order to avoid misinterpretations, I have to explain in which way communication between the sexes differs in the *salsa* scene: in spite of the definition of *salsa* as an erotic dance, most dancers reject the idea of *salsa* dancing as an easy means of finding a sex object (cf. Ward 1993: 21). [13] Some are very annoyed about men who are obviously more interested in chatting up women than in dancing. The easy communication with the opposite sex, on the other hand, was considered to be a great advantage of the *salsa* scene. Dancing *salsa* does not oblige one to engage in any verbal communication that exceeds the invitation to dance (and even that is often communicated without words), but nonetheless offers nearness and physical contact and a kind of non-verbal com-munication. I instance a male dancer who said: 'When I dance with a woman, it's a kind of communication – it's like a – non-verbal communication. I can feel whether the woman is in a good mood or not or maybe she has problems. This is an important element of dancing to me, this type of communication.'

This kind of contact is important to most dancers; some even regard it as a therapy for social problems or difficulties with the opposite sex. Many expressed ideas like the following, presented by a woman who had danced *salsa* for a year:

I'm actually a kind of eccentric, solitary person and, to me, *salsa* means to encounter an official setting where I can walk towards other persons or they can approach me – which is much more complicated in everyday life, I guess. This is somehow – I like this ritualized way of meeting and that it is temporary – if you want it to be so. You can always say: 'OK, it was nice, thank you and good bye!'

And thus – in my case – I always used to have exceptionally – highly problematic – relationships with men, I mean, actually highly neurotic, and therefore, for me, *salsa* is first of all a harmless and inoffensive way of meeting people, but something can happen. So, you have the chance, with a person you don't know at all, to smell and to touch this person or whatever.

A very frequent male dancer told me:

Because of *salsa* I feel more free and easy – facing women, too. I am more composed and relaxed dealing with women. With other women, too, not only with the ones I know from *salsa* dancing. For instance, with my female colleagues, I talk to them much more easily; we talk about all kinds of things.

It is beyond the scope of this account to decide whether the 'new old role model' of couple dancing in *salsa* and its perception by the dancers means a backlash in the fight against traditional gender models or a new rebellion, this time against the now prevailing ideology of gender equality. However, the departure from patterns of behaviour and values that are common in the world outside the *salsa* scene seems to enlarge the repertoire of behaviour and to open up new possibilities for relationships with members of the opposite sex for many dancers.

After presenting so many reasons for dancing *salsa*, I also have to mention that I heard a lot of complaining and grumbling about the negative sides of dancing and the *salsa* scene as well. Almost all complaints referred to obstacles that impede or make it difficult to dance: the 'wrong' music, not enough space on the dance-floor, careless dancers who disturb or even hurt others. Other major topics were the shortcomings of one's dance partner or the search for the right partner. This is mainly a problem for women. Some do not have the chance to dance as often as they would like to, while others criticize the skills of their dance partners. It seems that (at least in Hamburg) there is a larger number of female *salseras* than male *salseros* who are willing to dance and capable of dancing.[14] Many German women react to the lack of adequate partners in a way that is highly disapproved of by *Latinas*: instead of waiting for a man to ask them for a dance, women take the initiative and ask men. However, this is not always a solution, because men can reject the offer of a dance – and this can cause many bad feelings and much lamentation on the part of the female dancers.

Conclusions

This case-study demonstrates how one style of dancing can be practised for very different reasons and how it can convey different or even opposed meanings. *Salsa* is an element of the collective identity of Latin Americans outside their home countries; but it can also be an expression of the individuality and exotic particularity of Germans who want to distinguish themselves from their compatriots. The *salsa* scene is a transitory, unconstrained and non-obligatory group; but it is also perceived as 'home' by many of its members. The identification of dancers with *salsa* creates a space where the social, ethnic and economic differences of German society are more or less ignored and where persons meet who would probably never have met in other spheres. In this setting communication between men and women is facilitated, too; but dancing *salsa* nevertheless reinforces gender-role differences.

However, as contradictory as these characteristics of *salsa* and its adherents seem to be, they all are related closely to the surrounding German culture and its conditions of life. Thus, the study of *salsa* in Germany opens up a fresh look at German culture and the way it is perceived by its members. Their hunt for identity, exoticism, communication and different gender-role models reveals shortcomings, predicaments and dilemmas in their life outside the *salsa* scene.

Notes

1. I wish to thank Noel Dyck and Eduardo P. Archetti for their critical and constructive comments on earlier drafts of this chapter. The DJs Holger Hiller, Jörg Feikes and Michael Beyer provided valuable information on questions of music. Pirkko Remesch added significant and helpful empirical data to my ethnographic records. My special thanks to Richard-Michael Diedrich for the time and effort he spent on proofreading and commenting on the manuscript.
2. I understand the term 'explanatory system', following Charlotte Linde, as 'a system that claims to give a means for understanding, evaluating, and interpreting experience or accounts of experience and usually, as a consequence of that understanding, also gives, either explicitly or implicitly, a guide for future behaviour' (Linde 1987: 351). I prefer 'explanatory system' because it denotes a consciously known and shared folk theory, in contrast to 'cultural models', which may also be unconscious (D'Andrade 1987: 114).
3. By analogy with Noel Dyck's reflections about research into sports (2000: 22), I propose that ethnographic accounts of dance should consider not only performance but also interconnections between various levels of performance, for example professional presentations of the same dance form, children's dancing,

and official presentations. Moreover, the researcher should pay attention to all persons who play a role in or for the performance of a dance and who influence this by their respective targets and purposes: participants, spectators, organizers, hosts of ballrooms, etc.

4. For example, the Puerto Ricans Willie Colón, Hector Lavoe, Cheo Feliciano, El Gran Combo, Ismael Rivera, and Pete 'El Conde' Rodríguez, Dominicans like Johnny Pacheco, and, of course, Cuban musicians, like Celia Cruz, La Lupe or Gloria Estefan, played an important role.

5. However, the union of German professional dancing instructors presented in 2001 a dance called 'salsafox'. According to the dancing instructors 'salsafox' is a combination of disco-fox and *salsa*, a versatile and easy-to-learn dance-form which is suitable for all kinds of popular music. For persons who are acquainted with *salsa* dancing this claim sounds quite amazing: even talented dancers need weeks of intense training to acquire basic skills in *salsa* dancing and months or years to acquire some expertise. Furthermore the dance-form is closely connected to the music style of *salsa*; thus you can perform it to similar music styles like *mambo* or *son*, but if it comes to Latin pop, *merengue*, *bachata* or *rumba*, dancing *salsa* becomes a troublesome and unpleasant task with rather awkward results.

6. But African elements of dancing are not absolutely new for Europeans. These have invaded the European canon of movements since the beginning of the twentieth century via a number of dance fashions. Tango, ragtime, Boston, cakewalk, and Charleston or swing, as well as rock 'n' roll, twist and reggae are all influenced by African dance styles. Moreover, the African canon of movements is taught in classes for jazz dance and jazz gymnastics, let alone in African dance classes, which are offered even in the smallest towns. G. Klein mentions that there were about 1,500 institutions for teaching dance in West Germany at the beginning of the 1990s. Consequently, *salsa* beginners with some experience in one of these dance styles (according to Klein (1992: 9) usually women) have fewer difficulties in acquiring the *salsa* movements.

7. Almost simultaneously with the start of the *salsa* boom in the nineties, tango and swing regained popularity. Remarkably, these are performed in couples as well.

8. I wish to thank Pirkko Remesch, who designed and conducted this survey. He interviewed 109 people in November 2001.

9. This excludes the clienteles of discos for Latin music without a special emphasis on *salsa*, who are avoided by *salseros*.

10. A particular motive for these non-Latin and non-German dancers to join the *salsa* scene is probably the openness of this scene, which stands in contrast to many other spheres of German society. As opposed to the German mainstream culture, differences in ethnicity, nationality, language, profession and social

status are less important, for they are overridden by the relevance of individual dancing competence and physical attractiveness.

11. I have only fragmentary accounts concerning *salsa* in Latin America. Frances R. Aparicio states 'my upper-class upbringing [in Puerto Rico] limited my identification with *salsa* music' (1998: xi), and later adds that in 'Puerto Rico and other Caribbean countries, such as Venezuela, *salsa* music has emerged as a marker of race and class differences', *salsa* being the mark of young black men, rock 'n' roll of the white middle and upper class of young Puerto Ricans (1998: 69). Concerning Colombia, I was told that only non-white members of the lower classes and lower middle class dance *salsa* (oral communication by Jörg Feikes).
12. Diane Forsythe gives a good description of the predicaments of Germans over their national identity after the Second World War (Forsythe 1989).
13. The popular misunderstanding of dancing as a convention of sexual bargaining corresponds with widespread scientific misconceptions of dancing as 'the mechanization of the sexual impulse' (Mungham 1976: 92) or 'the unfortunate prerequisite to courting' (McRobbie 1984: 143).
14. In the empirical survey two-thirds of the respondents were female.

References

Alén Rodríguez, Olavo (1992), 'The Afro-French Settlement and the Legacy of Its Music to the Cuban People', in Gerard H. Béhague (ed.), *Music and Black Ethnicity. The Caribbean and South America*, pp. 109–18. Miami: North–South Center.

—— (1998), *From Afrocuban Music to Salsa*, Berlin: Piranha.

Aparicio, Frances R. (1998), *Listening to Salsa. Gender, Latin Popular Music, and Puerto Rican Cultures*, Hanover/London: Wesleyan University Press.

Archetti, Eduardo P. (1999), *Masculinities. Football, Polo and the Tango in Argentina*, Oxford/New York: Berg.

Birdwhistell, Ray L. (1970), *Kinesics and Context: Essays on Body Motion Communication*, Philadelphia: University of Pennsylvania Press.

Blacking, John (1985), 'Movement, Dance, Music, and the Venda Girls' Initiation Cycle', in Paul Spencer (ed.), *Society and the Dance. The Social Anthropology of Process and Performance*, pp. 64–91. Cambridge: Cambridge University Press.

Brake, Mike (1985), *Comparative Youth Cultures*, London: Routledge and Kegan Paul.

Brownell, Susan (2000), 'Why Should an Anthropologist Study Sports in China?', in Noel Dyck (ed.), *Games, Sports and Cultures*, pp. 43–63. Oxford/New York: Berg.

Calvo Ospina, Hernando (1997), *Salsa: Havanna Heat – Bronx Beat,* Stuttgart: Schmetterling-Verlag.

Colón, Willie (1999), 'Foreword', in Sue Steward, *Salsa. Musical Heartbeat of Latin America,* pp. 6–7. London: Thames and Hudson.

Cornelius, Steven (2001), 'Afro-Cuban Music', in *The Garland Encyclopedia of World Music,* Vol. 3, pp. 783–9. New York/London: Garland Publishing.

D'Andrade, Roy (1987), 'A Folk Model of the Mind', in Dorothy Holland and Naomi Quinn (eds), *Cultural Models in Language and Thought,* pp. 112–48. Cambridge: Cambridge University Press.

Duany, Jorge (1984), 'Popular Music in Puerto Rico: Toward an Anthropology of Salsa', *Revista de Música Latino Americana/Latin American Music Review,* vol. 5, no.2: 186–216.

Dyck, Noel (2000), 'Games, Bodies, Celebrations and Boundaries: Anthropological Perspectives on Sport', in Noel Dyck (ed.), *Games, Sports and Cultures,* pp. 13–42. Oxford/New York: Berg.

Eichberg, Henning (1986), *Die Veränderung des Sports ist gesellschaftlich,* Münster: Lit Verlag.

Forsythe, Diana (1989), 'German Identity and the Problems of History', in Elizabeth Tonkin, Maryon McDonald and Malcom Chapman (eds), *History and Ethnicity,* London/New York: Routledge, pp. 137–56. (ASA Monographs 27).

Frith, Simon (1988), *Music for Pleasure,* Cambridge: Polity Press.

Fritsch, Ursula and Knut Dietrich (1981), 'Europäisches und afrikanisches Tanzen – Durchdringung unterschiedlicher Bewegungskulturen?', in August Nitschke and Hans Wieland (eds), *Die Faszination und Wirkung außereuropäischer Tanz- und Sportformen,* pp. 70–84. Ahrensburg bei Hamburg: Verlag Ingrid Czwalina.

Günther, Helmut (1981), 'Das überlieferte Bewegungsverhalten', in August Nitschke and Hans Wieland (eds), *Die Faszination und Wirkung außereuropäischer Tanz- und Sportformen,* pp. 11–24. Ahrensburg bei Hamburg: Verlag Ingrid Czwalina.

Hanna, Judith Lynne (1987), *To Dance Is Human. A Theory of Nonverbal Communication,* Chicago/London: The University of Chicago Press.

—— (1988), *Dance, Sex and Gender. Signs of Identity, Dominance, Defiance, and Desire,* Chicago/London: The University of Chicago Press.

Kellermann, Paul (1985), 'Zur Konstitution sozialer Ungleichheit durch die gesellschaftliche Organisation von Arbeit und Bildung', in Herrmann Strasser and John H. Goldthorpe (eds), *Die Analyse sozialer Ungleichheit. Kontinuität, Erneuerung, Innovation,* pp. 280–306. Opladen: Westdeutscher Verlag.

Klein, Gabriele (1992), *FrauenKörperTanz. Eine Zivilisationsgeschichte des Tanzes,* Weinheim/Berlin: Quadriga-Verlag.

Linde, Charlotte (1987), 'Explanatory Systems in Oral Life Stories', in Dorothy Holland and Naomi Quinn (eds), *Cultural Models in Language and Thought,* pp. 343–66. Cambridge: Cambridge University Press.

McRobbie, Angela (1984), 'Dance and Social Fantasy', in A. McRobbie and M. Nava (eds), *Gender and Generation*, London: Macmillan.

Manuel, Peter (1985), 'The Anticipated Bass in Cuban Popular Music', *Revista de Música Latino Americana/Latin American Music Review*, vol. 6, no.2: 248–61.

Martin, Joel (1967), *American Dancing*, New York: Dance Horizons.

Mungham, Geoff (1976), 'Youth in Pursuit of Itself', in G. Mungham and G. Pearson (eds), *Working Class Youth Cultures*, London: Routledge & Kegan Paul.

Nettl, Bruno (1978), *Eight Urban Musical Cultures. Tradition and Change*, Urbana, IL: University of Illinois Press.

Nitschke, August and Hans Wieland (1981), *Die Faszination und Wirkung außereuropäischer Tanz- und Sportformen*, Ahrensburg bei Hamburg: Verlag Ingrid Czwalina.

Pacini Hernández, Deborah (1998), 'Popular Music of the Spanish-speaking Regions', *The Garland Encyclopedia of World Music*, Vol. 2, pp. 100–6. New York/London: Garland Publishing.

Polhemus, Ted (1993), 'Dance, Gender and Culture', in Helen Thomas (ed.), *Dance, Gender and Culture*, pp. 3–15. London: Macmillan.

Quintero, Sabina (1998), *'Salsa', Die Musik in Geschichte und Gegenwart. Allgemeine Enzyklopädie der Musik*, Vol. 8. Kassel: Bärenreiter.

Reed, Susan A. (1998), 'The Politics and Poetics of Dance', *Annual Review of Anthropology*, no. 27: 503–32.

Sachs, Curt (1937), *World History of the Dance*, New York: Norton.

Schenda, Rudolf (1986), 'Die Verfleißigung der Deutschen. Materialien zur Indoktrination eines Tugend-Bündels', in Utz Jeggle (ed.), *Volkskultur in der Moderne. Probleme und Perspektiven empirischer Kulturforschung*, pp. 88–108. Reinbek: Rowohlt.

Spencer, Paul (1985), 'Introduction: Interpretations of the Dance in Anthropology', in Paul Spencer, *Society and the Dance. The Social Anthropology of Process and Performance*, pp. 1–45. Cambridge: Cambridge University Press.

Steward, Sue (1999), *Salsa. Musical Heartbeat of Latin America*, London: Thames & Hudson.

Stokes, Martin (ed.) (1994), *Ethnicity, Identity and Music. The Musical Construction of Place*, Oxford/New York: Berg.

The New Grove Dictionary of Music and Musicians (2001), Vol. 6, London: Macmillan.

Thomas, Helen (ed.) (1993), *Dance, Gender and Culture*, London: Macmillan.

Ward, Andrew H. (1993), 'Dancing in the Dark: Rationalism and the Neglect of Social Dance', in Thomas, Helen (ed.), *Dance, Gender and Culture*, pp. 16–33. London: Macmillan.

Washabaugh, William (ed.) (1998), *The Passion of Music and Dance. Body, Gender and Sexuality*, Oxford/New York: Berg.

Wieschiolek, Heike (1999), '. . . *ich dachte immer, von den Wessis lernen heißt siegen lernen!' Arbeit und Identität in einem mecklenburgischen Betrieb,* Frankfurt/New York: Campus.

Wittman, Carl (1987), 'Loving Dance', in F. Abbott (ed.), *New Men, New Minds,* Freedom, CA: The Crossing Press.

Wulff, Helena (2001), 'Anthropology of Dance', in Neil J. Smelser and Paul B. Baltes (eds), *International Encyclopaedia of the Social and Behavioural Sciences,* Oxford: Pergamon/Elsevier Science.

7

The *Aikido* Body: Expressions of Group Identities and Self-Discovery in Martial Arts Training

Tamara Kohn

I must begin this chapter with a disclaimer. Aikido is a non-competitive martial art; it is generally not conceived of as a sport. This has been made clear by many of my informants who train in *aikido*, as well as in the many written sources that describe the practice and philosophy of *aikido*. Their identities as *aikido* practitioners are often framed in terms of the non-sport-like qualities of their practice. To them, 'sport' is a physical activity in which competition, rules, and goal/achievement are central attributes. As a friend and *aikido* teacher, Nobuo Iseri, told me, 'sport is a particular rite of passage and spectacle – part of the hero's journey'. *Aikido*, however, as it was designed by its founder in Japan earlier this century and as it is taught and practised in Japan as well as abroad today, is presented as non-competitive – there are no heroes (although there are masters), nor 'fights' with 'winners and losers'.[1] *Aikido* techniques are purely defensive. And yet the commitment, enthusiasm, 'club' solidarity, organizational politics, physical training and athleticism involved in and around *aikido* practice is reminiscent in many ways of that expressed in and around sporting practice. Issues raised around sport and sporting activity, for example about its position in daily life, the way it is used to define people's senses of self and other, and the way it appears to give a sense of direction and continuity in a fragmented contemporary world, are raised at least as meaningfully in the words and actions of aikidoists as they may be by baseball players or children kicking balls around a playing-field.

Aikido passes in and out of the realms of 'sport' and 'like sport', depending upon context and intent. For a clear example, consider the fact that the International *Aikido* Federation in Japan has become a member of the GAISF (General Association of International Sports Federations) in order to get official recognition outside Japan (www.*aikido*-international.org/index.php). We can understand from this how people involved in the political and institutional framing of the activity may instrumentally choose to describe *aikido* as 'sport', while the very same people may describe their art to their friends in terms of its 'non-sport', 'non-competitive' philosophies of practice. It is from the borderland of sport that this body practice knowingly traverses that I will attempt to contribute to themes raised in this volume.

One clear aim of this volume is to place the study of sport, dance, play and leisure squarely in the centre-court of the anthropological discipline rather than on the sidelines, and this is totally in keeping with the aims I have in studying *aikido* practice in the West. Indeed, I would suggest that there is not a subject of contemporary social anthropological interest that cannot be seen in a meaningful way through the practice, movements and words of my subjects. This is largely because *aikido* practice is a path, a 'way' or 'do' that reaches far beyond the mat for those who train seriously. It is, as we will see shortly, a philosophy of movement and of life entwined. It reaches far beyond the small group of *aikido* enthusiasts to touch on many levels of identity that are central interests in this discipline: issues of family, gender, ideology, religion, ethnicity, nationalism, the constructing and changing of 'self', etc. Because it is understood as a 'total practice' (much akin to Mauss's notion of 'total phenomenon' in his work on *The Gift* 1967 [1924]) I have found a wonderfully revealing self-consciousness and reflexivity exhibited by practitioners and teachers; a minefield for the participant observer and interviewer. Some aikidoists' ideas about the 'body' will be the focus of this chapter.[2] These ideas are shaped as much by felt movements in space[3] as by a vocabulary developed to aid people with their *aikido* practice. They are central to the understanding of the art as well as to a more general understanding of the ways in which 'bodies' are socially situated, socially inscribed and, indeed, I would suggest, inscribing. I will argue that it is this oft-expressed belief in the human capacity to shape a social world through individual body practice that can usefully inform our discipline's understanding of social process.

And yet, the work done so far by anthropologists and sociologists has generally fallen short of the mark when it comes to dealing with the depth of experience found in discourse about the sporting body (or, in my case, the *aikido* body). It scratches on the surface rather than thickly describing anything that may advance us in our study of human social engagement in a changing world. It avoids process and individual narrative in favour of structure and social anonymity. It tends to peer from the outside in order to tell us about how particular activities appear to slot into particular social structural frameworks and can thus be seen as a mirror reflecting a larger solid structure of value and institution (Snyder and Spreitzer 1978: 13).

Take, for instance, Bourdieu's study of sport, which argues that each sport has a special home in a particular social class. The sociologist's job, he suggests, is to find 'the socially pertinent properties that mean that a sport has an affinity with the interests, tastes and preferences of a determinate social category' (1990: 157). *Aikido*, he suggests, is the sport of the 'new petty bourgeoisie', to be contrasted with wrestling, which he would suggest belongs to the working classes. I have always admired Bourdieu's work; his words, particularly about the 'habitus', are convincingly descriptive, but that's the rub; they are *his* words. He appears to base his comparison of wrestling and *aikido* on a premise that the former emphasizes close and rough bodily contact, while 'in *aikido* the contact is ephemeral and distanced and fighting on the ground is non-existent' (ibid.). Furthermore, he suggests qualities for *aikido* like 'aerial', 'light', 'distanced', 'gracious' to take us beyond the sport and into larger relations of body and social position (ibid.). To ground these relations as he does, however, with inaccurate descriptions that come from an observer's *unfelt* vision of movement is potentially dangerous. I will soon attempt to demonstrate how *aikido* contact is far from ephemeral, how it is often practised 'on the ground' by people representing a huge variety of class backgrounds, and how it is characterized in very different terms from Bourdieu's by those who practise and teach it around the globe. The point to remember here is that one cannot build successful social theory by sitting on the outside looking in and playing with stereotypes that are not even recognized by the subjects of inquiry.

Many recent works on sport home in on 'rules' as indicants of social orders. For example, Horne, Tomlinson and Whannel's recent volume, *Understanding Sport* (1999) understands only the place of sport in particular political and social environments, for example the way it relates to work or to changes in industry, but not to the meanings it holds for the people who play or practise it. Other works situate sport as a form of leisure that becomes popular when it serves a particular function in a particular environment; either to take us beyond a 'civilizing process' (e.g. Dunning and Rojek 1992), or to offer excitement (Elias and Dunning 1986) and fun in a work-centred capitalist system (Clarke and Critcher 1985). These sorts of inquiries, along with those that analyse spatial arrangements or landscapes of sport (e.g. Bale 1994), describe arenas that are always meaningful for the analyst but not always for the people playing within them. As anthropologists I hope we can do more: searching for the *emic* making of meaning by playing for a while is surely our *forte*, so let us not just stop at opening the game box and reading the rules.

Coakley and Donnelly's recent edited volume, *Inside Sports*, provides a welcome exception to rule-bound surface study in its focus on experiences of 'doing' (1999). It examines identities that are forged through sport in terms of the ritual forms, functions and meanings of sporting events, and in terms of the relations outside the playing-field that are expressed. MacClancy's (1996) collection called *Sport, Identity and Ethnicity* also draws together various anthropologists' attempts to get inside the local meanings of sporting activities. It is by getting close to the experience of play and disciplined body practice and the indigenous philosophies of movement, power, harmony and so on embedded in such experience that we can justify occupying central seats in the anthropological academy.

We all teach our students about the way social anthropology developed over the last hundred years, and how a methodology of participant observation, born out of necessity on a Trobriand Island, became a defining feature of the discipline. It became a feature that allowed us to gaze for long periods of time into weird and wonderful exotic tribal worlds, to learn local dialects and befriend local people. After time we could empathize with their lives and describe their social structure and even the meanings attributed to everyday as well as to ritual action. This methodology also allowed us to return 'home' to gaze and engage with communities in our own complex societies. So, surely an anthropology of sport will dig deeper than sport studies have generally managed to do. Instead of just painting landscapes of sport – describing the arenas, forms, events, and rules – we should watch and listen and join in with the people who are players (or 'practitioners') and spectators and who tell us their ideas. Instead of stopping with *etic* structural descriptions, we should also collect *emic* narrations. The examples offered in this chapter will hopefully serve to highlight individual voices that are often caught in the act of *de*construction rather than reification of 'self' and 'society' – *re*formulation rather than just mirroring. Feeling one's own body and hearing one's own voice is part of the process that allows us to empathize with and understand people for whom meaning and nuance of activity itself is paramount. Participant observation is about speaking the body language and hearing people talk about their body practice and the social world it constructs in a natural way. Sport, dance, and other body practices 'are processes from which we derive *meaning*' (Hill 2002: 2), and the creative generation of sociocultural meaning may occur in a multitude of different public and private venues – on the pitch, in the locker room, beside the mat, in the pub after the practice, in front of a video made of a game or during a course, or on an *aikido* master's back porch in San Diego, California, over a hot bowl of noodle soup . . .

I would like to share just a few of the ideas that were ingested with that soup on one sunny day in November; but first I must give you a thumbnail sketch of *aikido*. This will offer a brief introduction to a history of the art, the current contexts of its practice around the world, and something of its essence or philosophy about movement and redirection of energy.

Aikido

Aikido was founded by Morihei Ueshiba (1883–1969), also known as *O-Sensei* ('Great Teacher') to his students. It developed out of Ueshiba's spiritual and martial informal and formal training in the early 1900s, integrating *judo*, sword, spear, and hard *jujutsu* practice with principles of Shinto and Zen Buddhism. *Aikido* is generally practised 'empty hand',[4] but as its techniques and movements are derived from the art of Japanese swordsmanship, students also practice with weapons. This 'modern manifestation of the Japanese martial arts (*budo*)' (K. Ueshiba 1984: 14) is a defensive practice that requires one to 'blend' or 'harmonize' with and then redirect the energy of an attack to throw or pin the attacker. *Ai* translates as 'harmony', *Ki* refers to 'spirit', and *Do* means way – hence *aikido* has be translated as 'the way of harmony of spirit'. In 1948 an 'Aiki Foundation' was established in Tokyo to promote *aikido*, the first public demonstration of the art was held in 1956, and around that time foreigners, many of whom learned of the art through their military experience, began practising. Some travelled to Japan to train, but the real spread occurred when O-Sensei sent a number of his disciples around the globe to establish the art abroad. Now there are thousands of *aikido dojos* around the globe, and hundreds of thousands of practitioners.[5] One of the earliest of O-Sensei's students to leave Japan was Kazuo Chiba, who brought *aikido* to England in the early 1960s – first to the north-east (Sunderland) and then London. Then he eventually settled in San Diego, California where he has established a very successful *dojo* that attracts students from all over the world, including Japan, who wish to study with such a fine master. In many respects, the San Diego *dojo* has become a pilgrimage site – a destination that people will travel far to for spiritual as well as physical training. Much of my material comes from several months training with and working with Chiba Sensei and his students.[6]

When it is practised today, either in Japan or the chilly north of England or the sunny beach towns of California, there are some who will insist, with the founder, that spiritual aspects of *aikido* are essential to its practice as well as to the development of the self in 'harmony with the universe'. There are others who will remain fairly unaware of the deep spiritual foundation of the practice and will focus instead on how the techniques embody an exceptionally powerful martial art and method of self-defence. And many more will hover somewhere in the middle, between the more ethereal and the more practical applications of *aikido*. Elsewhere I have discussed how the 'Japaneseness' of the art can be more or less important to people as well (Kohn 2001). The art has grown out of a rich and involved development in the Art of War in Japan, and traditions of dress, etiquette and style of transmission continue to bear the impress of the art's cultural background, particularly while Japanese *shihan* (masters) are still at the helm of the art's organizational structure. Americans and Europeans may initially be drawn to *budo* because of the enchantment and allure of the 'oriental', the power and the mystique of various Asian in-body disciplines and fighting arts (encouraged by a popular culture full of Teenage Mutant Ninja Turtles and Bruce Lee wannabes) (Donohue 1994). Yet they may be as likely to be drawn to *aikido* practice by accident or as a suggested means of physical training or even therapy, unconcerned and sometimes even unimpressed by the culturally grounded ritual and etiquette that occurs within the space of the *dojo*. Nearly all of these people who train for any length of time, however, will eventually come to understand their practice in terms of a number of key principles of movement that are very commonly related to analogous reactions and events in their everyday social world. It's this capacity to intertwine growing awareness of movement in the physical activity with strategies and understandings in social interactions with others that gives it centrality in the minds of those who practise – that ensures it is not classified as a peripheral leisure pursuit. If they don't peripheralize it, then we can't either.

Aikido practice is centred on learning a series of forms/movements (*kata*) in which the student must participate as the executor of the technique (*nage*– the one who has been attacked and who then throws or pins the attacker) and the receiver (*uke* – the one who attacks *nage* with a strike or a grab and then absorbs *nage*'s technique by rolling or break-falling) in paired exercises. In the *kata* of *aikido*, unlike those of other martial arts, emphasis is placed upon the correct 'feeling' of execution rather than visual correctness. It is often said that learning to receive the technique and safely fall or roll out of harm's way (*ukemi*) is the key to under-standing *aikido*, for in *ukemi* one conditions the body and learns the art of blending with and absorbing the energy of an attack. With *aikido*, even a small, physically weak person can learn to redirect the energy of a strong attack if he or she learns to apply basic principles of movement. Circular or spiralling movements are key in the understanding of how to execute *aikido* techniques. There are many different styles of *aikido* practice, both 'soft' and 'hard'. 'Hard' styles are generally more dynamic and 'martial' in their application, but all styles are based on the same principles.

These principles are clarified and taken into the body only through repetitive and reflexive practice over many years, but they are also simultaneously under-stood through a consciousness of their general applicability in the process of living from day to day. These understandings are shared and indeed 'taught' to others in social interactions, as well as in the essays submitted by students for their *dan* grade tests and in contributions to *aikido* and other martial arts books, magazines, newsletters, web pages and so on. The examples are limitless. I have thousands of them collected in notes, essays and published work. For instance I have books with titles like *Aikido for Life* (Homma 1990), *Herding the Ox: the Martial Arts as Moral Metaphor* (Donohue 1998), and *Aikido in Everyday Life: Giving in to Get your Way* (Dobson and Miller 1978), which all read like self-help or personal development manuals.[7] Other writing shares narratives of personal discovery, for instance Sharon Stone's story about 'blending' with the reality of her father's death (1985). And there is Dobson's infamous story about his experiences on a Tokyo train, when he was about to intervene physically with a violent drunken labourer using *aikido* techniques practised in the *dojo* when an old man totally calmed the distraught man down with kind and sympathetic words. As he says at the end of the story, 'I recognized that I *had* seen *Aikido* used in action, and that the essence of it *was* reconciliation' (Dobson 1985: 68–9).

During my time off the mat in San Diego, Marcus[8] told me how he often applies *aikido* principles to his verbally abusive boss by 'meeting at the point of attack' . . . entering and then blending with his aggressive energy and redirecting it to his weak point with a calm and centred response. Cal, surveyor, carpenter and body surfer, told me that at first he felt no relation between his *aikido* training and the other things in his life, but now he does – especially around issues of responsibility and respect. Denise showed me the clay sculpture she was working on and explained how her art is changing – how she now tries to take *ukemi* (receive) when she works the clay – to let the piece rather than her own will lead the form and to move naturally, often in unexpected directions.

Many themes emerge from these sorts of examples, but suffice it here to say that all these revelations are genuinely felt to have emerged from the embodied experiences on the mat. They were felt to be new revelatory responses to the world rather than old ones that *aikido* metaphor could slot into nicely. They were expressed by people from many occupational and cultural backgrounds (not just the 'new petty bourgeoisie' or the 'artsy fartsy' California set). It is for this reason that the bodily practice may be said to be inscribing of society as a whole, as well as something that transforms the individual body and spirit. We will return to this process of inscription later.

There is a growing body of literature on *aikido* and other martial arts practice by masters and their students as well as by a few anthropologists and sociologists who have begun to recognize the tremendous potential of exploring martial arts topics. Alas, with rare exceptions, these get whisked away into the Martial Arts sections of the Sport shelves in libraries and bookstores – hidden away from the general public and the academy. Exceptions include Zarrilli's descriptively and theoretically rich studies (e.g. 1998) of the South Indian martial art, *kalarippayattu*, which have found homes in anthropological volumes on modernity and performance, even if the writer ended up working outside the discipline in a department of the performing arts. Cox's Anthropology Ph.D. thesis on 'The Zen Arts' draws from fieldwork on the Art of Tea and the martial art of *kempo* in Japan, as well as from his own years of teaching *kempo* in Edinburgh (1998). Donohue is another martial artist, an anthropologist and eloquent writer who has attempted to come to terms with what he sees as an American attraction to the danger, wonder and excitement of martial arts practice, which answers to 'a variety of psychic needs' in the individual (1994: 3). But surely this approach (oddly Malinowskian) only explains something for the minority of martial artists I know who indeed do dream of samurai, play Bushido Blade on the Sony Playstation, blow the *shakuhachi*, burn Japanese incense, and watch Steven Segal movies when not rewatching Kurosawa films. Most people who train in *aikido* are not like this (particularly the women I know!). For the majority of practitioners, who begin with their own bodily discoveries and *then* buy into the cultural *accoutrement* . . . or not, we must listen more closely to their words and not be too hasty in looking for functions. We should savour and record the way new identities are forged out of bodily practice – the way in which culture (and indeed, a unique multiculturalism) is created through movement and association.

Aikido Body

After the group interview finished, the *kenshusei*, or inner circle of students training to be teachers of *aikido*, finished up the last of the pizza in the back room of the *dojo*, and Sensei smoked and drank some homemade sake. Dina, the most senior of the *kenshusei* in the *dojo*, said 'I'll tell you a really interesting thing that's happened to me since I've been training is that in the last three or four years I've been painting stuff that shocks me, because I've suddenly seen things differently. I mean, my parents will look at a painting and say, "Where did that come from?," and I'll say, "Oh, I did it", and they'll go: "WHAT?!" I mean, literally, I couldn't draw a stick figure as a kid, I had no ability to see any of that stuff and now it just comes out of me. But it has totally to do with *aikido* – something in the way I've seen.' Sensei responded 'That's very good. I see movement like a painting drawn with the stroke of brush. That's our speciality – try to eliminate everything unnecessary. The *aikido* body is something to do with that very much. How your body draws line in atmosphere – that's what I see – how much clarity, how much purity, how much force in the simple drawing of how you move. What is most important is that calligrapher's line.'

On another day he said, 'The *aikido* body can be seen in any first-class well-trained martial artist. *Aikido* body is alive, that's what I mean, basically. In order to be alive you must have centre . . . so that the left and right don't argue with each other. Upper portion body, lower portion body don't argue with each other. We say . . . The mountain doesn't laugh at the river because it's low. The river doesn't laugh at the mountain because of its stillness. Every function in the body has condition. And there has to be centre to cause link – to make it one single unit – for body to become alive. And everybody has it in youth, but most of the time they don't use it. As the notion of I – I, me, and mine – start to grow in a natural progression, the centre is sort of lost. And *aikido* training I consider one of the best ways to discover that organic order.'

In the words above, Dina, echoed by many others I've spoken to, introduced the notion that an *aikido* body is one that sees itself and its surroundings in a different and clearer way. Its development through focused training allows a perceptiveness that can be expressed in unexpected ways. This led to Sensei's discussing the *aikido* body as it moves through space as like a single stroke of a brush with a coordination and spirit that he suggests is natural in childhood but lost with the development of ego. *Aikido* training with the right spirit involves a peeling back of these egocentric layers to reveal qualities that appear paradoxical but may exquisitely coexist in the *aikido* body. Sensei said: 'In Japanese we say, heavier, lighter – same time. Stronger, weaker – same time. That is not paradoxical to us. Fast and slow same time.' It is suggested that in that moment of balance and clarity of movement, a healing or recovery takes place within the self, allowing creativity and freedom beyond the constraints of the various forms that are practised. A fellow student from the UK once suggested that most *aikido* practitioners have been physically or psychologically damaged at some point or other, and that their training is a healing process. Another spoke of layers and layers of 'crap' or excess that we as individuals accumulate through life and that we need to painfully (literally, through the pain of hard training) peel off and let go of. What is then revealed within is what Sensei calls 'the true body':

> In many ways, rightly or wrongly, our body is the product of our consciousness, and in order to discover what that is, requires close self-examination within our training. It is not a path where one adds more and more information, details, power etc. externally and endlessly, to the 'too much' that is already there (Chiba 1987).

The *aikido* body must look deep inside itself, recognize the excess and peel it off, absorb the negative energy of an attack and cast it away, all with a clean, centred and sure movement through space. Aikidoists further suggest that if the body can defend itself against a committed and potentially lethal attack, then it can also protect itself within the potentially disruptive and disordered social world it finds itself in.

Kenneth spoke of how supportive the *aikido* community could be to a person going through a 'hard time', and Sensei responded: 'That exactly relates to our problems with *aikido* body. As much as man, woman broken up, as much as nuclear family as community is broken down, that's what I mean by *aikido* body – *recovery* of *aikido* body. My kids come to see me and say, "You take care of your students better than us!" I say, "no, I don't make difference – whether my family or my *dojo* – that is all our body."' So here we see the *aikido* body may be situated within a community framework – this time offering a path along which perceived loss or disarray in the family or local community may be followed by recovery – a regaining of balance.

This recovery is felt to take place in the self as well as within society as a whole. *Aikido* is described as an 'antidote to modernity', a 'counterbalance to the worst tendencies in American culture of materialism and individualism/isolation'. Another describes it in terms of chaos theory:

It is a common example in chaos theory to say that the way a butterfly flaps its wings can change the weather in another part of the world. The interactions of conscious beings is even more complex and chaotic than weather, yet the nature of consciousness is to find order in chaos. The benefit to all of society from a few people who practice Aikido seriously is difficult to quantify because of those strange attractors in chaos theory (Fox, unpublished *yudansha* essay 1998).

So are we dealing here with ideas and aspirations of societal change shared by a small community of martial artists, or are we really describing, through these expressions, something that indeed impacts on a community larger than itself? Is it possible to know how the local impacts on the global or the self on the other and vice versa except through our informants' narrative? The questions posed here require that a meaningful relationship be drawn between various narrated *ideas* of embodied change and the visible and/or felt changes themselves.

The 'mindful body' (cf. Thompson 1996) is the house in which ideas and action, self and society meet and influence one another on an equal footing. We have seen above how change (in body, in social life, in work, in family), is felt by aikidoists to come about through the mundane repetitions of their lived body practice. This contrasts markedly with a perspective that sees societal innovation as being meaningfully located in the remarkable or new rather than in repetition. Anthropologists and historians have often seen innovation as a key to positioning individuals (the 'innovators') within a context of social process (cf. Ardener 1987; Hobsbawm and Ranger 1983). Perhaps 'the practising body' that repeats a relatively small number of basic throwing and pinning techniques over and over again for a lifetime of training is another such 'key' that unlocks new potentials and a fresh awareness of change. We can witness, through the narratives of aikidoists, how these changes happen at the individual as well as at the social level, simultaneously through imagination/reflection and through action.

And yet, while a global community of aikidoists experience change through repetition of a shared repertoire of movement, the resulting *aikido* bodies are not shaped in the same ways. Not all aikidoists who pick up a paintbrush will find a new ability to paint. Nor will all bodies apply themselves to their training with the same energy and attitude. One important ingredient in our study of thoughts on the body and society is the fact that 'we' inside this global community embody diversity. It is to perceptions of this diversity on a national level that I wish to turn to next.

National Body

I arrived at Sensei's house on 34th street after a couple hours of morning classes at the *dojo*. Mrs Chiba had made delicious bowls of noodle soup, and Sensei and

I sat at the big table on his back porch to talk and eat, the sound of a trickling pond and birds in the garden filling the silences.

TK: Sensei, can you recognize differences in training, attitude, and understanding between people from different nations that you work with?

CS: There are two types. One comes from cold harsh climate, and the other from warm and rich environments, like the Mediterranean. And I from my own experience, I understand these people from cold harsh environment are much stronger, much more resilient, and their concentration is very direct and pure. This is something very much to do with the diet system. People from cold climates can eat less food, and warm climates can eat much richer with variety and [greater] quantity. Those who eat simple are much stronger, and bigger.

TK: What about Californians, then?

CS: I have an interesting situation over here in San Diego. Most of my serious committed members come from East Coast . . . And from elsewhere . . . California people are very easygoing, very laid back, nice people, friendly, open, but not necessarily fit for this kind of training I conduct. This is a generalization, again . . . But you know Spanish are a little different from other Mediterranean people, I think. They have more macho men, you know. Very proud and straight back, well committed. [And in the UK:] I find the Celtic race very much closer . . . Scottish, Irish, Welsh . . . identical to Japanese. I always feel it's easier to work with those guys than the English themselves. I feel closer to those Celtic races. In social behaviour, in attitude to training, and so forth . . . And I have told you that when I was in London many years ago, I rarely had English students – very rare . . . I would say 30 per cent, that's about it. Most of my committed students were from India, Pakistan, Greece, Iran . . .

TK: You've described here a difference in martial attitude and commitment, and strength and concentration, but do you also see it, do you think, in their bodies, in the way they move?

CS: Their body is changeable and workable for me. It has more flexibility for change . . . openness, accepting new ideas . . . Something physically changes from one stage to another – the shift takes about four months. Consistent work about 3–4 hours a day, after four months you begin to notice changes. And often I have problems with those who have been training elsewhere before me . . . They are not doing it intentionally . . . but unconsciously there is resistance to change. I always enjoy, therefore, the fresh ones . . . wherever I go. See, whatever you learn from other teachers, that's fine with me. It can never be wasted. But it's like mixing wine and sake together. It makes two good drinks undrinkable! In general

American people are very open to change. They're not as stubborn as European people. And they have lots of time if they want to have time, . . . and still keep going on. Elsewhere, I know, it's very difficult to have time on your own. In Japan it's even more extreme. If you do use time people treat you badly – it's treated like a crime. Everybody's watching you.

In this brief excerpt of an interview with Sensei, we hear about a different level of understanding of the *aikido* body that emerges with a directed consciousness of national character. *Aikido* bodies are not just given a new shape and line through months and months of daily practice of *kata* (technique) and *ukemi* (receiving/falling). They don't just absorb, understand and then resolve problems with family and local community. Their strength, character, receptiveness to change and attitudes are also shaped by the environments they have been raised in, and these are seen, certainly by this one master, on the basis of forty years of experience, to vary significantly from place to place. He associates northern climes with simpler diets that feed the *aikido* body in a particularly strong and martial way. Relationships to time are also seen to vary between subcontinents – Americans are open to change, owing in part to the time that they are willing to give to individual growth and development, while in Europe and Japan time for such development is not seen to be as free.

Here I could segue into a discussion about time, leisure,[9] diet, and national character studies, but that would steer us away from our path, which seeks to describe the *aikido* body. Suffice to say here that the *aikido* body apparently ingests very different foods in different climes and times, it balances its practice on the mat with other tasks and pleasures in a multitude of ways and with different sets of priorities. Social distinctions of ethnicity, nation, gender, class may or may not shape *aikido* bodies: they may or may not insert themselves into people's 'actions and attitudes, their discourses, learning processes and everyday lives' (Foucault 1980: 39). These *potential* diversities enter the mat area, practise with a community of others that speak the same body language, and exit into a diverse and changing world of individual and social pursuits. The aikidoist's experience would suggest that while the world may impress itself (*à la* Foucault) on the body, the body may as easily turn around and impress itself through reflection and action on the social world.

The practising *aikido* body invites diversity and creates change, but it also is a site for the expression of unity. Such unity is achieved locally and globally. An aikidoist is part of a local club full of members that train and often socialize together several times a week. He or she is also a member of an international organization that will host large courses taught by senior teachers of the art (such as Chiba Sensei). Practice at these events draws people from many parts of the world on to the mat, and the space of the mat becomes a global village of bodies that silently share a language of movement and a quality of body contact. Off the mat, this 'community' of practitioners will discuss the quality of the training and the teaching, they will be able to watch others practising and identify and discuss the ways in which various people's bodies are changing or not. The ability to use an indigenous vocabulary to describe elements of training that are seen to be essential for good practice (for example 'contact', 'spirit', 'commitment', 'relaxation', and so on) reinforces a sense of community belonging. The shared language may, however, frequently be used to communicate disagreement around the quality of different performances.

Teachers will discuss these differences before making decisions about whether or not to promote a student after performative tests held at courses. Students will discuss these too. A student from Germany once argued with me for an hour about a test demonstration that resulted in promotion. He felt that the aikidoist's movements were 'too soft' and 'would not be effective' in a 'real-life situation', while I felt that the person who had tested had demonstrated real 'understanding' of *aikido* principles; he had trained with a 'good attitude' and with excellent 'fluidity of movement' and 'posture'. I wrote in my diary at that time that the martial artist was a 'typical German arrogant young male – macho and unrefined!'. These debatable generalizations around ideas of nation and gender that I privately scribbled explained in my mind at the time any differences of opinion that we had as individuals. We see here, how the ability to train together and share a verbal as well as a non-verbal language of *aikido* movement creates an *aikido* community. The capacity to relate those body movements to other aspects of social life (as demonstrated earlier in this chapter) also unifies the group. But community need not equal consensus!

What many practitioners call 'Little *Aikido*' takes place on the mat, it's about the mechanics of practice. 'Big *Aikido*', however, takes place in the world outside the mat. As we've seen above, the Little gives one vision to approach the Big in a different way, with different eyes and different sensitivities. The Big allows one to move, react, and learn with one's body in different ways when the 'Little *Aikido*' is practised. I have also been told about the difference between 'inner *aikido*' and 'outer *aikido*'. The 'inner' is the practice itself, and the outer is what has been called by one of my sources the 'spectacle' of *aikido*; the politics and organizational structure that supports the art, the testing, the essays that are written, the booklets and publications that are produced. The outer is the 'head of the beast' and the inner is the centre and heart. The two can never be free of one another – the head and body are one.

The *aikido* body is both an ideal entity (embodying a perfect line through space) and a real entity (inscribed by environment/national characteristics/individual background). It is both singularly contained in an individual and a composite of many significant others. The art is at core the same everywhere; the principles and the potentials are universal, but the individuals and groups that imbibe of it take it into themselves in ethnic, national, and age- or gender-specific ways. The '*aikido* body' becomes an exceptionally useful metaphor or tool to 'think with' in order to understand the relationship of bodily practice and everyday life, and one that is not generated by the analyst, but by the subject.[10] So it is at this point, *after* we are told about the body in our lived interactions with our informants, that it becomes meaningful for us as anthropologists to engage with theory on social change and the body. If we briefly return to Bourdieu's expectations of the aikidoists' habitus here, a truly *emic*, practitioner-generated understanding of aikidoists' experience would illustrate diversity rather than consensus in background. Such diversity would be seen both to generate and to be generated by a shared but often critically and comparatively observed and experienced 'body'. What is revealed and particularly meaningful from this example is an overwhelming consciousness of the body's power for change through practice.

I wish to end this chapter by emphasizing that regularly popping down to the local sports centre or a purpose-built *dojo* for some *aikido* practice is far more significant to a vast number of practitioners than would strike the untrained or unpractised eye. It is a 'way' more than a leisure pursuit. It is because of the many levels of understanding that so many practitioners share – about the way the body should react on the mat, the relation of inside and outside, the place of *aikido* in today's fragmented society, and so on – that it generates such dedicated practice and reflexive discussion and argument. It is because of the richness and challenge found in the many apparent paradoxes embodied in the practice (the heavy but light, the soft but hard, the strong but weak, the non-competitive but hierarchical, the way of the warrior as a way of peace, and so on) that students of *aikido* all over the world often make their practice a lifelong pursuit. The practice of the art is felt to be a central key of their experience, rather than confined to the casual periphery at which one often finds 'leisure' located in the popular imagination. Change at several levels is observed and felt from such embodied repetitive practice. It is for these reasons as well that social anthropologists can study this martial art as a 'total phenomenon' and place it in the centre of the discipline. As Steven said, over the divide from the men's changing-room after a particularly challenging session, 'Maybe it's the elusiveness of *aikido* that brings us back every day.'

Acknowledgement

I would like to thank the editors of this volume for their useful feedback on the text. I am also extremely grateful for the time, thoughtful contributions to and support of my work offered by T.K. Chiba Sensei and Coryl Crame Sensei (as well as by their students in the San Diego Aikikai and North County Aikikai respectively).

Notes

1. An exception is a style initiated by one of Ueshiba's students, Tomiki, that integrates *judo* and *aikido* techniques into a special competitive sport that is currently quite popular, particularly in Japan (while the non-competitive 'traditional' form is more popular in the West) (Reid and Croucher 1983: 194–5).
2. See Kohn (2001) for a discussion about how the learning of *aikido* is felt and communicated through bodily practice.
3. The trick, of course, is how we are to describe these as anthropologists. Movements can be recorded on film and even with a Laban-like notation for individual techniques and their variations, but the feeling of contact, and the way in which the attack leads the form, and the like must come from the attempts from practitioners to verbalize their experiences.
4. In common with *karate* – *kara*, 'empty' + *te*, 'hand'.
5. In the early 1960s, four disciples went to Europe, two to the States and one to Australia. Now there are *shihan* based in 14 countries around the globe, including North and South America, Europe, New Zealand, Thailand, and Malaysia. Tamura Sensei has a huge following in France, and has clearly exercised great organizational skill to stimulate this! A rough estimate of membership indicates that there are over 17,000 aikidoists in France, 10,000 in the UK, and 26,000 in the USA.
6. This fieldwork took place during my research leave in autumn 1999, and it draws largely from participant observation both on a number of practice mats in the area and off them. I also engaged in formal and informal interviews with aikidoists, as well as focus-group discussions. I often captured informants' words with audiotape and their silent movement on the mat with a digital video recorder. My 'field' here, however, consists of a body practice and the people who engage in it, rather than a place that is situated in geographical space. Thus I have also augmented my findings from San Diego with spoken ideas and bodily expressions recorded from my ongoing personal training experiences in the art over the last decade.
7. Additional recent titles of this genre found on Amazon.com (but not examined more closely!) include *Corporate Aikido: Unleash the Potential Within Your Company to Neutralize Competition and Seize Growth*, and *Leadership Aikido*.
8. Please note that names of most informants have been changed to preserve anonymity.
9. Ideas about leisure, time and *aikido* are the focus of a paper I presented at the American Anthropological Association meetings 2001 in a session co-organized with Simon Coleman entitled, 'The Discipline of Leisure: Embodying Cultures of "Recreation"'.

10. Artists and art critics have been through the same crises over form and meaning and voice that social anthropologists have over the last forty years or so. If our subject of inquiry was traditionally situated and observed in a remote village and then described using our own words in books and articles, theirs was traditionally produced in solitary studios and then exhibited and 'shared' from the walls of museums. Our subject is blossoming because the field can be in our neighbourhood, and the voices of our informants can sing with stronger voices than our own. One of the great revolutionaries in the art world is Allan Kaprow, the creator of 'the Happenings' of the 1960s. In his performance art he dispenses with the museum and creates art, with the participating public, in the 'real world' outside. By placing it there and by inviting participation in an art form that only exists while it is being produced (it cannot be collected), profound questions about the sometimes paradoxical relationship between life and art can be explored (see Kaprow 1993). I think it is an example of pure providence that Allan Kaprow is married to Coryl Crane, the first *aikido* instructor I worked with and lived with in the San Diego area, who is one of Chiba Sensei's most senior students. Is it mere coincidence that her words, and those of many other aikidoists I've spoken to, celebrate relationships between life and martial arts through daily practice?

References

Ardener, E. (1987), '"Remote Areas": Some Theoretical Considerations', in A. Jackson (ed.), *Anthropology at Home*, London: Tavistock.

Bale, J. (1994), *Landscapes of Modern Sport*, Leicester: Leicester University Press.

Bourdieu, P. (1990), *In Other Words: Essays Towards a Reflexive Sociology*, Stanford, CA: Stanford University Press.

Chiba, T. K. (1987), 'On the Art of Training', *Sancho: Aikido Newsletter of the San Diego Aikikai*, Vol. 5, No. 1, April.

Clarke, J. and C. Critcher (1985), *The Devil Makes Work*, London: Macmillan.

Coakley, J. and P. Donnelly (eds) (1999), *Inside Sports*, London: Routledge.

Cox, R. (1998), 'The Zen Arts: An Anthropological Study of the Culture of Aesthetic Form in Japan', Ph.D. thesis, University of Edinburgh.

Dobson, T. (1985), 'A Kind Word Turneth Away Wrath', in R. S. Heckler (ed.), *Aikido and the New Warrior*, pp. 65–9. Berkeley, CA: North Atlantic Books.

Dobson, T. and V. Miller (1978, *Aikido in Everyday Life: Giving In to Get Your Way*, Berkeley, CA: North Atlantic Books.

Donohue, J. J. (1994), *Warrior Dreams: The Martial Arts and the American Imagination*, Westport, CT: Bergin and Garvey.

—— (1998), *Herding the Ox: The Martial Arts as Moral Metaphor*, Hartford, CT: Turtle Press.

Dunning, E. and C. Rojek (eds) (1992), *Sport and Leisure in the Civilizing Process*, London: Macmillan.

Elias, N. and E. Dunning (1986), *Quest for Excitement*, Oxford: Blackwell.

Foucault, M. (1980), *The History of Sexuality – Volume 1: An Introduction*, Harmondsworth: Penguin.

Heckler, R. S. (ed.) (1985), *Aikido and the New Warrior*, Berkeley, CA: North Atlantic Books.

Hill, J. (2002), *Sport, Leisure and Culture in Twentieth-Century Britain*, New York: Palgrave.

Hobsbawm, E. and T. Ranger (eds) (1983), *The Invention of Tradition*, Cambridge: Cambridge University Press.

Homma, G. (1990), *Aikido for Life*, Berkeley, CA: North Atlantic Books.

Horne, J., A. Tomlinson and G. Whannel (1999), *Understanding Sport*, London/ New York: E. and F. N. Spoon.

Karow, A. (1993), *The Blurring of Art and Life* (ed. J. Kelley), Berkeley, CA: University of California Press.

Kohn, T. (2001), 'Don't Talk – Blend: Ideas about Body and Communication in *Aikido* Practice', in J. Henry and C. W. Watson (eds), *An Anthropology of Indirect Communication*, pp. 162–78. London: Routledge.

MacClancy, J. (ed.) (1996), *Sport, Identity and Ethnicity*, Oxford: Berg Press.

Mauss, M. (1967 [1924]), *The Gift*, New York: Norton.

Reid, H. and M. Croucher (1983), *The Way of the Warrior: The Paradox of the Martial Arts*, Woodstock, NY: The Overview Press.

Snyder, E. and E. Spreitzer (1978), *Social Aspects to Sport*, Englewood Cliffs, NJ: Prentice-Hall.

Stone, S. (1985), 'Blending with Death', in R. S. Heckler (ed.), *Aikido and the New Warrior*, pp. 70–7. Berkeley, CA: North Atlantic Books.

Thompson, E. (1996), 'The Mindful Body: Embodiment and Cognitive Science', in M. O'Donovan-Anderson (ed.), *The Incorporated Self: Interdisciplinary Perspectives on Embodiment*, London: Rowman and Littlefield.

Ueshiba, K. (1984), *The Spirit of Aikido*, Tokyo: Kodansha International.

Zarrilli, P. B. (1998), *When the Body Becomes All Eyes: Paradigms, Discourses and Practices of Power in Kalarippayattu, a South Indian Martial Art*, Oxford: Oxford University Press.

8

The Embodiment of Male Identities: Alliances and Cleavages in Salvadorean Football

Henrik Ronsbo

Introduction

Football[1] had never been on the research agenda when I started my fieldwork in Western El Salvador in 1995. It was forced upon me. Forced by the time and energy spent on football grounds by young men. Not that the game was new to me when I started playing with them. I have played it since childhood and continue to do so in a minor league in Copenhagen, and I spend inordinate amounts of time following my team in the Danish Championship. In short, nothing that follows in this essay should divert the reader from the fact that for myself, as well as for the rest of the persons mentioned, the most important part of the game is to win matches – playing together! However, as groups of men try to do so, they also entrain a variety of social processes that are worth exploring from an ethnographic point of view. In this essay, I will explore these social processes by describing how young men, when playing football, and other villagers, when watching it, embody personal and social identities.

In order to do this, this essay contains two separate ethnographic pieces. The first piece describes the ongoing adjustments in alliances between young men, who on a daily basis play on their respective home grounds in the municipality of Santo Domingo de Guzmán in Western El Salvador. In these daily tournaments, personal alliances are created, broken and maintained as the young men team up to play for money, and although the game is a leisure activity undertaken in the afternoon, the prize money makes a difference for the winners. The other ethnographic piece explores the multiple fields of personal and social identifications that are created during the municipality's annual football tournament. In this tournament teams from different territorial units within the municipality (*cantones* and *barrios*) as well as teams from neighbouring municipalities play against each other, the final being played during the village's *Fiesta Patronal* in August. This piece will take the form of situational analysis of a match played in 1996 between two village teams, a match that sparked off a debate on the history of and identification with the indigenous and non-indigenous communities of Santo Domingo.

What I shall also demonstrate is that, although such a description of village sports may appear to be a novelty, it does in fact resonate with a well-established Mesoamerican ethnography of male sociality as developed in the literature on religious brotherhoods.[2] These studies focused on the brotherhoods' function in the maintenance of corporate village communities, but gave only a little attention to the understanding of the ways in which the embodiment of personal and social identities shaped male worlds.

In order to unfold this ethnography of masculinity, I introduce the concepts of regulative ritual, performative reflexivity and embodied identity. I argue that with these concepts we are able to explore the everyday adjustment of personal alliances within male peer groups and link this arena to the description and analysis of how communal identity is practised and debated by men as well as women – community members as well as non-members. What brings together these two arenas of description and interpretation is the practice of football with its attendant discourses on the style and genre of play, bodily expression and gesture. That is, through the concept of embodied identity we are provided with an important nexus between body and discourse – between personal biography and the social history of communities.

Studying Male Sociality

Football, no doubt, plays a prominent role in the creation of social and individual identities in Central America. Despite this, we know very little about the social history of the game. Questions such as the relationship between the formation of conscript armies, the rise of male migration to public works and agro-industrial enclaves and the spread of football and baseball in rural communities have not been addressed so far. The relationship between the emergence of the bourgeois national imaginary and the introduction of national championships remains unexplored, and while North American and European ethnographers have foregrounded dances, rituals, and religious brotherhoods, the 'natives' of Mesoamerica have increasingly focused their emotional and physical attention on sports such as football, baseball and volleyball.

It is beyond the purpose of this essay to analyse why sports in general and football in particular have never received the attention they deserved from ethnographers working in Mesoamerica. However, two explanations are worth considering. Firstly, from the point of view of regional ethnography most sports were never seen as belonging to the realm of 'regional culture', and hence they were not seen as worthy of ethnographic description.[3] The fact that sports follow the same rules globally blinded anthropologists to the ways in which such rules were explored and inscribed differently in various regional contexts. Secondly, during most of the twentieth century Mesoamerica was almost exclusively the ground of North American ethnographers. As a consequence it was sent fieldworkers unfamiliar with the game of football, its history, its tactics, the way it is practised and how it is experienced. Not surprisingly we must turn to 'native' ethnographers to find descriptions and analysis of Latin American football as a social and cultural phenomenon – and then we only find them in a South American context (Archetti 1999; Altamirano 1984; DaMatta 1982).

In order to argue that football matters we must, however, make a detour to regional ethnography itself. In particular to the parts thereof that have been engaged in exploring the intersection of male sociality and communal organ-ization. By discussing two key works in the regional ethnography, this essay advances the argument that the study of local sports not only enriches our under-standing of sports, but also contributes to the tradition in Mesoamerican ethno-graphy that has been dedicated to the study of religious brotherhoods.

From the 1930s, the community study was the preferred methodology in Mesoamerican ethnography. The indigenous community was the site of fieldwork and, more often than not, it also framed the key ethnographic question – how have indigenous villagers been able to maintain communal identity and 'separate cultures' during more than five hundred years of colonial and post-colonial domination? During the second half of the twentieth century, the answers to this question were framed by two opposing paradigms. The first took its point of departure in the agrarian community as a vestige of a pre-Columbian cultural tradition. Isolation and remoteness explained its existence, and hence ethnographic material could, if properly collected, provide answers to questions framed by archaeologists working in the region.[4] Communities were seen as small-scale social structures that had survived from a complex pre-historical civilization to a historical one. Quite naturally, proponents of this argument focused their attention upon the indigenous communities of Guatemala and Southern Mexico. The oppos-ing model was historicist, and based on an eclectic political economy. Eric Wolf's seminal article from 1955 on the nature of closed corporate and open peasant communities stipulated that both these were shaped by European colonization and the surplus extraction it was based upon (Wolf 1955). Community, he argued, was a way of resisting and accommodating the pressures of an exploitative political and economic state formation, or to use William Roseberry's phrase, 'communities were the precipitates of capitalism'. These two models divided historians and anthropologists for several generations, not only in the United States but also in Central America and Mexico.

The civil wars of Central America swept away these models. Previously com-munity had been seen either as a deeply rooted cultural paradigm (Vogt 1993) or as the outcome of a long history of domination and resistance. The civil wars shattered the ethnographic field of community studies,[5] and during the 1990s a new ethnography took shape that focused on social organization and the creation of meaning in volatile situations of conflict and mobility. Reading the older ethnography with these more current questions in mind enables us to break down the duality of cultural essence versus social history that framed discussions within regional ethnography from the 1950s to the 1980s. To move beyond the duality, as this essay intends to do is, however, not tantamount to asserting that the duality was unproductive or erroneous. Rather, we should pay attention to what these particular research paradigms were able to illuminate, and to what fell outside their view (Roseberry 1994).[6]

Frank Cancian's monograph *Economics and Prestige in a Maya Community – The Religious Cargo System of Zinacantan* of 1965 is a seminal work in many ways.[7] Cancian frames the general question of communal resilience in the face of 'modernization' as a study of the development of religious brotherhoods in Zinacantan.[8] By providing 'rules under which a man may enhance his public image' (1965: 135), the religious brotherhood (*cofradía*) 'legitimizes the wealth differences that do exist and thus prevents disruptive envy' (1965: 140). In this monograph, Cancian describes in detail the hierarchical structure of the brotherhoods and the services (*cargos*) undertaken in them. Such 'services' include the participants' devotion to a particular Saint, the rituals they perform in his/ her honour, the costs they incur when organizing services, the ascendance of particular individuals within the institutions during their lifetimes and the historical evolutions of the institutions themselves. Participation in the brotherhoods thus facilitates community integration; but the different ways in which men participate are not analysed. Issues of disagreements over styles of performance in terms of drinking, smoking, dancing and eating are theoretically irrelevant, according to Cancian. The mere participation of men makes the difference.

In 1983, Robert Wasserstrom published a monograph on the same religious brotherhoods, but his ethnography bore the title *Class and Society in Central Chiapas*. The book was a historicist critique of the Harvard Chiapas Project in general, and it was read partly as a rebuttal of Cancian's ahistorical and funct-ionalist monograph from the point of view of political economy.[9] Wasserstrom details the development of the 'wider field of force' within which the communities of Chiapas were situated from the sixteenth to the twentieth centuries, and argues that hierarchically organized male religious services became the way in which some highland communities – unlike others – were able to withstand pressure from external political and economic elites. Wasserstrom thus understood religious brotherhoods as institutions through which native peoples of Mesoamerica acted within and reflected upon larger social orders characterized by domination.

In this way, Wasserstrom's analysis of *cargo* service was no less functionalist than was Cancian's. Whereas Cancian saw ritual as the product of communal hierarchy (Cancian 1965: 51), Wasserstrom saw it as the product of a regional social hierarchy. Male identities as embodied through dancing, drinking and smoking were analysed not in terms of how they organized and adjusted relations between men,[10] but in terms of how they expressed hierarchical socio-economic relations. Both of these are of course relevant concerns; but what is intriguing is how the argument between the culturalist Cancian and the historicist Wasserstrom rested upon a silenced subtext of male sociality.[11] From the monographs emerges a picture of men drinking and dancing for no apparent reason. It is in order to throw light upon this silenced subtext of male subjectivities that I will discuss the notions of regulative ritual and reflexive performance in the following section.

Ritual and Performance

Football is a rule-based activity (a game) where the struggle between two opposing sides to gain control of the ball (the play) generates a social field in which social and individual identities are embodied. Through practices such as motion, gesture, contact and oral communication, relations are created between the participants – players as well as spectators. In this field participants interpret bodily performances as statements within broader discourses on social identity such as masculinity, ethnicity and religion or class (Archetti 1999). Bodies are objects of interpretation and sites of enunciation. In this way a football game becomes a space in which personal and social identities are created, organized and adjusted. To state, however, that football is merely a rational and communicative behaviour places it outside the realm of ritual, and so renders it distinct from the practices undertaken in for example religious brotherhoods. It is this proposition about the nature of football that I would like to challenge in the next part of this essay.

Fundamental to the classic definition of ritual is that it involves a magical act that does not have an effect in itself, but is supposed to evoke the potency of some other entity in order to produce a desired effect in the form of disruption or restoration of order. Recently, a critique of the classic reading of ritual, termed the regulative interpretation, has been proposed. According to this, ritual is not a means, but a way in which to formulate ends (Gose 1994).[12] The merit of this interpretation is that it takes its point of departure in the interwoven character of magical, symbolic and rational technical behaviour; thus, according to Gose: 'ritual depends on, and interacts with, other kinds of purposive activity, and becomes much more comprehensible once we stop treating it as a type of activity that must be coherent unto itself' (Gose 1994: 7). This view of ritual also emerges from Gerald Sider's analysis of customs among fishermen in Newfoundland. Sider sees custom as Gose sees ritual, as a regulator of social relations. Customs provide:

a context in which people can do things that it would be difficult to do directly; they may provide a context in which to coordinate and co-adjust a multiplicity of emotions and interests; and especially, as the loci for intentional, forward-looking actions, they may keep the need for collective action, collective adjustment of interests, and collective expression of feelings and emotions within the terrain of the co-participants in a custom, serving as a boundary to exclude others (Sider 1986: 94).

These intentional and reflexive aspects of ritual can be expanded by drawing on Turner's (1987) definition of ritual as a type of performative action: 'Cultural performances are not simple reflectors or expressions of culture or even of changing culture but may themselves be active agencies of change, representing the eye by which a culture sees itself and the drawing board on which creative actors sketch out what they believe to be more apt or interesting "designs for living"' (1987: 24). While disputing the view that ritual is a reflection or a model of and for culture,[13] Turner proposes that we see the performance as an social agent *sui generis* that by proposing new 'designs for living' may reorganize everyday life. I propose that we unpack Turner's notion of 'design for living' by using William Roseberry's assertion that such designs provide ways of 'living through, talking about and acting upon orders characterized by domination' (Roseberry 1994: 361). Such a focus on social orders and social relations is consistent with Turner's own definition of performative reflexivity: 'Performative reflexivity is a condition in which a socio-cultural group [. . .] reflect back upon [. . .] the relations, actions, symbols, meanings, codes, roles, statuses, social structures [. . .] and other socio-cultural components which make up their public "selves"' (Turner 1987: 24).

What runs through the texts of Gose, Sider and Turner is an awareness of ritual and performance as forms of practice that not only produce a set of specific social relations but also create a space of reflection, thereby making ritual and performance a subject of social agency *sui generis*. Although both Cancian and Wasserstrom in their monographs on religious brotherhoods detail the paths of dancers, their forms of drinking, the burning of firecrackers, the smoking of cigarettes and the sharing of meals, they still reduce the institution of the brotherhood to a function in a larger cultural structure or a longer social history. The implication of this view is that we are unable to account for the changes in the styles, gestures and coding of male social relations. In addition, we are unable to perceive the possibility of failure and misunderstanding in performative practices. Finally, we are unable to understand football as a performative space that shares a variety of features with religious brotherhoods in the ways in which they both structure the field of male–male social relations while generating the community as a non-gendered social field, characterized by male social agency.

Football and Young Males

Playing football in the village of Santo Domingo is a male activity organized by three separate peer groups. Two of the groups play on their own separate grounds on a daily basis. These are the upper moiety, whose team is known as *Las Vegas*, and the lower moiety, which has a team without name. The third team of the village, the *ladino* team, known as *Fuerza* (the Force), practise weekly on a field south of the village. The following description refers to the practice of playing in the lower moiety of the village. It is based on my own participation at least twice a week during the year I lived in the village; and in form and content these practices were similar to what took place at the same time of the day in the upper moiety.

Every afternoon around four o'clock male members of the lower moiety aged between 12 and 30 years assemble in order to play football. Their ground lies next to the river that separates the village from *cantón* El Caulote, one of four rural subdivisions of the municipality. Prior to the matches the men hang out by a small shop at the entrance to the village, drinking soda, smoking cigarettes if somebody has any, and shouting at the female youth from the *cantón* who pass in and out of the village in the afternoon. The girls pass by with soaked corn, which is ground in one of the mills in the village, or they bring fruit for relatives in the village. But they might also be on their way home with groceries bought in the regional capital of Sonsonate, or coming from afternoon classes in the village school. The river crossing with its shop thus forms a point of social interaction. Here the boys and men, who come from *cantón* el Caulote, meet with the village lower moiety youth, forming what is known as a *mara*. A *mara* is a group of men that spend their afternoons together. The core of the *mara* are the young men around 20; but older *bolos* (drunkards) who try to collect enough money to buy their next bottle of alcohol are also around. Around four o'clock somebody starts to blow a whistle, and more of the lower moiety youth begins to appear, and everybody, normally around twenty of them, moves down to the football ground that lies on the river bank just below the shop.

The ground is around seven metres wide and twice as long. It is closed off towards the river by large stones that have been removed from the ground and towards the village by the rising *peña*, and the rocky substrate breaks through the surface in several places. The overall quality of the ground makes rebounds unpredictable and running hazardous. Its maintenance is a major issue, around which the *mara* organizes itself. Sewage runs over it, and an underground pipe was installed in early 1996, only to be ruined a few months later, when a military bulldozer rolled on to the ground to remove a large tree. The goals, which are made of cane, are small, only about two by three metres, and the rapid game played is very much akin to three- or four-person indoor football, although here the keeper can hold the ball, and tackling is allowed and even cherished. Furthermore, with six to ten people on the field, the game is much more physical than indoor football. There is very little room to dribble; almost any move is hindered by an opposing player. The unpredictable rebounds from the ground as well as those from the rocks and stones surrounding the ground and the tree in the middle – all these factors turn the game into long intervals of coordinated struggle for the ball, only broken by the occasional strikes at goal. Overall, the lack of space and the poor ground support a style of football in which technical aspects such as passing the ball around among team members or dribbling past an opponent are absent. Consequently, the more physical form of play in the air becomes the favoured arena for the display of individual excellence. The clustering of players and the speed of the game are reflected in the name given to this kind of football: *rapidfútbol* or 'fast-football'.

Teaming up is the first activity that takes place after the *mara* moves down to the ground. One player, often a senior within the peer group, holds a coin of one *Colon* in the hand. He moves around chatting, pushing, and throwing dirt or mud at other players, while he throws the coin up in the air to signal that the team is open for contributing participants. Others put their *Colons* in, and when the team leader has a *Colon* from each participant, the team is closed. This money, together with that of the opposing team, forms the prize money. Some players without money may solicit a sponsor to enter a team. A successful afternoon in which the same team wins several consecutive games may provide a player with an income equivalent to a quarter of a day-labourer's pay. This alone is a good reason to be careful when joining a team.[14]

A game is normally played as two halves of 10 or 15 minutes each. It is one long outburst of energy until one of the teams has a lead of several goals, following which the pace slows down and the game draws towards its end. The ruggedness of the ground means that luck always plays a considerable part; hence the only way to prevail in the game is by using energy to push the play towards the opponents' goal, which brings one into a position to score. It is a game where physique rather than technique prevails. Participants do not refer to this mode of playing as constituting a particular style, nor do they refer to the ground in order to explain its presence. Rather, to explain the specific characteristics of their style of playing, participants call upon a racialized class discourse. Local residents argue that since 'the Indian is *recio*' (has stamina, resilience and strength) this shapes his particular style as a player. The same discourse validated the self-perception among ex-servicemen in the village,[15] that they had superior qualities as soldiers, and has since the early twentieth century supported the notion that indigenous men have superior qualities as day-labourers. In this way football embodies a racialized class discourse, and it creates a space in which a specific indigenous masculinity is performed.

With matches in which physique and endurance are essential assets and with money to win, it is attractive to play with men who can be trusted and will commit themselves. For this reason, the core of any team is made up by *comadines*, i.e. young men that trust in each other. These alliances are also marked in everyday verbal exchanges, where young men refer to each other using the kinship terms of *primo* or *hermano* (cousin or brother) in order to signal close emotional relations.

In this way, everyday football organizes alliances within the peer group. When changes in favoured teams appear, it inevitably signals changes in the personal alliances and relationships of trust. A case of this emerged around a group consisting of three unmarried men between eighteen and twenty-three that played together. The three men came from two neighbouring, but unrelated, households in the lower moiety. Two of them – Manuelito and Pollo – are cousins on their mothers' side, and in 1995–96 they both lived in the household of Manuelito, owing to the death of Pollo's mother. The third man – Toro – was their closest friend, to whom they always referred as *hermano* (brother).

During the spring of 1996, Toro developed an amorous relationship with a woman from *cantón* el Caulote, going as far as proposing to form a household with her. Because of this relationship, the whole group broke its alliance with a man from Caulote, with whom they had played over a longer period and who months earlier had assisted in the construction of the house of Toro's parents. The Caulote player claimed fatherhood over the woman's two children (he was also married to another woman), and during the following months a dispute developed involving allegations of witchcraft, physical assaults and, of course, fierce matches on the football ground.

To state that the football ground was the only space in which this conflict was displayed is wrong. However, everyday football games provided the field in which these four young men could express the emerging cleavage and the peer group could adjust itself accordingly. The embodiment of the cleavage entailed separateness in the pre- and post-match period in which the peer shared a space of consumption of water, cigarettes and fruit. It entailed the formation of separate teams on the ground, and loud cheering when opponents of the rival managed to win games or at least to place a fierce tackle, and it ended with a violent threat during a night vigil in which a *corbo* (machete) – the icon of *ladino* masculinity – was wielded.

The maintenance or severance of a personal alliance thus entails everyday choices on the part of the participants. These choices are made mostly around the game of football, when choosing between the better player and the more reliable *comadines*. Nevertheless, there also exists the split-second decision whether to spare an opponent or to tackle him fiercely, to shout or shut up. The peer group participates in these ongoing adjustments, aligning itself according to perceived loyalties. In the case mentioned above it entailed that the *mara* divided itself into a Caulote fraction and a village fraction.

The alliance between Pollo, Toro and Manuelito was strengthened in the years following my first fieldwork in Santo Domingo. From 1997 when Pollo left to 1999 when Manuelito as the last one departed, the three men managed to move from El Salvador to the USA, at first as illegals, though later under the Post-Mitch legislation[16] they all obtained legal residence. After several moves between different households, Pollo and Manuelito now live together with Manuelito's older brother in Seattle, and on several occasions, they have tried to persuade Toro to move to Seattle. When the woman over whom the dispute had erupted in 1996 moved to Miami to live with Toro in the summer of 2001, it would have seemed as if the alliance had been dismantled. That, however, is far from the case. Bi-weekly or monthly telephone calls serve to maintain the male alliance, and as young Salvadoreans organize their migrancy, there is nothing to prevent the three men and the woman from forming a household in Seattle or Miami.

In this way the alliance forms an important livelihood resource not only within the social field of the village, but also within the space of transnational migrancy in which the *comadines* who played together now share and adjust experiences, expectations and emotions. The alliance provides an important livelihood resource in the institutional sense of the concept, and it increases the leverage young men have in their ongoing discussions and conflicts with the seniors of their kingroup over the consumption of their labour and income.[17] The young males' alliances always represent an alternative in terms of consumption as well as production, and seniors know this when bargains are struck as to the division of the income that these unmarried men provide to their households in Santo Domingo.

But football is also played at the level of the municipality in tournaments where teams from different territorial units with different ethnic affiliations compete, and on these occasions football becomes a reflexive performance set apart from everyday life, opening a space for reflections upon social relations and orders of domination.

In order to understand the significance of the game that I will analyse in the following section, one has to know the historical context. During the seventies and into the period when the Salvadorean social conflict became a fully-fledged civil war (1979), inhabitants of the upper moiety were active participants in the political movements of the Left. In late 1979, an attack was organized on a coffee plantation where land-poor villagers had worked in the seasonal coffee harvest for several generations. During the attack, one assailant was captured, and he apparently disclosed the names of other members of the group. This led to several abductions from the village carried out by the army, and it culminated on 26 February 1980 with an army attack. On that day 24 men, all living in the upper moiety, were killed. While some died in a shootout during the attack, most of them were capt- ured, tortured and finally executed. In the following months approximately thirty more were 'disappeared' and killed by the army in coordination with the civil patrol of the village. Apparently, *ladinos* were particularly active in the patrol. Survivors claim that *ladinos* helped the army locate certain individuals, and they claim that *ladinos* displayed contempt towards the recently widowed women who were forced to subsist through the production of *comales*, clay plates of pre-Columbian origin used for roasting *tortillas*.

Owing to these historical animosities between the upper moiety and the *ladinos*, great expectations were attached to the game between Las Vegas and Fuerza. The draw for the 1996 football tournament had placed the two teams in the same group. The match was played on the ground where Fuerza practice, a ground owned by the organizer of Fuerza Leopoldo Contreras, one of the richest *ladinos* in the village. Before the match, more than a hundred people had assembled around the ground. Given the importance of the match, a marimba band from a neighbouring village had been hired for the day's matches, three in all. Of these the most important was the Fuerza – Las Vegas game. The spectators were standing around the ground on three sides. The small *ladino* crowd supporting Fuerza was standing at the far end under a tree, with the municipal marimba band at their side. The majority – the Las Vegas supporters – were along one side, and the general crowd was at the opposite end to the *ladinos*. The crowd was largely male, but the women that were present participated actively in the cheering that went on, while they sold various kinds of beverages. The core of the *mara* from the upper moiety was sitting around the team-owner, a young man who had lost one leg during the war. He collected fees from players and paid the referee, and he managed the players' cards, with names and pictures, which were handed over to the referee prior to the match – a standard procedure prior to any organized football game.

The selection of the team is a drawn-out negotiation between the team-owner and the senior players. Long discussions are carried out in the evenings before a game over the issue of who should play. Issues like who has a decent pair of boots, who has shin-guards, who feels fit affect the selection process. In this way the team becomes a collection of the individuals who on this particular day consider themselves the strongest and therefore the best representatives of the moiety.[18] Fixing on a team in this way is highly divergent from the alliance negotiations that take place during everyday football, although this does not alter the style of the game. Instead of having a team bound by strong personal alliances, which guarantees a strong collective performance based on the strength of those alliances, the Las Vegas team in the annual tournament is a collection of individuals, whose participation in the team is based on their self-perception as fit and strong, and whose main purpose is to show excellence as representatives of the moiety. In European football jargon this would be termed a 'lack of technical and tactical skills', but such a description does not capture the specificity of the style. The focus on individuals representing the moiety has the effect that team tactics become less relevant. This is manifested in the lack of passing in midfield, and the lack of defensive coordination between midfield and defence. Only in the final matches of the tournament, when a midfielder was brought into the team from outside the village, were collective principles introduced into the play of Las Vegas. On this team of individuals, nobody but the outsider could organize the play. What I conceived as almost total chaos during most of the matches was, however, the way this team played the game; it was a display of individuals embodying the moiety, and hence the hours of subsequent analysis were spent on individual rather than team performance.

However, let us turn to the game. After ten minutes Fuerza scored. It was a dubious goal – nobody knew if the ball had passed the line, but finally, under pressure from players from Fuerza, the referee awarded them the lead. However, with the support of most of the spectators, Las Vegas played themselves back into the match. The ground was in their favour. It was a Sunday, and it had been raining for a week. The players of Las Vegas have all grown up and developed their style and skills on a ground that is similar to the one described in the previous section, one that favours play in the air. It was this style that served the team that afternoon. It was the physical strength of the Las Vegas players against the much more technically and tactically developed game of Fuerza, and, with a soaked pitch, Las Vegas managed to move the ball forward rapidly during the following minutes, made the equalizer, and had a chance at the frame. When the first half was over, the game was tied at 1–1.

During the first half, there had been several incidents. These incidents are interesting inasmuch as they demonstrate the fragility of the distinction between spectator and player; or rather, they demonstrate that these categories represent different enunciative positions within the match seen as performance. When Las Vegas made the equalizer, the *mara* from the upper moiety invaded the pitch amid great shouting and cheering. Later on, ten minutes before halftime, a fight almost broke out between Leopollito – the oldest son of Leopoldo Contreras – and the oldest surviving son of a man killed the day the army attacked the village. Another orphaned son invaded the pitch, followed by as many as ten, and they all attacked Leopollito. Some players separated them, and the game went on. A little later, a Las Vegas player had a free run towards the goal, but was grabbed by the shirt by Leopoldo and forced down. Some *mara* ran on to the ground, but since the incident took place at the other end, it would have meant crossing most of the ground to get to Leopoldo. Leopoldo was penalized with a yellow card and, just after the free kick was taken, a young man – another orphan – ran on to the pitch and shouted, 'You killed our fathers – today we will win over you!' However, it was not to be so. During most of the second half Las Vegas were under pressure and unable to control the game, and towards the end, Fuerza made another goal against a now very tired and disintegrating Las Vegas team.

It was a historic game. This was underlined in the evening, when the team discussed whether it could continue its weekly training. Leopoldo Contreras owns the ground, and, as he left after the match in the afternoon, he was heard shouting, 'From now on these *Indios comaleros* won't be allowed in.' Everybody, Leopoldo apparently too, felt Las Vegas had won the game.

By using the term *Indios comaleros* Leopoldo Contreras referred to an important mode of subsistence among indigenous families in general, although he may in particular have referred to the widows against whose children he had played. During the eighties these households subsisted on the work of the mothers and daughters, who mined clay on the land of the indigenous community and used this to produce *comales*. The term is derogatory, and encapsulates the notion of the *Indio* as dirty, bound to the earth, illiterate and archaic. Despite these connotations of the word *indio*, all the men took great pleasure in reliving the match incidents in narrative form. The match as well as the stories around it thus offered a field in which interlocutors could co-adjust their feelings and emotions and express their wish to end the *ladino* landowners' dominance of village politics, a dominance that had persisted for more than sixty years.[19]

It is important to take into consideration the fact that the expression of such emotions of belonging and assertions of membership took place within a context where individual identities are far from clear. Although a discourse of race exists, it is not clear how this discourse translates into the present forms of social organization. Nor is it clear how particular individuals align themselves in relation to such organizational patterns. Intermarriage between village families of indigenous origin and poor *ladino* families from the *cantones* are widespread. The pleasurable retelling of stories related to the match therefore became an important vehicle for individual expressions of belonging to the village and asserting membership of an otherwise often non-distinct indigenous community.

Another theme in the debates that started during the match and continued during the following days was that of private and public consumption. The debate was centred around the location of the marimba band during the matches that afternoon. Although the municipality paid the band, it was placed at the most distant corner of the ground, where the group of richer *ladino* families from the municipality had parked their pick-ups and four-wheelers. Here they were drinking canned, imported beers and had a barbecue. To the community of Santo Domingo, this was indicative of the ways in which the *ladino* group appropriated communal funds for their own purpose. Through their attire, consumption patterns and location at the ground they embodied their separate and superior position within the village and the municipality, while openly displaying their ability to appropriate municipal funds for their own entertainment, and the point was not missed by the Las Vegas players. As they drank their jar of *chicha*,[20] they continuously denounced and commented on the abuses and corruption committed by the *ladino* leadership of the village; and these denunciations continued in the days that followed.

The match also opened broader reflections upon the social relations that pertain between the indigenous and *ladino* communities and between these and the outside world. Since Las Vegas was made up of young men from the village's upper moiety, the team and its players not only represented the moiety, but authentically embodied it. The team of Fuerza, on the other hand, was made up largely by outsiders, thereby representing the *ladino* population without any claims to authenticity. The criterion of selection for Fuerza was not that of authentically representing a territorial unit but that of skill, and the logic behind team composition was that of winning. Only four players came from the *ladino* sector of the village, two players were drawn from the lower moiety, and a few players came from *cantón* El Zope, which lies south of the village, while the rest were players from outside the municipality, some even playing in second-division teams, such as *Los Tiburones* (the Sharks) from Acajutla. Leopoldo paid all the players varying amounts of money, in particular the outsiders who, during the match, had made a difference. These received between thirty and fifty *Colons* for one game, equalling one to two days' wages for a day-labourer.

In our conversations over the following days, Leopoldo Contreras defended himself, arguing that the village ought to support his team during the rest of the tournament – thereby in effect stating that he was a member of the community; but nobody in the community perceived it that way. The argument among the male population was that Leopoldo won, as he always does, by drawing in outsiders, and to the indigenous community and in particular to the upper moiety he thereby declared that participation with co-residents was less important than the strength that could be derived from outsiders with particular skills. The Las Vegas players, on the other hand, although annoyed by the loss, were proud that they had put up an even struggle with a team put together for the sole purpose of winning, which therefore did not express the efforts of individual community members. Thus the game created a reflexive space in which the civil war had been re-enacted. Most players of Las Vegas were sons of the men that were killed in the early eighties, and inasmuch as they regarded Leopoldo Contreras as the key organizer of patrol activities in the eighties, the game had provided an opportunity to imagine the settling of the old score. Behind these various arguments there lies a structural homology between the violent confrontations of the early eighties and the football match. In the match as well as in the early eighties *ladino* political leadership had been successful in winning confrontations with the indigenous community by relying on external skill and force.

Conclusion

From an ethnographic point of view, it is difficult to maintain the position that football is an irrelevant practice, largely void of symbolic mediation. As I have shown in this essay, the football game between Fuerza and Las Vegas was a performance set off from everyday life. The framing of the match I have analysed, the scaling of social conflict it provides and the density of meaning in the composition of the opposing teams and the different styles with which they played, all led to the emergence of the match as a vehicle for reflection upon the different types of relations that the *ladino* and the indigenous community maintain with the outside. The match mimicked the violent relations of the early eighties, when *ladino* patrol members supported by outside army and police forces killed the men of the upper moiety. The match thereby afforded a possibility for restating in commentary and public discourse individual allegiances to the community as well as distrust towards 'outsiders', as resident *ladinos* are called.[21] It furthermore offered a possibility for people to state that the *ladino* political leadership was corrupt, and that it appropriated communal funds for personal use, as was the case with the marimba band. The match as a reflexive performance thus generated a set of embodied identities that served as the point of departure in a critique of the legitimacy of *ladino* dominance. This analysis of football points towards the serious shortcomings that we can now say characterized earlier analyses of male sociality. The lack of analytical engagement with male performances such as dancing, drinking and praying naturally led to the conclusion that participation could only take place within the institution. The analysis of football demonstrates that participation in bodily performance encompasses not only the bodily motion as such, but also the commentary upon this. There is ample space to revisit regional ethnographies with this theoretical adjustment in place.

Football – a form of bodily performance introduced only some forty years ago – has become the dominant way in which communal and indigenous identity is claimed and asserted in public. Commentaries upon the performance of the village teams Fuerza as well as Las Vegas place the practice of football at the centre of the reflexive space that produces community. It is a reflexive space in which enunciative positions for discourses upon the social relations that divide the village into different communities is provided. Hence, it forms a space in which to maintain as well as to act upon orders of domination through embodied as well as discursive practice. Although Las Vegas did not win the game that rainy afternoon, it was a perceivable possibility, and that possibility was noted not only by the young players from Las Vegas, but by Leopoldo Contreras as well.

However, football also provides material for the analysis of male–male social relations within the group of young men. Through their everyday performative practices on the football field, they organize themselves in groups that provide them with resources with which they can manoeuvre on the wider field of relations between juniors in the community; but it also provides them with resources that enable them to face seniors within their own extended kingroups, resources such as solidarity and trust expressed through gesture and bodily contact. Clearly, much as football matters to me as a native of Copenhagen – it also matters as much to me as an ethnographer of Santo Domingo.

Notes

1. The game of football is known as 'soccer' in the United States.
2. Religious brotherhoods are known as *cofradías*, *hermandades* and *guachivales*. The brotherhood organizes and sponsors the celebration of a patron saint's day through reverence paid to a particular image or figure possessed by the brotherhood. This image they care for daily or weekly through masses and offerings that are undertaken in correspondence with a particular religious calendar. As part of this calendar, annual visits to neigbouring villages are undertaken with small copies of the image (*hijos*). These visits are a palimpsest of sixteenth-century parish organization in the region, and today they constitute a regional indigenous space within the *mestizo* state of El Salvador.
3. Sports were relevant inasmuch as they were regional, as in the Mesoamerican case, where the existence of pre-Columbian ball courts was proposed as a key marker of the Mesoamerican cultural region (Kirchhoff 1943).
4. See Vogt (1993: 2) for an example of this perspective on ethnographic material.
5. Studies began to focus on contexts that were different from the highland community of western Guatemala. Communities of Nicaraguan agro-industrial labour (Gould 1990), Misquito rebels (Hale 1994), Salvadorean refugees (Hammond 1998), indigenous intellectuals (Campbell *et al.* 1993) and even extinct communities (Binford 1996) became sites of ethnographic studies. The mass displacements of the indigenous population in the Guatemalan Highlands called for wider regional (Stoll 1993; Wilson 1995) as well as more thematic analysis. Transnationalism (Kearney 1996), racism and gender (Nelson 1999; Casaus Arzú 1992), state formation (Stepputat 1999a,b, 2000) and indigenous movements (Warren 1998) were some of the subjects that emerged in ethnographies during the 1990s. As these new areas of description and analysis surfaced, community studies moved away from the explanation of community resilience through deep structure or long history, towards more situated ethnography focusing on everyday life and politics (Watanabe 1992).
6. During the land invasions of the 1950s in Guatemala, as well as during the period of modernization in the Central American economies in the 1960s, the dualism outlined above framed questions of importance for anthropologists, activists and policy-makers. What had generated indigenous mobilization during the 1940s? What were the likely responses of the rural population in an expanding market economy during the 1960s? And what would those responses entail for the indigenous communities as economic, cultural and political subjects as the political climate became radicalized and violent during the 1970s and 1980s?
7. From a theoretical point of view the monograph has become synonymous with the culturalist model outlined above.

8. From a methodological point of view it is outstanding inasmuch as it applies a rigorous positivist methodology based on the empirical verification of functionalist propositions concerning the integrative functions of male religious brotherhoods in an indigenous community.

9. Such an interpretation was hardly surprising. In his introduction, Wasserstrom characterizes the publications coming from the Harvard Chiapas Project in the following way 'absent from all these discussions is the problem of . . . how Indian communities . . . became what they are today and how the past has determined their present position in national society' (Wasserstrom 1983: 5).

10. In an illuminating description of a particular ritual (Cancian 1965: 59–61), participants voice disagreement over the levels of acceptable intoxication during the performance of ritual. In this case. Cancian provides no analysis of the discussion.

11. Male sociality includes a variety of social interfaces or relations, such as indigenous men *vis-à-vis ladino* men, juniors *vis-à-vis* seniors, stay-at-homes *vis-à-vis* migrants, landholding men *vis-à-vis* land-poor men.

12. This view of ritual goes against not only the classic definition of ritual proposed by Malinowski and Evans-Prichard, but also the hermeneutic definition proposed by Geertz. It points towards a view of ritual as deeply enmeshed in everyday embodied practice.

13. A statement that can only be read as a rebuttal of the Geertzian view of ritual.

14. According to the players from the upper moiety, this betting going on was the reason why they had chosen the name of Las Vegas for their team. The name referred not only to the team but also to the field – thereby creating a transnational space of ludomania.

15. Many of the village men, including the orphaned boys, joined the Salvadorean army during the 1980s in order to support their families.

16. Under post-Mitch legislation an annual residence permit was given to Central American residents from Guatemala, El Salvador, Honduras and Nicaragua.

17. For a more extended analysis of the gendered forms of livelihood and the intra- and inter-generational tensions generated by these, see Ronsbo 1999.

18. Prior to several games senior players excused themselves with fatigue.

19. The *ladino* group took over control of the municipality following the 1932 uprising in Western El Salvador known as La Matanza. During this uprising an unknown number of indigenous and *ladino* villagers were killed by the army. Estimates range from 3,000 to 30,000. Until the 2000 municipal elections, *ladinos* had always controlled the municipality. In 1999 the left-wing party FMLN won the elections. The new mayor was the youngest of five brothers of whom two died during the attacks on the village in early 1980.

20. *Chicha* is a fermented and slightly alcoholic beverage made of corn or rice, typically associated with indigenous culture.

21. This despite the fact that they have resided in the municipality since the 1890s.

References

Altamirano, Teófilo (1984), *Presencia andina en Lima Metropolitana: un estudio sobre migrantes y clubes provincianos*. Lima, Peru: Universidad Católica del Perú, Fondo Editorial.

Archetti, Eduardo P. (1999), *Masculinities. Football, Polo and Tango in Argentina*. Oxford: Berg Publishers.

Arzú, Marta Casaus (1992), *Guatemala – linaje y racismo*. San José, Costa Rica: FLACSO.

Binford, Leigh (1996), *The El Mozote Massacre: Anthropology and Human Rights*. Tucson, AZ: University of Arizona Press.

Campbell, Howard *et al.* (1993), *Zapotec Struggles: Histories, Politics, and Representations from Juchitán, Oaxaca*. Washington DC: Smithsonian Institution Press.

Cancian, Frank (1965), *Economics and Prestige in a Mayan Community – The Religious Cargo System in Zincantan*. Stanford, CA: Stanford University Press.

DaMatta, Roberto (1982), *Universo do futebol: esporte e sociedade brasileiro*, Rio de Janeiro: Ediçoes Pinakotheke.

Gose, Peter (1994), *Deathly Waters and Hungry Mountains – Agrarian Ritual and Class Formation in an Andean Town*. Toronto: University of Toronto Press.

Gould, Jeffrey (1990), *To Lead as Equals. Rural Protest and Political Consciousness in Chinandega, Nicaragua, 1912–1979*. Chapel Hill, NC: University of North Carolina Press.

Hale, Charles (1994), *Resistance and Contradiction. Miskitu Indians and the Nicaraguan State, 1894–1987*. Stanford, CA: Stanford University Press.

Hammond, D. (1998), *Fighting to Learn. Popular Education and Guerrilla War in El Salvador.* New Brunswick, NJ: Rutgers University Press.

Kearney, Michael (1996), *Reconceptualizing the Peasantry: Anthropology in Global Perspective.* Boulder, CO: Westview Press.

Kirchhof, Paul (1943), 'Mesoamérica, sus límites geográficos, composición étnica, y carácteres culturales', *Acta Americana*, Vol. 1.

Nelson, Diane (1999), *A Finger in the Wound. Body Politics in Quincentennial Guatemala*. Berkeley, CA: University of California Press.

Ronsbo, Henrik (1999), 'Indians and Baseball Caps: Ethnicity and Everyday Life in a Salvadoran Village', Ph.D. dissertation, Institute of Anthropology, Copenhagen University.

Roseberry, William (1994), 'Hegemony and the Language of Contention', in Gilbert M. Joseph and Daniel F. Nugent (eds), *Everyday Forms of State Formation: Revolution and the Negotiation of Rule in Modern Mexico*, Durham, NC: Duke University Press.

Sider. Gerald (1986), *Culture and Class in Anthropology and History. A New-foundland Illustration.* Cambridge: Cambridge University Press.

Stepputat, Finn (1999a), 'Repatriation and Everyday Forms of State Formation in Guatemala' , in Richard Black and Khalid Koser (eds), *The End of the Refugee Cycle? Refugee Repatriation and Reconstruction.* New York: Berghahn Books.

—— (1999b), 'Politics of Displacement in Guatemala', *Journal of Historical Sociology*, vol. 12, no. 1.

—— (2000), 'At the Frontiers of the Modern State in Post-war Guatemala', in Alberto Arce and Norman Long (eds), *Anthropology, Development and Modernities: Exploring Discourses, Counter-tendencies and Violence.* London: Routledge.

Stoll, Peter (1993), *Between Two Armies. In the Ixil Towns of Guatemala.* New York: Columbia University Press.

Turner, Victor (1987), *The Anthropology of Performance.* New York: PAJ Publications.

Vogt, Evon Z. (1993), *Tortillas for the Gods. A Symbolic Analysis of Zinacanteco Rituals.* Norman, OK: University of Oklahoma Press. (1st Edition, 1976.)

Warren, Kay B. (1998), *Indigenous Movements and their Critics. Pan-Maya Activism in Guatemala.* Princeton, NJ: Princeton University Press.

Wasserstrom, Robert (1983), *Class and Society in Central Chiapas.* Berkeley, CA: University of California Press.

Watanabe, John M. (1992), *Maya Saints and Souls in a Changing World.* Austin, TX: University of Texas Press.

Wilson, Richard (1995), *Maya Resurgence in Guatemala. Q'eqchi' Experiences.* Norman, OK: University of Oklahoma Press.

Wolf, Eric R. (1955), 'Types of Latin American Peasantry: A Preliminary Discussion', *American Anthropologist*, Vol. 57: 452–71.

Part IV
Embodying the National

9

The Irish Body in Motion: Moral Politics, National Identity and Dance

Helena Wulff

The Free Presbyterian Church bans sex because it might lead to dancing! – Belfast joke

At the Belfast Festival in 1996, the Dublin dance theatre company, CoisCéim, performed a dance piece titled *Straight with Curves*. Inspired by Auguste Rodin's sculptures 'The Kiss' and 'The Thinker' the piece featured a short section with naked dancers. This provoked a group from the Free Presbyterian Church[1] to demonstrate with banners inside the theatre, marching up and down the aisle and praying during the performance. The Government and Morals Committee and the Free Presbyterian Church of Ulster Government issued a press release condemning the nudity in *Straight with Curves*. The protest was reported in the Belfast papers, which, according to the press officer of the dance company, only increased the ticket sales. 'Nudity had not been done before in Ireland', she told me in an interview, and also that they had not had this kind of reaction anywhere else (for instance, in the Republic of Ireland, Scotland, London or Marseilles, where they had been on tour with this dance piece). It should be pointed out, however, that although nudity is not uncommon in Euro-American dance theatre, it is usually aimed at an audience more or less accustomed to it.

In the Belfast *Telegraph* Neil Johnston (1996) sent out a careful warning before the opening night of *Straight with Curves*:

I have already given some coverage – or perhaps the more appropriate word would be uncoverage – to the dance show which opens at the Old Museum arts centre tonight. It is by the Cois Ceim [sic] dance company from Dublin, and includes, towards the end, a couple of scenes full of nudity. Only a couple of minutes, you understand, and all done in the best possible taste. Still, I thought you'd like to know.

A couple of days later, Robin Greer (1996) reported somewhat ambivalently in the Belfast *Newsletter*:

It is sad indeed when the human condition becomes so perverted with sexual obsession that all appreciation of beauty and art is extinguished and people can focus only upon the possibility of a few fleeting moments of nakedness. Unencumbered by original sin, the rest of us in the comradeship of damnation trotted into the Old Museum Arts centre for the much-trumpeted return of Dundalk-based [2] dance troupe Coisceim [sic]. Straight With Curves was a beautifully graceful work, stylistically pure and simple, maybe just too much, so occasionally reaching the point of sterility. It was a piece to be appreciated rather than really enjoyed . . . Well done our friends the protestors. They have ensured that a rather good show that might otherwise have been overlooked will be a complete sell-out.

Under a headline announcing 'All kissing, cavorting and steamy dance' Amanda Verlaque (1996) wrote a rave review in the *Irish News*, praising *Straight with Curves* as 'exquisite and accessible', 'sexually explosive' and a 'funny, touching' piece.

All this testifies to the power of dance to unleash strong emotions, often of an erotic nature, that are normally held back in daily life. Despite a common assumption that dance is a marginal social practice, dance is in fact, and has often been perceived as, so prominent and disturbing as to call for control both on political and religious grounds. This has especially been the case in colonial situations, although such control has tended to spur resistance in the form of the making or revival of ethnic and national dances (Wulff 2001a). The Kalela dance is a classic anthropological example of a 'tribal' marker in Northern Rhodesia (Mitchell 1956). European folk dances have been analysed on the one hand as a form of ethnic resistance to dictatorial nationalism, and on the other hand as a component in nation-building (cf. Löfgren 1993; see also Daniel 1995).

The purpose of this chapter is to investigate moral politics in relation to Irish bodies in motion, mainly in dance theatre performances and dance competitions,[3] but also in *Riverdance*, the Irish dance show, and liturgical dance. I find a notion of moral politics useful here, because at the same time as it relates to earlier anthropological attention to morality (e.g. Overing 1985; Howell 1997a) it takes a step further by sharpening the focus on the processes of negotiations and public debate over morality. For moral politics is not only about moral values and attitudes, but even more about the management of open confrontation over moral issues.

When dance performances provoke moral debate in the wider society in Ireland, North and South, such debate is usually ignited by religious indignation emanating from particular wings of Catholicism or Protestantism. This debate is enacted in large part through the media; but, as I will show, by way of a number of different strategies. Since moral politics and dance are associated with questions of national identity, character-building and the nation in Irish society, I will bring in those topics, too.[4] Notions of the body are moreover often discussed in terms of sexuality and touch, which have an impact on dance. An understanding of moral politics, national identity and dance has to be contextualized in Irish history, which is characterized by the long colonialism in the South but also by structures of resistance, as well as the central role of the Catholic Church in the state. These situations still contribute to cultural contradictions and otherness. I will suggest that certain features of Irish dance originate in everyday movements and dispositions that have been shaped by social conditions in Irish society.

One striking feature of Irish society is the presence of otherness. The legacy of colonialism in the South of Ireland is a prominent part of this circumstance, which Luke Gibbons (1996: 147) has described in terms of to 'have known otherness from the inside'. This, as well as the conflict in the North, continues to produce otherness and divisions within Irish society. An Anglo-Irish identity is, for instance, something that is still commented on in terms of being 'not Irish', even self-referentially. Although the Dublin choreographer John Scott thus talks about 'a deep sense of Irishness inside me', he does admit that he is '. . . considered a foreigner, an Anglo-Irish, not really Irish. I feel a bit like an outsider in my own country'.

When otherness within Irish society raises issues of morality that produce moral politics, Michael Walzer's (1994) conceptualization about two different but interrelated types of moral arguments uncovers an exceptional situation of the geographical proximity of conflicting moral orders. Walzer suggests that there is a 'thick' argument, which is rich and local and maximizes the sharing of standards, and a 'thin' moral argument, which is abstract, detached, and general, often pertaining to justice in places abroad. My point is that a thick moral sharing and a thin awareness of other moralities co-exist in Irish society, but that the latter often concerns other moral orders within Ireland, North and South. Analytically, what is perceived as an other moral order within Irish society nowadays nonetheless does depend on the vantage point. Morality is perspectival and to some extent con-textual.

Otherness Within

Taking the universality of moral sensibility as a point of departure, Signe Howell (1997b: 4–5, 7, 9) discusses moral reasoning in terms of an awareness of altern-ative values to one's own morality and the problem of moral choice. Howell makes the case for a comparative study of indigenous moralities. Anthropologists have much to contribute to this approach, such as an understanding of the shifting 'relationship between moral values and practices' as well as a search for both implicit values and explicit ones. Howell recommends the anthropological approach to look for ethical breaches and sources of definitions of what is regarded as right and wrong. Values change, not least contextually, and there may well be conflicting values in one society, even if they are not perceived in that way. Conflicting values may, as Howell says, also be introduced through the encounter with a foreign moral order.

It seems likely that the English view of the Irish as 'unruly', which was still prevalent in the late nineteenth and early twentieth centuries, had an impact on how Irish competitive dancing style and regulations evolved in tandem with ideas of national identity and morality. This especially concerned the characteristc stiff upper body and straight arms, which are accentuated by the contrast with the speedy and intricate footwork in competitive Irish dancing. Hall (1995, 1996) explains this posture puzzle, as he calls it, in terms of a combination of physical education, the requirements of competitions, and the policy of nationalism. Some older people I have interviewed in the dancing community were quite explicit about the fact that the stiff posture came about from the beginning as a way to train the Irish in manners. It was considered good for the Irish character to keep an erect posture (Wulff, in preparation). This echoes Foucault's (1979) famous argument about how the power of discipline moulds docile, political bodies that display more ability but in fact are controlled.

It is important to note that this otherness from the inside, which Gibbons writes about, did not cease when colonialism ended in the South of Ireland, nor has it been limited to that part of the island. The opening vignette about the scandal at the Belfast festival may be seen as having been caused by a particular group, the Free Presbyterian Church, which does not represent the majority of the population. It constitutes one aspect of Northern Ireland. Another side of this scandal is that, if we accept that Northern Ireland has recently become a more conservative society in certain respects than the Republic, it is likely that the dance theatre company knew very well that it would attract sensationalism by featuring naked dancers in Belfast. For even though, as I mentioned above, nudity aesthetics is a part of Euro-American dance theatre and has been for a long time, it does guarantee attention of one type or another, whether scandalous or successful.

In April 2001 Dance Theatre of Ireland presented their new production *A Question of Distance* in Dublin. This piece explores relationships, space and proximity in a playful way. In one scene, a male dancer and a female dancer moved slowly towards each other on stage. They started taking off one garment after another until they were completely naked. During an enchanting moment, as the erotic energy grew, they were standing contemplating each other. Then they walked by each other without touching, put on each other's clothes and left the stage in different directions. Later in the performance, another naked male dancer entered holding a folding rule. As he was moving on the spot he was trying out different angles with the folding rule in relation to his limbs, one after another. He returned twice during the performance, once more with the folding stick, but now dressed, and in the background repeating the movements and spaces he had made when he was naked, thereby in fact changing them.[5] But he also appeared naked a second time, together with a fully dressed woman dancer who complimented him verbally for his face and eyes, thereby emphasizing his nudity and those parts of the rest of his body that would normally have been covered by costume.

The dance piece did very well: not only did it sell tickets, but people who had seen it once came back to see it again. They were, if not accustomed to the nudity, at least somewhat prepared that this kind of aesthetics is a possibility in contemporary choreography. The reviews were excellent – however, the nudity was only hinted at, if at all mentioned. When I tried to find out why the electrifying atmospere that had been created by the nudity did not make it to the newspapers, I was told that it was a way to protect the dancers. It is also probable that the critics did not want to admit in public that they had been touched by this aspect of the performance. This nudity was thus kept in a rather small circle in the Dublin contemporary dance world. Still, it was a public event and definitely much more erotic than line dancing, the American style of dancing in a line wearing cowboy hats and boots. This dance form was the target of protests from the Free Presbyterian Church in Belfast at the same time.

'Occasions of Sin'

In May 2001 I attended a dance festival in Belfast, The Belfast Week of Dance. It was a collaboration between Dance Northern Ireland (an association that promotes dance classes, performances, and community projects) and the Belfast City Council as a part of an initiative from the World Health Organization for active living in European cities. There were dance displays in public places such as in a square, in a shopping mall and at a hospital, workshops on dance styles from *salsa* to Irish dancing, tea dances for senior citizens, a disco dance competition for children and young teenagers, and line dancing. The festival culminated in a gala cabaret to which the Reverend Ian Paisley had been invited. He did not show up, however. Whether he really was busy campaigning for the upcoming election, or suspected that he was in fact invited to attract attention to the festival, rather than to his own concerns about it, we will never know.

I happened to be present at the office of Dance Northern Ireland the day after the billboards of the Belfast *Telegraph* had announced Paisley's condemnation of line dancing. On the front page of this newspaper, it said that Paisley had issued a statement in April to be read at all Free Presbyterian congregations, declaring that line dancing might lead to hell. 'Line dancing is as sinful as any other type of dancing, with its sexual gestures and touching,' Paisley was quoted as having said. However, a line dancing teacher then explained in the article that line dancing is performed with almost no touching (Harper and Grattan 2001). Neither does this dance form contain specific sexual gestures. Compared to most other contemporary popular dance forms, such as *salsa* and disco dancing, line dancing is quite innocent in this respect. There are even those who look upon it as 'the risible pastime of a nerdish minority' according to Eamonn McCann (2001) in his critical but entertaining article inside the same edition of the Belfast *Telegraph*.

At the office of Dance Northern Ireland, the staff were amused over Paisley´s attack on line dancing: 'He can't be serious! He's taking the piss!' But when they tried to call Paisley in order to invite him to the festival gala cabaret, and got hold of someone at his office, the joking mood changed into a sharp tone of voice. They wanted to thank him, they said, for the publicity for the dance festival. Incidentally, the dance festival was not mentioned in the Belfast *Telegraph*, neither had it been mentioned on the BBC local television news nor on the radio news, which reported on the latest Paisley condemnation for a UK audience. The line dancing decree had probably been conceived as a part of Paisley's election campaign, and just happened to coincide with the Belfast Dance Week. The coverage of Paisley's protest against line dancing in the Belfast *Telegraph* did not, however, pass without rebuke from readers, who, in letters to the editor, criticized Ian Paisley for being a fundamentalist and not reading the Bible properly, since in it dance is actually referred to in positive terms.

In his article, with the headline 'Yee-haw! Paisley bid to pluck lusty line dancers from the jaws of Hell', Eamonn McCann (2001) uses the expression 'occasions of sin' ironically. Although there may be many different kinds of 'occasions of sin', this expression, I have noticed, is still a part of the vocabulary in the Irish competitive dancing world with reference to Catholic clerical disapproval of dancing in the past.[6] And as Brennan (1999: 125) writes: 'The Catholic archbishops and bishops of Ireland issued a statement on the "evils of dancing" on 6 October 1925, which was to be read at masses during the Ecclesiastical Year. They advocated the strict supervision of dancing and warned of the 'occasions of sin' involved in night dances.' Already in the 1920s the media had an impact on moral debate. Both Breathnach (1983) and Brennan (1999) have found the editorial titled 'Irish Morals' in the *Irish Times* in March 1929 which supports the idea of the dangers of drinking, let alone dancing, since the latter may incite sexual misconduct. This, but above all the clerical disapproval, paid off. Within a few years, in 1935, the state thus implemented the Public Dance Hall Act as a way to stop informal dancing at the crossroads,[7] in barns and houses. Dances should thus only be held in licensed dance halls, which would not only ensure morality – but also bring in tax money (see also Inglis 1998a).

There are many stories about the Catholic Church denouncing crossroads dancing, telling about priests going to crossroads and setting fire to dancing platforms or driving their cars backwards and forwards over them (MacMahon

1954 in Brennan 1999), and even beating couples who were sitting down in the grass between dances with a stick, so they would get up and dance instead.[8] Brennan (1999) reports police raids on dances held in homes, such as dances for workers who had helped out on a farm or just for domestic merrymaking, and subsequent court cases, but also a widespread cheeky resistance among the people, both to the Public Dance Hall Act and to other attempts to restrict dancing: 'Despite such opposition, dancing continued unabated' (1999: 121), she points out. There were impromptu dancing and dancing endurance tests. People danced on flag-stones and halfdoors, and at so called 'sprees' at home and at wakes.[9] The night before someone was emigrating, it was common that an American or Australian wake, with dancing, was arranged.[10]

The clergy's banning dance for causing frivolous sexual behaviour, or at least suggesting the idea of such conduct, is nothing unique to Irish society. Another example of religious leaders protesting against dance occurred in the 1950s in Sweden, when Protestant bishops engaged in a moral panic over what they saw as the misbehaviour of the youth that went to public dances (Frykman 1988). What is unique in the relationship between dance and religion in Ireland compared to other countries is that the clerical condemnation of dance has taken place at the same time as there has been a remarkable closeness between the Catholic Church and the dance world. Priests and nuns have been visible in the dance theatre world in the Republic of Ireland in capacities such as founding directors and board members of dance companies, as well as dance enthusiasts. Other aspects of the links between religion and dance in Ireland are nuns contributing a choir to a dance performance, inviting ballet companies to schools, and taking pupils to ballet class (Fleischman 1998).

Building Character, Building Nation: Dance and Sport

National identity, dance and morality have a long and complex history in Ireland. The nationalist cultural revival that the Gaelic League introduced in the late 1800s should be seen in a wider European context, where such movements were common at the time, even though the contents of the movements varied (Löfgren 1993). In Ireland, the nationalist cultural revival movement thus started with the founding of the Gaelic Athletic Association (GAA). However, the main idea was to support the Irish (Gaelic) language, even though other cultural forms were also taken into consideration, among them dance. It became a priority to distinguish Irish dancing from foreign, primarily English, dance. In order to accomplish this, the Gaelic League set up dancing classes and competitions, and in 1929 it established the Irish Dancing Commission, which continues to regulate competitive Irish dancing style and costumes, as well as examining teachers and adjudicators.

Looking at dance and sport in a comparative perspective, each through the other discipline, might reveal new sides in both disciplines and contribute to wider theoretical discussions at the same time. There is also a growing number of points of intersection between dance and sport, such as the new discipine of 'dance sport' (cf. Ballett International 2000). In an exchange between dance and sport, professional dancers take an interest in the mental training developed for athletes, for example, and choreographers are inspired by sport when it comes to both form and content (see for example Jamison 2001 on the tribute to Florence Griffith Joyner by the Alvin Ailey American Dance Theater), while gymnasts and figure skaters ask choreographers to compose their routines.

Competitive Irish dancing has been analysed by Hall (1995) as a sport, an aesthetic sport where the style of performance is important, by contrast with purposive sports (cf. Best 1978) where the end is emphasized rather than the manner of getting there. Adjudicators consider 'the presentation' of Irish dancers when they decide their scores. Writing about Argentinan football as a microcosm of moral values, Archetti (1997) describes the conflict of values between winning and beautiful playing: male football players and fans are deeply involved emotionally, on the one hand to prioritize winning and on the other to succumb to a search for beautiful football. Brutish playing is the local aesthetic style which is preferred for winning against a foreign team, while elegant playing will produce happiness. This thus tends to be regarded as morally superior. Football is an integral part of male Argentian national identity, and its outcome is closely connected to feelings of honour and shame.[11]

Sport as a means for building character starts with children, as Noel Dyck (2000: 149) shows in the case of Canadian community sports for children. Dyck relates how moral precepts such as 'hard work', 'team play' and 'playing by the rules' are associated with such early discipline. The British notion of 'fair play' as an element in character-building and nation-building through sports in ex-colonies is commented on by Appadurai (1996) with reference to cricket and decolonization in India (see also Brownell 1995; 2000). In the case of Turkish wrestling, Stokes (1996) argues, however, that this moral education includes not only chivalry but also deceit, since both are aspects of social life. As MacClancy (1996: 11) points out, with reference to the politicization of sports in Northern Ireland along the sectarian divide (see also Sugden and Bairner 1993), 'sports can divide as much as it may unite'. This obviously applies to many other sport situations, as well as to dance.

When it comes to Irish competitive dancing, the attempt to build character goes back to childhood and circles around the idea of national identity. In the Irish dancing community, there is a tendency to regard Irish dancers from the Republic of Ireland as better solo dancers than other dancers from other countries, even those of Irish descent from the diaspora. To learn Irish dancing is to acquire a way to embody the history of Ireland. Hard work and fair play are considered important, as well as team play during team dances, which are less prestigious, however, than solo dances. There is moreover a good deal of rivalry that often is expressed through suspicions of politics, such as mothers trying to influence adjudicators. It does happen that dancers sabotage each other's steps by bumping into a rival on stage during competitions or pretending to fall when they do not feel that they are doing their best, and then getting a chance to dance again (cf. Wulff, in preparation). Irish dancing competitions thus divide some and unite others in a changing pattern of victories and defeats around negotiations about Irish national identity.

The latest brick in Irish nation-building involving dance is *Riverdance*, the Irish dance show, which developed out of competitive dancing and has been hailed as the modern version of traditional Irish dancing. This commercial show broke through unexpectedly as an interval entertainment in the Eurovision Song Contest in 1994, hypnotizing millions of viewers, and then catapulted into a global hit. But it also triggered a host of Irish commentary and critique concerning authenticity and national identity. One common reaction in Ireland to *Riverdance* has been that the show has 'made Irish dancing sexy' through softer costumes and less rigid steps and a somewhat more relaxed posture than in competitive dancing.

Riverdance is usually associated with the crescendos of the signature section and the long Chorus Line of Irish dancers pounding out their unison steps. This long line may be an influence from Broadway shows, but the prominence of the percussive step beat also brings to mind the annual sectarian marches in Northern Ireland. This well-known type of Irish marching and movement has been studied by Jarman (1997) in terms of ritual events. Jarman (1997: 10) talks about the impact of repetition and rhythm as they engage both body and emotions: 'the rhythmic repetition of sounds, whether liturgy, singing, chanting or music helps to create a sense of collective identity where before there was only a collection of individuals' (see also McNeill 1995).

The Irish Body, Sexuality and Touch

It could be argued that the body is always in motion: there is movement even in a body that is standing still or lying down – through the heartbeat. In the growth of studies of the body, and especially of the body as culturally constructed,[12] there is still a lack of problematization of the body in motion (cf. Reed 1998).This topic has, however, been dealt with to some degree in dance scholarship, including dance anthropology, usually together with issues on gender and sexuality.[13] There is also an orientation in dance and movement studies that looks at the relationship between physical surroundings, such as architecture, and everyday movement.

Bodies in motion and space are central in Ness's (1992) analysis of the *sinulog* dance in Cebu City, the Philippines. Ness ties dance movements and space to everyday movements like walking, as well as to the urban landscape of Cebu City. In Lewis's (1992) study of Brazilian *capoeira*, dance movements are similarly traced to everyday movement.

Applying Bourdieu's (1977) celebrated concept of habitus to the practice of dancing discloses how dispositions such as perceptions and actions are inscribed into a dancer's body. These dispositions influence not only the dancing but also the social life of dancers, as well as how dancers move when the are *not* dancing (cf. Wulff 1998). Such dispositions also involve non-dancers, which prompted me to ask the choreographer John Scott: 'How do the Irish move?' I wanted him to describe Irish everyday movement such as walking, the Irish movement habitus. 'They stoop', he said and went on: 'They don't move their hips. We're shy too, but very dramatic. But there is a reticence.' There is moreover an idea among Irish choreographers that not only do people in general move differently, that is in a more stiff manner, in the North than in the South, but also that Catholics move more softly than Protestants. Choreographers who work in schools in the North in cross-border projects, as a part of community schemes to promote understanding between the two groups, commented on this, saying that Catholic children were easier to teach dance and movement sequences than many Protestant children, who are somewhat more restricted. Catholic children pick up the rhythm faster. The fact that there is a certain difference in agility between the two groups is especially obvious when they come together to dance, according to these choreographers, who included both Catholics and Protestants from the North as well the South.

Touch is basically a mode of communication, but there are many different meanings of communicating through touch, such as magical, healing, arousing, loving, murderous, and polluting, which Synnott (1993: 180–1) enumerates. Although tactility varies culturally, as well as individually, Synnott emphasizes the human need for touch, which is yet paradoxically 'strangely taboo'. During my fieldwork on dance in Ireland, North and South, I have often listened to discussions on the lack of touch in Irish society. There seems to be a yearning for closeness across what is perceived as a distance.

When the dance scholar and writer Diana Theodores (1996: 204) worked as a dance critic in Ireland in the 1980s and early 1990s she observed 'the *solitariness* of Irish dancing, with its historic resistance to physical touching' (or, as one Irish choreographer joked, 'Ireland: country responsible for the extinction of the *pas de deux*'). 'In Ireland, we've never been in touch with the body', the choreographer Michael Keegan-Dolan told me in an interview when we were discussing Irish dance styles and everyday movements. Keegan-Dolan continued to talk about 'the Irish fear of touch' and 'a lack of touch, a lack of sexuality', arguing that this comes across in how Irish people move. He attributed all this to 'this obsession with the Catholic Church'. A sociological commentator on recent changes in Irish morality and sexuality, Tom Inglis (1998a, 1998b), has written about the abstention from sexuality in the past (1998a: 29, 31–8) explaining how marriage used to be restricted to one son who would inherit and one daughter who would get a dowry. So family and the civilizing society had to be built around 'strict regulation of dating, dances and all contact between the sexes'. This moral monopoly of the Catholic Church was supported by the alliance with the state. Now the views of the Catholic Church on sexuality clash with audacious media images, producing cultural contradictions in Irish society. Still, there are other kinds of media messages about sexuality, Inglis points out.

There are also different kinds of dance broadcast on television. Father Dermod McCarthy, who works for RTÉ (Irish television), told me about liturgical dance, television and morality: 'There's a great nervousness in Church circles about dance on the altar, among some senior Church people because they think it has to do with sexuality, the body. They're afraid of the body, you know.' He went on to say that 'to me, we were made of both body and soul'. One of the highpoints of his career had been the installation of Kevin McNamara as archbishop of Dublin in 1985: in this solemn ritual of status elevation (cf. Turner 1995[1969]) in front of a full cathedral of Irish dignitaries and on live television – there was dance on the altar! At the request of the new archbishop, six women in modest blue dresses and four men in white shirts and blue trousers performed the *Gloria*.[14] It was the first time liturgical dance had been used at the installation of an Irish bishop. Father McCarthy contrasted this ceremony with the long and sometimes boring install-ation ceremonies to which Irish people have been accustomed. This particular event acted as an injection of inspiration. From then on many groups around the country came together to do liturgical dance. People even came from abroad to study physical gesture as a mode of prayer. When the next archbishop was to be installed in 1988, however, Father McCarthy was told that 'there will be no dance at my ordination'! That effectively killed liturgical dance – at least for the time being. Now traditional Irish dancing is included in events such as the Easter Vigil that was broadcast from Cork in 1999. For, like many Irish people before him, Father McCarthy does not give up in his pursuit of dance: 'If I'm not in the cathedral, I can still do it on television!'

Conclusions: Culture of Contradictions

In his programmatic volume *The Anthropology of the Body*, Blacking (1977: 23) makes the point that 'the moral element is a critical factor in many bodily activities and experiences'. Looking at it from the other angle, Howell (1997b: 9) char-acterizes core moral values as 'intellectually and emotionally embodied'. The emotional nature of morality is stressed in Archetti's (1997) study of the passions in Argentinian football. It is through such moments of effervescence, he says, which often are sparked off by a crisis, that new norms are created.

This chapter has examined instances of moral politics, the management of open confrontation over moral issues about dance in some wings of both Catholicism and Protestantism, in Northern Ireland and the Republic of Ireland. I have spent a lot of time on religious critique and prohibition of dancing, yet dance theatre performances and dance shows, and even liturgical dance and dance competitions, are more or less statements of moral politics in themselves. It may seem as if moral politics about dance starts when some religious wing or conservative archbishop reacts negatively to a dance performance, while in fact the moral politics start with the dance performance. It is therefore particularly interesting to consider the condemnation of line dancing and the subsequent media debate that took place in the North at the same time as nude dance theatre was shielded from media attention in the South. The success of this nudity aesthetics can be seen as a crisis for the dance critics in a Catholic society with a tradition of sexual modesty. The critics solved the situation by creating a new norm: nudity should not be mentioned in the newspaper. They thereby avoided exercising the moral power of the media, which according to Inglis (1998b) is now almost as pervasive as that of the Catholic Church used to be.

We have seen the Irish body in motion as a site for contestation and resistance, going back to colonialism and cultural nationalist revival. Is there then a 'post-colonial' Irish body (at least in the South) formed by traces of suppression? Remember choreographer John Scott's description of the Irish 'stoop' and claim that 'there is a reticence'. Incidentally, the English are known to show 'reserved' characteristics in their everyday movement as well as their dancing – but in combination with a 'magnificient' or 'majestic' attitude (cf. Wulff 1998, 2002). In line with this, the 'very dramatic' quality of Irish movments would have started as a creative resistance, but by now has developed into a distinctly Irish style thriving on its own.

The study of Irish society inevitably moves into issues of religion and morality, which contribute to cultural contradictions as well as to experiences of otherness within. So do notions of national identity, here mostly dealt with as features of competitive Irish dancing and *Riverdance* in the South. Both dance forms have represented and created different versions of Irish national identity and, on a wider scale, played some role in the building of an Irish nation, first as a part of the Gaelic cultural nationalist revival and now as a part of Ireland as a modern European nation.

Acknowledgements

I would like to thank Andrew Finlay for an astute reading of an earlier version of this paper and Fr. Dermod McCarthy for a prompt reply to a query about it. I would also like to thank Eduardo P. Archetti and Noel Dyck for perceptive editorial comments. This study was made possible by a Social Science Faculty grant from Stockholm University and a research grant from the Bank of Sweden Tercentenary Foundation.

Notes

1. Such protests are not uncommon, however. Whenever there is nudity or a suggestion of what could be interpreted as immoral at an art gallery or in the theatre, the Reverend Ian Paisley is expected to come around. A theatre director in Belfast told me: 'We always joke that if Paisley, if they, didn't come, we´d have to take out costumes – and dress up, get actors to do it!'
2. The dance company, CoisCéim, comes from Dublin, not Dundalk.
3. There are dance competitions in different dance forms ranging from ballet and contemporary art dance to ethnic dance and social dance in many places around the globe. The kind of dance competitions I am writing about here, in Irish traditional dancing, are the purpose of the training in that dance form, and are very widespread in Ireland. There are local competitions almost every month and annual national and world championships in Irish dancing in Ireland. This dance form is taught (nowadays voluntarily) as a subject at school in Ireland. The preoccupation with dance competitions in Ireland goes back to a tradition of informal improptu dancing competitions in the back yard, in a pub or at a fair, which sometimes turned into endurance tests (cf. Brennan 1999; Wulff, in preparation).
4. This chapter is a part of my study 'Dance in Ireland: Memory and Modernity in a Postcolonial Age'. My focus is on *Riverdance*, traditional and competitive Irish dancing and contemporary dance theatre. Fieldwork consists of multilocal stints of participant observation and interviews when dance events such as performances, festivals and competitions take place, usually in Dublin, sometimes in Belfast and occasionally in other places around the island. Some of the dance productions I refer to were performed before I started my study on a part-time grant in 1998. These I have seen on video, sometimes together with dancers and choreographers, who then commented usefully on the dancing and on political and cultural circumstances in relation to it.
5. Interestingly, repetition tends to imply some kind of change (cf. Stokes 1997; Jarman 1997; Wulff 2001b), whether through improvisation, mistake, or other circumstances or action.

6. According to Breandán Breathnach (1983), who was an authority on Irish traditional music, the first case of clerical condemnation of dancing in Ireland dates back to 1670. O Cuiv (1952: 52–5 in Breathnach's translation) depicts how a Sister Anastasia gives a speech to a parliament of women in Cork about the evils of dancing: 'It is dancing that excites the desires of the body, in the dance the onset of evil enters the mind; in the dance are seen frenzy and woe, and with dancing thousands go to the black hell'.

7. Crossroads dancing used to be the only way for young men and women to meet in the countryside in Ireland. This romantic memory has become a key metaphor in Irish society, because there is also a widespread belief that it was referred to in a famous radio speech in 1943 by Eamonn de Valera, the Prime Minister, about an ideal Ireland. Having had an opportunity to listen to a copy of the tape I know that de Valera never said 'comely maidens dancing at the crossroads'. Still, this phrase keeps being repeated both fondly and ironically in various contexts in Ireland (cf. Brennan 1999; Wulff 2001b). The reason for this is that the original speech as printed in the *Irish Press* differs from what de Valera actually said on radio. It was Fr. Dermod McCarthy, who works for RTÉ, who told me this and arranged for me to listen to the tape and read the printed version of the speech.

8. From an interview with dance teacher Josephine McNamara in the television programme *Emerald Shoes: The Story of Irish Dance* (1999).

9. Breathnach (1983: 33) refers to 'the charges of dreadful misbehaviour at wakes in Ireland' which included dancing. There was dancing at wakes all over Europe, however, because of a widespread belief that music and dancing might put the dead to rest properly instead of risking harming the living. Breathnach also mentions the graveyard dance, which took place at night. To the accompaniment of drums masked naked dancers excelled in 'loud laughter and devilish songs or incantations' which 'not uncommonly ended in drunkeness and debauchery'.

10. Fintan O'Toole (1999: 10) notes that these occasions were called 'wakes', since there was the idea that the emigrant was 'passing away to another side, probably for ever'. One of the scenes of *Riverdance* features an 'American Wake'.

11. Aware that sport competitions do not always imply winners and losers, Mac-Clancy (1996) mentions Melanesian football and Native Americans playing lacrosse, games that go on until an equal score is achieved. A considerable amount of sport and dance is moreover non-competitive and recreational, even though people may compete against themselves, aiming to become better at favourite pastimes such as swimming, riding, or *salsa* or Irish dancing.

12. Some milestones in the rapid development of the anthropology and sociology of the body focus on the body as a site of culture, such as Blacking (1977), B. S. Turner (1984), and Featherstone *et al.* (1991) and on embodiment,

such as Csordas (1994). Mary Douglas' (1970, 1976) classic work on the body as social and natural symbol and Scheper-Hughes's and Lock's (1987) programmatic article. Since then Howes (1991) has contributed a study on the senses, and Lutz and White (1986) one on emotions. Csordas' (1995) argument for embodiment as a phenomenological paradigm in anthropology has been quite influential. There are feminist anthropologists such as Martin (1987) theorizing the body in terms of reproduction in a patriarchal order. Wacquant (1995) deals with bodily capital among boxers in Chicago and Brownell (1995) shows how gender, body and the nation are interconnected in China through sports.

13. There is thus Hanna's (1988) cross-cultural review of dance and monographs such as Cowan's (1990) on body politics in Greek dance and women's dancing as being in danger of balancing on the border of indecency. This is also the problem of the belly dancers in Cairo that van Nieuwkerk (1995) writes about.

14. The *Gloria* is an abbreviation for *Gloria in Excelsis Deo*, the first line in Latin of a hymn of praise to God, which is an integral part of the Catholic Mass on most Sundays and solemn occasions during the liturgical year. In musical settings of the Mass by great composers such as Bach, Beethoven, Mozart, Britten, and so on, the *Gloria* is the celebratory and festive highlight.

References

Appadurai, Arjun (1996), 'Playing with Modernity: The Decolonization of Indian Cricket', in A. Appadurai, *Modernity at Large: Cultural Dimensions of Globalization*, pp. 89–113. Minneapolis, MN: University of Minnesota Press.

Archetti, Eduardo P. (1997), 'The Moralities of Argentinian Football', in S. Howell (ed.), *The Ethnography of Moralities*, pp. 98–123. London: Routledge.

Ballett International (2000), *The Yearbook: Dance is Sport*, Special Issue, Berlin: Friedrich Berlin Verlagsgesellschaft.

Best, David (1978), *Philosophy and Human Movement*, London: Allen and Unwin.

Blacking, John (ed.) (1977), *The Anthropology of the Body*, ASA Monograph 15. London: Academic Press.

Breathnach, Breandán (1983), *Dancing in Ireland*, Milton-Malbay, Co. Clare: DalgCais Publications.

Brennan, Helen (1999), *The Story of Irish Dance*, Dingle, Co. Kerry: Brandon.

Bourdieu, Pierre (1977), *Outline of a Theory of Practice*, Cambridge: Cambridge University Press.

Brownell, Susan (1995), *Training the Body for China: Sports in the Moral Order of the People's Republic*, Chicago: Chicago University Press.

—— (2000), 'Why Should an Anthropologist Study Sports in China?', in N. Dyck (ed.), *Games, Sports and Cultures*, pp. 43–63. Oxford/New York: Berg.

Cowan, Jane K. (1990), *Dance and the Body Politic in Northern Greece*, Princeton, NJ: Princeton University Press.

Csordas, Thomas J. (ed.) (1994), *Embodiment and Experience: The Existential Ground of Culture and Self*, Cambridge: Cambridge University Press.

—— (1995), 'Embodiment as a Paradigm for Anthropology', *Ethos*, 18(1): 5–47.

Daniel, Yvonne (1995), *Rumba: Dance and Social Change in Contemporary Cuba*, Bloomington, IN: Indiana University Press.

Douglas, Mary (1970), *Natural Symbols: Explorations in Cosmology*, London: Cresset.

—— (1976), *Purity and Danger: An Analysis of Concepts of Pollution and Taboo*, London: Routledge and Kegan Paul.

Dyck, Noel (2000), 'Parents, Kids and Coaches: Constructing Sport and Childhood in Canada', in N. Dyck (ed.), *Games, Sports and Cultures*, pp. 137–61. Oxford/New York: Berg.

Featherstone, Mike, Mike Hepsworth and Bryan S. Turner (eds) (1991), *The Body: Social Process and Cultural Theory*, London: Sage.

Fleischman, Ruth (1998), *Joan Denise Moriarty: Founder of Irish National Ballet*, Dublin: Mercier Press.

Foucault, Michel (1979), *Discipline and Punish: The Birth of the Prison*, New York: Vintage.

Frykman, Jonas (1988), *Dansbaneeländet: Ungdomen, Populärkulturen och Opinionen*, Stockholm: Natur och Kultur.

Gibbons, Luke (1996), 'Identity Without a Centre: Allegory, History and Irish Nationalism', in L. Gibbons (ed.), *Transformations in Irish Culture*, pp. 134–47. Cork: Cork University Press in Association with Field Day.

Greer, Robin (1996), 'Straight Way to a Sell-out', *Belfast Newsletter*, 20 November.

Hall, Frank (1995), 'Irish Dancing: Discipline as Art, Sport, and Duty', Unpublished Ph.D. thesis, Indiana University.

—— (1996), 'Posture in Irish Dancing', *Visual Anthropology*, 8: 251–66.

Hanna, Judith Lynne (1988), *Dance, Sex and Gender: Signs of Identity, Dominace, Defiance, and Desire*, Chicago: University of Chicago Press.

Harper, Smyth and Gary Grattan (2001), 'Dancers on Road to Hell: Paisley', *Belfast Telegraph*, 16 May.

Howell, Signe (ed.) (1997a), *The Ethnography of Moralities*, London: Routledge.

—— (1997b),'Introduction', in S. Howell (ed.), *The Ethnography of Moralities*, pp. 1–22. London: Routledge.

Howes, David (ed.) (1991), *The Varieties of Sensory Experience: A Sourcebook in the Anthropology of the Senses*, Toronto: University of Toronto Press.

Inglis, Tom (1998a), *Lessons in Irish Sexuality*, Dublin: University College Dublin Press.

—— (1998b), *Moral Monopoly: The Rise and Fall of the Catholic Church in Modern Ireland*, Dublin: University College Dublin Press.

Jamison, Judith (2001), 'The Ecstacy, and Agony, Linking Dance and Sport', *The New York Times*, 2 December.

Jarman, Neil (1997), *Material Conflicts: Parades and Visual Displays in Northern Ireland*, Oxford: Berg.

Johnston, Neil (1996), 'Folk Roads to a Classical Debut', *Belfast Telegraph*, 18 November.

Lewis, J. Lowell (1992), *Ring of Liberation: Deceptive Discourse in Brazilian Capoeira*, Chicago: University of Chicago Press.

Löfgren, Orvar (1993), 'Materializing the Nation in Sweden and America', *Ethnos*, 3–4: 161–96.

Lutz, Catherine and Geoffrey White (1986), 'The Anthropology of Emotions', *Annual Review of Anthropology*, 15: 405–36.

McCann, Eamonn (2001), 'Yee-haw! Paisley Bid to Pluck Lusty Line Dancers from the Jaws of Hell', *Belfast Telegraph*, 16 May.

MacClancy, Jeremy (1996), 'Sport, Identity and Ethnicity', in J. MacClancy (ed.), *Sport, Identity and Ethnicity*, pp. 1–20. Oxford/New York: Berg.

MacMahon, Bryan (1954), *The Vanishing Ireland*, Dublin: O'Brien Press.

McNeill, William H. (1995), *Keeping Together in Time: Dance and Drill in Human History*, Cambridge, MA: Harvard University Press.

Martin, Emily (1987), *The Woman in the Body: A Cultural Analysis of Reproduction*, Boston: Beacon Press.

Mitchell, J. Clyde (1956), *The Kalela Dance*, Livingstone, Zambia: Rhodes–Livingstone Papers No. 27.

Ness, Sally Ann (1992), *Body, Movement and Culture: Kinesthetic and Visual Symbolism in a Philippine Community*, Philadelphia: University of Pennsylvania Press.

O Cuiv, Brian (ed.) (1952), *Párliament na mBan*, Dublin: Instidiud Ard-Leinn Bhaile Atha Cliath.

O'Toole, Fintan (1999), *The Lie of the Land: Irish Identities*, London: Verso.

Overing, Joanna (ed.) (1985), *Reason and Morality*, ASA Monographs 24, London: Tavistock.

Reed, Susan A. (1998), 'The Politics and Poetics of Dance', *Annual Review of Anthropology*, 27: 503–32.

Scheper-Hughes, Nancy and Margaret M. Lock (1987), 'The Mindful Body: A Prolegomenon to Future Work in Medical Anthropology', *Medical Anthropology Quarterly*, 1(1): 6–41.

Stokes, Martin (1996), '"Strong as a Turk": Power, Performance and Representation in Turkish Wrestling', in J. MacClancy (ed.), *Sport, Identity and Ethnicity*, pp. 21–41. Oxford/New York: Berg.

—— (1997), 'Voices and Places: History, Repetition and the Musical Imagination', *Journal of the Royal Anthropological Institute*, 3(4): 673–91.

Sugden, John and Alan Bairner (1993), *Sport, Sectarianism and Society in a Divided Ireland*, Leicester: Leicester University Press.

Synnott, Anthony (1993), *The Body Social: Symbolism, Self and Society*, London: Routledge.

Theodores, Diana (1996), 'Report – A Dance Critic in Ireland', *Dance Chronicle: Studies in Dance and the Related Arts*, 19(2): 191–211.

Turner, Bryan S. (1984), *The Body and Society*, Oxford: Basil Blackwell.

Turner, Victor (1995[1969]), *The Ritual Process: Structure and Anti-Structure*, New York: Aldine de Gruyter.

van Nieuwkerk, Karin (1995), *'A Trade Like Any Other': Female Singers and Dancers in Egypt*, Austin, TX: University of Texas Press.

Verlaque, Amanda (1996), 'All Kissing, Cavorting and Steamy Dance', *Irish News*, 20 November.

Wacquant, Loïc J. D. (1995), 'Pugs at Work: Bodily Capital and Labour Among Professional Boxers', *Body and Society*, 1(1): 65–93.

Walzer, Michael (1994), *Thick and Thin: Moral Argment at Home and Abroad*, Notre Dame, IL: University of Notre Dame Press.

Wulff, Helena (1998), *Ballet across Borders: Career and Culture in the World of Dancers*, Oxford/New York: Berg.

—— (2001a), 'Dance, anthropology of', in N. J. Smelser and P. B. Baltes (eds), *International Encyclopedia of the Social and Behavioral Sciences*, pp. 3209–12. Oxford: Pergamon/Elsevier Science.

—— (2001b), 'The Link to the Land: Memory and Place in Irish Dance', Paper for the Anthropological Association of Ireland Spring Conference, National University of Maynooth, 11–12 May.

—— (2002), 'Aesthetics at the Ballet: Looking at "National" Style, Body and Clothing in the London Dance World', in N. Rapport (ed.), *British Subjects: An Anthropology of Britain*, pp. 93–110. Oxford/New York: Berg.

—— (in preparation), 'Winning the "Worlds": Irishness and Modernity in Dance Championships in Contemporary Ireland', in H. Donnan, D. Meagher, and J. Ruane (eds), *Multiple Modernities: Traditional Ireland in a Postmodern Age*, London: Pluto Press (in preparation).

Television Programme

Emerald Shoes: The Story of Irish Dance. UTV (1999).

10

Football, Nation and Identity: German Miracles in the Postwar Era

Werner Krauss

During my fieldwork in Portugal, I began to take an interest in football from an anthropological perspective. While elaborating on my field notes and thinking back, it struck me that I had used football as a means of establishing contact and entering into conversation with other males in cafés. There always seemed to be some football match on TV wherever I happened to be, I often found myself reading one of the two daily football newspapers, and soon I was able to display a certain minimal understanding of the ins and outs of Portuguese football. This new knowledge proved to be beneficial in every way: locals were both pleased and astonished at my newly acquired expertise in Portuguese football. On the other hand, German football was not entirely unknown in Portugal: Beckenbauer, Müller, Netzer, the 'blonde angel' Bernd Schuster, who had played in Spain, were all familiar names and respected players.

But just what were we really discussing in our frequent conversations about football? It was more than just a game. We found ourselves entering into contact by presenting ourselves – implicitly – as members of various (footballing) nations. We were entering into dialogue via football, while at the same time a process of 'othering' was being set in train: two individuals having a chat in a bar are transformed into members of different nations. Conversations and thoughts about the omnipresent game run on and meander from one topic to the next; the most varying issues are assembled within a common semantic framework. At stake here are questions of victory and defeat, economics, politics and personal pride, or even, as a Portuguese football newspaper put it in headlines (in the context of disputes within the national squad), *Guerra e Paz*, 'War and Peace'. In fact, the semantics of football are shared across borders, with national identities being negotiated, asserted and assigned in the specific idiom of football. In discussions between informants and anthropologists, including those on football-related topics, a certain jockeying for power always tends to manifest itself. In my own case I became acutely aware of how this played out: I found myself being categorized in terms of perpetually recurring stereotypes, both in the world, as a human being, and in concrete situations. Sooner or later discussions turned to Hitler and Beckenbauer, the 'Führer' and the 'Kaiser' (as Beckenbauer is known), the 'world destroyer' and the 'world champion' respectively. From here it is but a short ride to the so-called 'German virtues', such as combativeness, discipline, order/subordination, punctuality, and the will to triumph. And football, according to the well-known dictum of the English player, Gary Lineker, is 'when 22 men play and in the end the Germans win' (Schulze-Marmeling *et al.* 1999: 218).

Clearly, these are all widely held stereotypes that are repeated time and again in conversations between anthropologists and informants. But in these discussions, I also became uncomfortably aware of the fact that I was not only a member of a 'footballing nation', but also a 'nervous system' that reacted very sensitively to the possible assertions hidden in such apparently anodyne conversations. I was astonished with myself. In what sort of a relationship do football, nation and identity stand to one another? To what extent am I as an anthropologist also susceptible to the power effects of discussions on football? By power effects, I mean the fact of being personally identified with supposed national characteristics and virtues conjured up by such footballing talk, characteristics that are thus imposed upon me whether I like it or not.

Upon returning home, I began to examine this phenomenon from the perspective of the cultural sciences, using the example of my own culture, that of Germany as footballing nation. I started by organizing a seminar at the university entitled 'Anthropology of Football', and then a series of lectures to which I invited German academics in the field. My aim was to replace the generally ironic tone of much commentary on football in Germany by bringing in intellectuals and scholars, while at the same time analysing football as a key hallmark of German culture with the same intellectual rigour as is applied to other anthropological themes. The fact that I was personally fascinated by the subject was of course helpful, as was the fact that I possessed an astonishingly broad knowledge of football, knowledge that I had – it must be acknowledged – acquired in a part-icularly intellectual manner: my personal footballing background had always been of a somewhat discursive nature. As a son of the Protestant bourgeoisie I had been banned as a child from playing the 'proletarian sport' of football – my footballing skills are thus limited to those acquired in the course of a former leisure-time activity. As a resident of a province that could not lay claim to having produced a first-division club, I was unable to identify with any top local team. My team was thus the national squad, my elixir TV transmissions and, above all, the daily sports report in the newspaper – a habit I have maintained to this very day. As a member of the first postwar generation and as someone who was socialized by the student unrest of the early 1970s, football was for me, as for many of my generation, practically the only opportunity I had in which to give positive vent to my sense of national identity: 'We' had either won or lost. Apart from this footballing context, we otherwise simply spoke of 'the Germans' whenever it was a question of national affairs. Understanding why and how this negative sense of identity was able to transform itself into a positive identity precisely and exclusively in relation to football was the starting-point for my anthropological enquiry into football.

Outline

In the present chapter I shall thus seek to address the relation between nation/ nationalism and sport in a theoretical light, and further develop an interpretation of research on 'football cultures' (Feixa and Juris 2000). Following this, I shall present an overview of the history of German football from its origins to the imperial era, and from its existence during the national-socialist period through the postwar epoch down to the present day. This history centres, in large measure, on that of the German Football Association (GFA), which, with its 6 million members, is the world's largest and richest football organization (Menzen 2000: 363).

The so-called 'Miracle of Berne' in 1954, when Germany became surprise world champions by beating Hungary in the final, marks the beginning of Germany's rebirth as a gradually more self-confident nation following the Second World War. I shall illustrate the emergence of a collective sense of 'we', of the notion that 'we're back' (*wir sind wieder wer*) attributable to the 1954 victory using a number of examples drawn from the literature and the media. In conclusion, I attempt to show, on the basis of examples of several great 'footballing heroes', how the myths of national identity are able to be maintained via football while at the same time continually having to be adapted to new circumstances. The choice of footballing 'heroes' is always of a somewhat speculative – or subjective – nature. My personal choice included Fritz Walter, Uwe Seeler and Franz Beckenbauer, as they had all been designated as 'honorary captains (*Ehrenspielführer*) by the GFA, and as such were invested with great symbolic significance. In contrast to these players, I finally decided to add Stefan Effenberg to my list because, although he was not any less successful, he famously attracted the wrath of the GFA.

Football and Nation as Ritualized Performance

What type of relation exists between a sport and a country's reputation in the world, between football and the self-perception of a nation?

According to Anderson (1993), nations are 'imagined communities' – in the sense that all communities that extend beyond face-to-face encounters are 'imagined'. This does not, however, imply that it is a case of 'fabrications', i.e. of false facts – even where the respective inventions have no basis in reality. Rather, nationalism is akin to an act, a practice, a creation. As such, according to Anderson, nationalism cannot be treated like other 'isms', such as fascism or liberalism, but rather in terms of categories such as 'parentage' or 'religion'.

This approach to understanding the phenomenon of 'nationalism' contains a thread leading directly to sport in general, and, in this case, to football. Sports, and in particular modern, professional sports, are often portrayed and analysed in terms of a ritual, or something similar to this, by many authors.[1] New theories tend to stress that rituals are not only about reinforcing a community, but also about moulding and creating communities and meaning in a continually changing world. Sporting competitions, such as world championships or the Olympic Games (cf. Rudie 1998: 113), are thus seen as 'ritualized performative practices (that) embody creativity and constraint', and have 'to be thought of as simultaneous, co-present, and co-dependent, and embodied in different forms of participation' (Crain and Hughes-Freeland 1998: 2f.).

This 'embodiment' occurs through permanent repetition of myths, through the ritualization of social activities and their propagation, and the simultaneous commentary generated by media specialists such as commentators, public relations representatives and officials. The media thus assume a distinctive role, and in particular the modern mass media, such as radio, press and TV: 'The processual approach to ritual also permits a further illuminating comparison between the unrealities of ritual and media, which helps us to think about the ways in which we frame reality/-ies and how variable framings alter our roles, our self-images, our identities' (Crain and Hughes Freeland 1998: 3). The nation as an 'imagined community' is in need of such ritualized performances, such continual repetitions at the interface of constraint and creativity in order to become real, in order to become encoded in bodies, and thus to bring forth national bodies. Archetti (1997, 1999) has described this process convincingly using the example of football's significance for the hybrid identity of Argentina and, entirely in line with Anderson's view, has depicted the veneration of Maradona in terms of a religious phenomenon. Here embodiment is expressed in the imagination of a 'Criollo style of football', in the same way that Lopes (1997) has detected a 'Carioca style' in Brazilian football. Football engenders bodily styles, gaits for negotiating the world that at the same time reflect national characteristics, from *el pibe* in Argentina, to 'fair play' in England and 'virtue, discipline and combativeness' in Germany.

Not least of all, Anderson's definition of nationalism contains a further thread that leads directly to football. He speaks of the 'miracle' of nationalism, which is based on the capacity to transform chance occurrence into destiny. A cliché of German footballing language (and it is one of the ritualistic characteristics of football that it has created its own rhetoric, and even its own idiom) runs: 'People go to watch football matches because they don't know how the game's going to end.' And as often as not, the outcome is determined by what we refer to as 'chance' or 'luck'. Such an explanation was proffered in the now-famous 1986

World Cup match between England and Argentina, where the referee failed to spot Maradona's handball, thereby allowing Argentina's goal and sealing England's 'fate'. As it was, and as Maradona himself famously put it, 'the hand of God' that was at work here. In the same way that the nation, not religion, is, in many countries, able to bring forth 'miracles', it is in the context of sport that these 'miracles' are enacted and experienced – whenever chance is transformed into destiny, players into heroes or saints, tactics into national virtues, and football into an identity-engendering myth.

As such, I have placed the notion of miracles at the heart of my analysis of German identity and football. The starting-point for such analysis is the now proverbial 'Miracle of Berne', which led to Germany's being crowned world champions in 1954. The miracle consisted in the fact of defeat on the battlefield and victory on the playing-field, being placed in a symbolic relation after the event. It was the media – radio, TV and tabloid press – who were originally responsible for creating, supposedly 'by chance', a symbolic connection between football and postwar Germany, and later between football and the 'economic miracle' in the 1960s and the 'miracle of reunification' of a divided Germany after 1989.

According to Anderson, nationalism has not produced any great thinkers – 'no Hobbes, no Marx, and no Weber' (1993: 15). But it has produced great footballers: a Maradona, a Pelé and a Beckenbauer. Media stagecraft has engendered, propagated and modified national myths. These national football myths are, in turn, adopted by a variety of social groups, which seek to direct and to use them for their own agendas. We are here dealing with a kind of national 'grand narratives' (Lyotard 1984) that are hegemonic and tend to suppress other competing narratives.

The question of the relation that exists between football and a country's reputation and self-perception is answered differently in each country, reflecting the contextual variations that exist from one place to another. The hegemonic German 'football narrative' is situated in the specific context of the organization and, often enough, domestication of popular sporting activities.

A Century of German Football

In January 2000 the largest football association in the world, the German Football Association (GFA), celebrated its centenary. The occasion was marked by special TV broadcasts, while the GFA itself organized a large exhibition (Brüggemeier *et al.* 2000), and the tabloid press, officials and politicians stressed the social significance of football as a form of 'cultural heritage' (*Kulturgut*) and as a bearer of Germany's reputation abroad. The hymns sung in praise of the irrepressible triumphal march of the game, the numerous anecdotes related with regard to individual players and clubs, and the three world championship victories of the national side somehow became condensed into a single 'grand narrative' in which football, nation and cultural identity became seamlessly interwoven. Nevertheless, this national celebration was also marked by certain critical undertones. Indeed, critics noted the astonishing fact that, for the most part, this 'national discourse' covered a mere half-century, beginning with a commemoration of the victory in the 1954 world championships, the 'miracle of Berne'. But what of German football in the first half of its hundred-year existence: in what sort of social context had it existed, and how had the GFA conducted itself under national socialism? The oft-evoked integrative character of football was contrasted to a 'political history' of the GFA in two book publications[2] and various newspaper supplements; book titles such as *Hitler's Forwards* (Fischer and Lindner 1999), and headlines such as 'The Führer's Players' (Dieckmann 2000) are an allusion to the more shadowy fifty years of the GFA. Indeed, GFA officials found themselves obliged, at least for formality's sake, to refer to the 'brown patches' in the GFA's history during their celebratory speeches. Yet in the same breath, the oft-evoked separation between sport and politics was then used to enact a simultaneous discursive distinction between the 'political mistakes' of the German nation and its 'healthy' core, a sportively active German youth. In the following, I shall briefly sketch the history of the GFA in terms of the continuity that organized football has permitted in imagining a national identity unscathed by two lost world wars.

The GFA to 1945

The connection between sport and politics is inextricably bound up with the history of the GFA from its very inception. Imported from England at the beginning of the last century, football first had to establish itself in competition with the widely popular gymnastics movement.[3] National unity and cultural identity found themselves intimately linked in the teachings of the 'father of German gymnastics' (*Turnvater*), F. Ludwig Jahn (1778–1852), who liked to present physical exercises and his disciplined programme of bodily training under the *leitmotif* of 'for the Fatherland.' Current-day sports club names, such as *Germania*, *Teutonia* or *Turn- und Sportverein* (Gymnastics and Sporting Association) are a throwback to this history. The competing football association managed to establish itself by adapting to this ideology, and footballers went to war in 1914 with the same degree of enthusiasm for the German fatherland as the gymnasts. Despite the myth of a 'proletarian sport' propagated by many left-wing commentators, it was primarily office employees who were gripped by football fever. Henceforth, football played its part in contributing to the 'propagation of German values around the world', with English football terminology being Germanized and, on the football pitch, the notion of 'war in times of peace' being put into action. The switch from playing-field to battlefield was preprogrammed at the very inception of the GFA, and defeat on the latter resulted more in sulky isolationism than in a radical rethink of the GFA's nationalistic roots. The German programme ran along the lines of *Teutsch, treu und tüchtig* ('German, faithful and virtuous'), and even the rising profess-ionalism of the game in the inter-war period was vehemently opposed: football was not motivated by money, but by the Fatherland.

When it finally occurred, the *Gleichschaltung*[4] of German football to the rising tide of national socialist ideology was carried out, as was to be expected, in a spirit of pre-emptive obedience: clubs were 'cleansed' of Jewish players and officials; in football, German youth was expected to be shaped by the *Führer*'s will; and, at least at the level of the GFA, barely any resistance to fascism at all was displayed. Hitler himself attempted to make football an instrument of his own aims, and the German national side's tactics were closely aligned to corresponding political ambitions in times of war. In spite of this, Hitler only attended one game involving the German side, leaving in an agitated condition after the Germans had lost 2:0 to Norway. Following total defeat in the Second World War, what building-blocks for a German national identity remained? How were phrases, stories, and continuities capable of being shaped from an 'imagined community' as total nightmare, without at the same time once more invoking guilt?

As in numerous other areas of society, a good many officials who had backed national socialism politically 'survived' in the GFA. In doubtful cases this decision was often justified by reference to the oft-cited formula that they had helped to save football in 'difficult times', and thus defended the 'apolitical' ideals of the German game. Victory on the pitch in the postwar period facilitated this manner of reasoning, while making German football the perfect vehicle for establishing a sense of continuity and a new national identity in spite of losses on the battlefield.

Continuity in the Postwar Period

In the period 1945 to 1954 Germany found itself excluded from international football life. The victorious nations set out to destroy the Nazi-backed sport apparatus together with Nazi political institutions. Locally, football enthusiasts began to organize new associations in which other sports were increasingly incorporated and in which other 'aberrant' ideals also gained currency, and a number of fascist officials were banished. While at the local level certain reformist tendencies began to unfold (as they continue to do today), at the national level a movement to restore conservative tendencies won the day. The refounding of the GFA also meant the return of a large number of former national socialist officials, and its first president, Bauwens, is credited with the following words: 'Considering the high ideals we represent, democracy is irrelevant' (Heinrich 2000: 167). The ideals being referred to were those of the imperial era of *Turnvater* Jahn's gymnastics movement, a period in which bodily training for the Fatherland was both preached and practised.

This continuity is also evident in postwar debates surrounding the unstoppable march of professionalism in German football. The core of the GFA's ideology continues to be that of an amateur sport movement, in spite of the fact that this ideology is clearly no longer consonant with the times and the GFA itself has assumed the position of an all-powerful arbiter within the media domain. Yet although all national team members have long since become millionaires, it is still considered not only an 'honour' but also an 'obligation to the Fatherland' to play and do battle for Germany.

In the postwar period, the GFA soon became the richest and largest sporting association in the world in terms of members, while football itself increasingly began to be seen as the national sport. Two further world championship titles in 1974 and 1990 were to follow the 1954 triumph, and Germany soon began to be seen as one of the leading footballing nations on the international stage. In official speeches on the occasion of centenary celebrations, talk of football as a form of 'cultural heritage', of football's importance for youth and for Germany's reputation in the world was much in evidence. Domestically, too, the GFA seemed to be 'imagining' a potent national German identity: the heart of Germany was represented as being made up of its sporting associations, which had sprung up from student associations in the imperial era, and which had been taken over by football following the tradition of the gymnastics clubs. Beyond day-to-day politics, it is in just such a social arena that sociability and 'high ideals' of one form or another tend to be upheld in today's Germany. In high-minded political speeches, sports clubs continue to be depicted as an antidote to the 'brutalization of youth', to youth involvement in neo-nazi or left-wing groups, as well as to drug abuse and other miscellaneous 'threats'. A thoroughly conservative management board in the postwar period ensured not only that game fixtures continued to be organized with a typically German degree of thoroughness, but also that these various ideals from the imperial era continue to survive in today's world: football as a 'national cultural commodity', as body and mind training, and as a rampart against evil at home and abroad.

The collusion of powerful football officials with the media, TV and the tabloid press helped to bridge the ideological gap between the battlefield and post-war Germany, while simultaneously ensuring continuity via the ritualized staging and performance of the (football) nation Germany and its ideals. This 'national narrative', which keeps threatening to negate or to assimilate all other diverging narratives, is based on the notion of a separation between sport and politics, which, as this short sketch has indicated, was in no way present at the outset of the GFA's existence. The discursive evocation of this separation, however, enables the chance element of football matches to be incorporated within the narrative of the 'destiny' and 'essence' of nationhood, while simultaneously maintaining a sense of continuity.

The Miracle of Berne

The 'national narrative' is only really able to deploy its full impact where there exists a receptive audience. The oft-cited 'Miracle of Berne' is the subject of a short story by the author Friedrich Christian Delius entitled *The Sunday I became World Champion* (2000), in which the nature of the miracle in question is once more evoked, here in an autobiographical vein. The background to the story is provided by an evocation of the narrator's life as a young boy in a Hessian village, in 'darkest' provincial Germany in 1954, shortly after defeat in the war, and in the context of the newly developing Cold War. The child's father is a vicar, and the church bells peal out warnings of great, incomprehensible powers, as do tales of the ominous threat from the 'East' – barely beyond the nearby hills – that dissect geography into Good and Evil. The 1950s are depicted as a mute period full of ineffable mystery for a child growing up in a world of silent war-returnees. Delius describes a typical Sunday visit to the local church, and the difficulty he experiences in seeing himself as part of the long lineage of fathers and forefathers:

> Stone memorial plaques for the dead soldiers of 1870/1871 hung over the heads of church visitors. *They fought for King and Fatherland*, beside which the names of those who, in 1914–1918, *fell as heroes in the battle for Germany's Honor and Survival, Never may their names be forgotten, may it remain holy to us all*. The name of my father's father was also chiseled into a stone tablet in Westphalia; I was lucky that my father had only been taken prisoner for almost three years by the French, without suffering any serious wound, thanks to *God's blessing* (Delius 2000: 49).[5]

Yet the narrator's joy that his father returned alive is somewhat diminished by the fact that he remained for ever unapproachable in his black frock – the vicar can here be taken as a metaphor for the silence and unapproachableness of the war-returnees, who often remained incapable of expressing their experiences in words.

   The narrator's emancipation and self-discovery in these postwar days still full of memorial plaques and an unapproachable father finally occurs one Sunday afternoon in front of the wireless set in his father's holiest of studies, after he has been permitted to follow the transmission of the World Cup final in Berne between Germany and Hungary: '*Schäfer crosses, header, defended, Rahn had to take a shot from outside the penalty area, Rahn shoots! Goal! Goal! Goal! Goal! Goal for Germany!*' The legendary radio commentary by Herbert Zimmermann is replayed in the story in such a way as to rekindle the full weight of its moving impact on many Germans right down to the present - even those who weren't even born at the time. The internal dialogue with the crackly, ecstatic voice on the wireless in this cramped provincial German backwater is a typical example of 'embodiment', of a rising sense of national identity in postwar Germany. In the very instant of the final whistle, the commentator anticipates the whole sense of ambivalence marked by the combination of jubilation and Germany: *'At this moment we shouldn't forget, though, that it's a game, a game, but the most popular game in all the world . . .'* – but the young listener contradicts: '... it had long since ceased to be a game, because for me, as I had shamefully and secretly wished, I'd become world champion, and I didn't want to have that taken away from me by soothing words' (2000: 115).

'I had become world champion': the radio ushers in a world beyond the reach of that of the narrator's father, one marked by Wilhelmian ideals, by Protestant bans, and by lost wars. This identification is accompanied by a sense of confusion at the transgression of a taboo – a confusion that also comes to the fore across background noises as the trophy is being presented: the narrator listens as the national anthem is played, hearing it in two different versions at one and the same time – the banned first verse with its notorious lines of *'Deutschland, Deutschland über alles'*, and the official postwar anthem, with the third verse to the same tune, 'Unity, Law, and Freedom'. This confusion soon takes a grip of the narrator as he tries to make out the celebratory cheering of the crowd droning from the radio set – he hears 'hey!' and 'yes!', but also *Heil!* These (phonetic) shifts are not only occurring in the narrator's postwar mind, but also quite patently within the stadium itself, and those in charge of the radio transmission make haste to put a stop to them: *'This was a joint radio broadcast by all stations of the Federal Republic of Germany . . . Your reporter was Herbert Zimmermann. The broadcast has come to an end. We return you now to Germany'* (2000: 116).

We're Back: Media, Stars and Football

Back to Germany. For the GFA's centenary celebrations, the organization's president, Egidius Braun, wrote:

> The game of football has always been a mirror image of trends in contemporary history. (. . .) In this regard I am naturally reminded of Germany's 3:2 World Cup final victory over Hungary in the 1954 championships at Berne: millions of individuals in our country, filled with guilt, insecurity and self-doubt were able to gain a new sense of self-worth: 'We're back.' Fritz Walter and the others were shining examples to us all (in Brüggemeier *et al.*, 2000: 5)

The football president here gives us a clear example of how a football match is transformed into a historical watershed, how chance becomes destiny, and players become heroes and bearers of national characteristics. 'We're back' – this act was never actually accomplished on the football pitch, nor in the stadium, but via a separate act of interpretation that placed a complex and contradictory reality in a novel semantic optic using the image of a miracle. The close connections between football stars, the media and powerful officials in Germany have helped to create such a potent myth that the GFA president is not the only one to believe the latter to be a mirror image of contemporary history – while forgetting that he and others like him were responsible for creating the myth in the first place.

Nationalism is embedded within a cultural nexus, and in many cases its heroes are not great thinkers or theoreticians, but football players. In the myths accreted around it, national identity assumes the character of an event staged by the media, with nation as 'imagined community.' Such mythical heroes of German football include the captain of the 1954 squad, Fritz Walter, his successor Uwe Seeler, the 'Kaiser', Franz Beckenbauer, and even – although he is seen as something of a fallen hero – Stephan Effenberg.

Fritz Walter and the Heroes of '54

In a TV broadcast in January 2000 on the sportsmen of the century, the entry of the surviving players of the 1954 squad proved to be the highlight. Gaunt-looking men of my father's generation stared blankly into the TV cameras, while photos of their deceased teammates were faded in: dead comrades were being commemorated. In this spooky sequence, the true character of the Miracle of Berne once again became apparent – the miracle consisted in the shift from the battlefield to the playing-field. The men who had once marched off in order to found a thousand-year empire (*tausendjähriges Reich*) had returned home beaten, mute, embittered, and humiliated. They had not only lost their youth, but their ideals, their faith, and their hopes had also been exposed as false. Germany was shattered. 'Mourning dead comrades' was only possible at a distance, in a shifted optic – outside the playing-field such mourning continued to be politicized, with false ideals and false ideologies becoming mixed up with mourning for fallen comrades who had fought for a wrong cause. The very same men, who perhaps are only able to mourn today, are those who became the victors on the football pitch immediately after the war.

A further highlight was provided by a video clip of the former captain, the now critically ill Fritz Walter, in his opening greeting. With serious mien he quoted a saying of the then national coach, Sepp Herberger: 'Men, remember what the boss always said: "You're not only playing for yourselves and your team, but also for the reputation of Germany in the world."'

The deciding goal scored by Helmuth Rahn was also replayed, one of the few remaining images of this game. The sound recording from the radio broadcast, which millions of Germans had originally heard (there were only a few thousand TVs at the time) and which has frequently been rebroadcast to latter generations, was added to the images. This special TV broadcast not only presented the myth in words and images, but implicitly its whole fabrication as a media collage, too, while the aged Fritz Walter, the hero of Berne, fulfilled, with his last ounce of energy, right to the very end, his function as a representative, hero and bearer of this myth. The TV presentation also included a whole host of his successors, bearing equally serious-looking miens and an aura of heavy responsibility.

Uns Uwe

Fritz Walter's immediate successor as captain of the national side in the 1960s and beginning of the 1970s was Uwe Seeler. *Uns Uwe*, as he was affectionately christened, and thus etched in the national consciousness, is considered a paragon of the 'good German' to this day. On the pitch he embodied the image of the remorseless battler/slugger and midfield player, and off it, of the honest employee.

While the year 1954 heralded the transition from radio to TV, the latter medium was initially confined to the mere reporting of facts. This being so, footballers were almost always apprehended in their capacity as footballers, rather than as public figures, on the TV screen. In consequence, the public was dependent on other sources to 'get a closer picture' of their heroes.

For me, as a youngster, 'Our Uwe' was one such hero. Radio commentaries, and later, sports news on TV were key features punctuating Saturdays between washing the car and weekly baths. It was the era of so-called 'collectors' cards', which, following the example of holy images, transformed the pictures of football stars into much sought-after collectors' items, while at the same time foreshadowing the first moves towards a greater commercialization of football. I also began to read avidly the newly available biographies of football stars, or football novels geared to youth, such as the now proverbial *Eleven Friends* by Sammy Drechsel (1955), a well-known sports reporter.

The book, *Uwe Seeler – Golden Goals* (Becker 1960), is still to be found on my bookshelves today. It contains short chapters illustrated by black and white photos that seamlessly transform the footballer's career into an exemplary life of the 'good German'. A description of his best goals and greatest successes is followed by a series of chapters entitled 'Training is everything', 'The friend', 'Uwe in everyday life', 'Uwe's private life'. The text praises Uwe's 'tireless combative spirit', 'iron discipline', the 'good comrade-in-arms' he always was, and his willingness both to lead and to take orders. The only females who get a mention are his mother and his spouse. The function of the former is seen as ensuring that her son gets onto the field (rather than, as in the previous generation, the battlefield) in good time. His wife, too, is seen as fulfilling merely a maternal role: one picture shows her shortly after having given birth, with the couple's newly-born daughter in her arms, and with husband Uwe standing by her. In the corresponding text passage, she explains how she always has to cook stew for 'her Uwe' – the classic dish provided to German soldiers. Supposed quotes attributed to her state that she is 'always ready to make sacrifices'. Frau Ilka even apparently had to sacrifice her honeymoon: 'Uwe had a match to play at the time!' (Becker 1960: 96).

The portrait of Uwe Seeler in his civil life in postwar Germany credits him with martial virtues. But also with national ones: it is underlined on several occasions that 'our Uwe' has always withstood the temptation of 'big money', having turned down offers to play for Madrid or Milan. He prefers to play 'for us', and indeed (almost) for free. In his everyday life, he worked as a representative of a sportswear firm, and as a result put in extra voluntary training shifts: 'Take a leaf out of his book!' as the author unambiguously commands with an exclamation mark. 'Our Uwe' is part of a longer tradition that precedes the 'Miracle of Berne' – a tradition that goes back to the founding of the German empire with its interweaving narrative of competitive sports and love of Fatherland.

'Kaiser Franz' Beckenbauer

The following head of the national side was none other than Franz Beckenbauer. He was lucky enough to achieve something twice over that eluded 'Our Uwe': he was world champion on two separate occasions – once as a player in 1974, and then as manager in 1990. Beckenbauer became the first media star of German football, something he has remained down to the present – to the extent that satirical spirits have characterized him personally as a 'medium'. In his external image and staged role, Beckenbauer stands for the new self-confidence of Germans following the *Wirtschaftswunder* (economic miracle), something for which Uwe Seeler still had to toil and struggle. His style is seen as light-footed, elegant and technically well-versed. As a midfield player and sweeper he always tended to be surrounded by so-called 'combative players' or 'water carriers' who did the 'work' for him – such players remained vital, and embodied those apparently indispensable martial virtues.

Beckenbauer entered into a close relationship with the media from the very outset of his career, and the media were quick to get him on board. He was the first German footballer to do advertising for consumer goods on TV, while his divorce and remarriage provided good material for gossip columns. But especially his visits to the opera, ballrooms and other public festivities were avidly raked over in the tabloid press – a place where his name was increasingly encountered owing to his often touching attempts at social climbing, from the football pitch to the cultural scene. Beckenbauer the footballer no longer embodied mere martial virtues; he rendered football acceptable in high society in a Germany where memory of the military past was gradually fading.

Even after his career had come to an end he retained a leading position within German football as an omnipresent commentator on TV and in the tabloid press, and as an official at his home club, Bayern Munich, which, as a player and then as president, he transformed into one of the most successful clubs in Europe.

When, shortly before the World Cup finals of 1986, German football appeared once more to be languishing in crisis, the popular press practically elected him national manager, and he promptly proceeded to lead the team to victory in the competition in 1990. The image of him wandering across the pitch in solitary contemplation amidst celebrating crowds of enthusiastic football fans was transported across the world. With typical media self-staging he seemed to be visualizing himself as someone spoilt by good fortune who appears to be floating above all and sundry. It is precisely this mixture of happenstance, skill and media stagecraft that led to his being baptized the 'Kaiser' at a very early date – and to some extent, quite appropriately. Kaiser Wilhelm II himself was venerated as someone capable of standing above things and factions in similar fashion; he was another early master in the use of the media, and, as Kaiser Franz, he was also not without a certain preposterousness, although he tended to make far more serious blunders.

Thus, following the 1990 victory and a year after the 'miracle of the reunification', Beckenbauer the speechifier announced that a unified Germany would remain unbeatable for generations to come – a phrase that was avoided at all costs on the political front in order to spare the world the scary prospect of Germany as a reawakened great power – and a footballing prognostic that in any case proved to be completely false.

Perhaps aside from Hitler, Beckenbauer is the most famous German worldwide. This suspicion also appeared to edge its way into Beckenbauer's mind when, following the FIFA decision that Germany would be allowed to host the 2006 world championships, he told the media about his experiences around the world as sports ambassador for Germany. In enthusiastic tones he explained how he had been received as a head of state in a good number of countries he had visited. In many countries he was also, he claimed, the only German whose name was known – apart from Hitler, as he noted with some confusion. But this association directed his attention back to his own task, to what he saw himself, or rather German football, as needing to accomplish in the world: 'Football is still the best ambassador for Germany's reputation in the world.'

The fact that football had become a multibillion dollar business and that Beckenbauer was acting on behalf of a media and GFA consortium in a bid to secure the right for Germany to host the 2006 World Cup finals was never called into question. Beckenbauer expressed his condolences to the defeated candidate, South Africa, while adding that it was precisely the elements of organizational capacity, discipline, order and security that predestined Germany to the task – virtues that South Africa would acquire in time.

'Middle Finger' Stefan Effenberg

Stefan Effenberg is known as the *enfant terrible* of the present-day German football scene. His nickname of 'middle finger' derives from a hand gesture made during his substitution in a 1994 World Cup match in the US, a gesture interpreted as obscene. In the first-round match against Spain, the national side had played in a purely tactical and defensive style. Effenberg was subject to hefty abuse by those German fans present in the stadium at the time of his substitution, to which he reacted by raising his finger in a gesture of contempt – an incident that was subjected to copious comment in the popular press. Leading GFA officials found themselves forced to act, and sent Effenberg home during the competition as a punishment for his improper behaviour. He was considered to have conducted himself in a manner unworthy of a representative of Germany abroad. His penalty can only be explained in terms of 'honour, Fatherland, propriety' – values which, beyond the confines of football, the GFA still considers itself to be responsible for upholding.

But this was not all: Effenberg is managed by his wife, Martina. She stated in the press that she found it ludicrous that her husband had been sent home – after all it was he who had been abused and insulted by the public, and he had the right to defend himself. She then threateningly declared that German football would live to regret such a moralistic sanction, and sold the story to the press. Following on from this, she arranged for her husband (who played in Italy) to join the German team Mönchengladbach, and then Bayern Munich. These clubs were interested in Effenberg's skills as a player, and Martina Effenberg negotiated the most expensive contracts for her husband that had ever been agreed upon at that time. In the press, which soon began to praise Effenberg's sporting abilities once more, Martina Effenberg instead was caricatured as a money-grubbing, vengeful, man-eating woman, and headlined her as a *Flintenweib* ('gunwoman') – a term that had seemed to have died out in Germany, and that had been used between the wars to pour scorn on Jewish and/or socialist women. In a psychoanalytical inter-pretation of institutionalized military practices of German soldiers, Theweleit (1977) interprets *Flintenweib* as a metaphor simultaneously conveying fear of and brutality against women. Martina Effenberg evoked these 'male fantasies' once more when she managed to assert herself in the all-male preserve of German football, in the cliques of ageing functionaries, brokers and club-presidents. Because of this she was subjected to sexist verbal abuse by the press on behalf of public opinion.

In contrast, her husband was asked to rejoin the national side by a contrite GFA. This he refused to do, noting that the same old men who had recently thrown him out were still holding down the same positions: it wasn't worth playing for Germany.

The 'Effenberg Affair' shows that the connection between football, national identity and German 'values' is occasionally endangered, while at the same time bringing to light the 'darker' underside of the oft-touted virtues. The aggressive campaign against Effenberg's wife is a throwback to an age many believed to have been well and truly forgotten, an age of homophobia and the ambivalent sexism manifest in a mixture of misogyny and pin-ups in army barracks as well as in football changing-rooms.

Long since established as a key actor in the billion-dollar football business, the GFA is currently in danger of losing its identity-building role to the footballers themselves, while assuming that of a pure business corporation. The discursive hegemony is constantly in need of refashioning, something that is proving to be increasingly difficult in an age of globalization, with the shifting sands of national identity under the influence of the European Union, the close interconnection between football broadcasting rights and the introduction of private or pay TV. Yet on the other side of the ledger, leading German politicians have recently been calling for a legislative clause that ensures public sector TV channels have the right to broadcast matches involving the national side. And the securing of the right to host the 2006 World Cup finals in Germany will in all likelihood mark a new chapter in the continuing saga of the relationship between nation and the rest of the world.

The German Miracle

Football is a ritualized performance that is re-enacted every week at the club level and whose spectacular pinnacle is assured by national team games – at least in Germany. Continutally new occasions present themselves for 'chance events' on the pitch to be reinterpreted as national destiny. The regularity of national and international tournaments furthermore guarantees that the narratives and myths are able to be continuously rewoven. The prerequisites for converting victory on the football field into a national myth include the supervention of 'miracles', instances of divine intervention in the normal workings of the world, plus the availability of heroes capable of doing destiny's bidding in an exemplary manner and a media willing to herald the miraculous 'good news' and to repeat it *ad infinitum.*

The example of Germany as (footballing) nation brings this cultural tendency to light in dramatic fashion: national identity and the expression of galvanizing sayings such as 'we're back on the march' have been shown to be directly connected to the rhetorical and media-based treatment of the game of football. The 'Miracle of Berne' in 1954 marks a historical watershed, while at the same time enabling reference to be made to traditions dating to before the Second World War.

In this chapter I have tried to use a variety of examples to show that not only has football played a central role in the construction of a German postwar identity, but also its 'official' version has tended to contain conservative, if not openly reactionary traits. Yet these traits are at the same time contradictory: it may strike one as odd that players for the German national side continue to receive orders from officials always to sing along to the national anthem – most players apparently don't even know the words. The same is true of the public, which instead prefers to sing the 1950s cabaret hit entitled, 'Such a wonderful day as today' (*So ein Tag, so wunderschön wie heute*). Television commentators, too (at least on public broadcasting channels) tend to make great efforts to give a non-biased presentation of the facts, even for national games, and proffer commentaries with all the panache of newscasters. Although this has changed in recent years, in comparison with many other countries the association of emotion and nation continues to be perceived as somewhat suspect in Germany, and almost always encounters criticism. It is precisely this ambivalence that characterizes German football, and it is also a hallmark of nationalism that no one is ever quite sure as to whether football helps to tame or merely to conceal its destructive power.

Football is more than a game and a harmless cue for 'chitchat' or light conversation. On the contrary, it provides an inexhaustible topic of conversation; it can act as an incentive to speak that those it has 'grabbed' are barely able to resist. The conversation never reaches a terminal point, partly because there is always a new match to comment on, but also because football represents a discourse on (national) identity, which is itself an imagined reality.

Notes

1. For an overview of theories on 'football cultures' see Armstrong and Giulianotti (1997) and the review article by Feixa and Juris (2000), and for sports in general see Dyck (2000).
2. Heinrich (2000) and Fischer and Lindner (1999).
3. For the history of German football see Heinrich (2000) and Eisenberg (1997).
4. A political term for bringing into line social, political and economic organizations.
5. Translations of Delius by Werner Krauss

References

Anderson, Benedict (1993), *Die Erfindung der Nation. Zur Karriere eines folgenreiches Konzepts*. Frankfurt/New York: Campus Verlag. (First published in 1983 as: *Imagined Communities. Reflections on the Origin and Spread of Nationalism*. London: Verso Edition and NLB).

Archetti, Eduardo P. (1997), '"And Give Joy to my Heart". Ideology and Emotion in the Argentinian Cult of Maradona'. in Gary Armstrong and Richard Giulianotti (eds), *Entering the Field. New Perspectives on World Football*, pp. 31–51.Oxford: Berg.

—— (1999), *Masculinities. Football, Polo and the Tango in Argentinia*. Oxford: Berg.

Armstrong, Gary and Richard Giulianotti (eds) (1997), *Entering the Field. New Perspectives on World Football*. Oxford/New York: Berg.

Becker, Robert (1960), *Uwe Seeler und seine goldenen Tore*. Munich: Copress-Verlag.

Brüggemeier, Franz-Josef, Ulrich Borsdorf and Jürg Steiner (eds), (2000), *Der Ball ist rund. Ausstellungskatalog*. Essen: Klartext.

Crain, Mary M. and Felicia Hughes-Freeland (1998), 'Introduction,' in Mary M. Crain and Felicia Hughes-Freeland (eds), *Recasting Ritual. Performance, Media, Identity*, pp. 1–21 London/New York: Routledge.

Delius, Friedrich Christian (2000 [1994]) *Der Sonntag, an dem ich Weltmeister wurde*. Reinbek: Rowohlt.

Dieckmann, Christoph (2000), 'Führers Kicker', *Die Zeit*, 16 March 2000.

Drechsel, Sammy (1955), *Elf Freunde müßt ihr sein*. Stuttgart/Vienna: Thienemanns Verlag.

Dyck, Noel (ed.) (2000), *Games, Sports and Cultures*. Oxford/New York: Berg.

Eisenberg, Christiane (1997), 'Deutschland', in Christiane Eisenberg (ed.), *Fußball, Soccer, Calcio. Ein englischer Sport auf seinem Weg um die Welt*, pp. 94–129. München: dtv.

Feixa, Carles and Jeffrey S. Juris (2000), 'Review Article: Football Cultures,' *Social Anthropology* Vol. 8, Part 2: 203–8.

Fischer, Gerhard and Ulrich Lindner (1999), *Stürmer für Hitler. Vom Zusammenspiel zwischen Fußball und Nationalsozialismus*. Göttingen: Verlag Die Werkstatt.

Heinrich, Arthur (2000), *Der deutsche Fußballbund. Eine politische Geschichte*. Cologne: PapyRossa.

Lopes, José Sergio Leite (1997), 'Successes and Contradiction in "Multiracial" Brazilian Football', in Gary Armstrong and Richard Giulianotti (eds) *Entering the Field. New Perspectives on World Football*, pp. 53–86. Oxford/New York: Berg.

Lyotard, Francois (1984), *The Postmodern Condition: Report on Knowledge*. Manchester: Manchester University Press.

Menzen, Michael (2000), 'Der DFB und seine Präsidenten', in Franz-Josef Brügge-meier, Ulrich Borsdorf and Jürg Steiner (eds), *Der Ball ist rund, Ausstellung-skatalog*, pp. 360–1 Essen: Klartext.

Rudie, Ingrid (1998), 'Making Persons in a Global Ritual? Embodied Experience and Free-Floating Symbols in Olympic Sport', in Mary M. Crain and Felicia Hughes-Freeland (eds) *Recasting Ritual. Performance, Media, Identity*, pp. 113–35. London/New York: Routledge.

Schulze-Marmeling, Dietrich, Hardy Grüne, Werner Skrentny and Hubert Dahlkamp (1999), *Fußball für Millionen. Die Geschichte der deutschen Nationalmann-schaft*. Göttingen: Verlag Die Werkstatt.

Theweleit, Klaus (1977), *Männerphantasien. Frauen, Fluten, Körper, Geschichte. Band 1*. Basle/Frankfurt: Stroemfeld/Roter Stern Verlag.

11

Playing Football and Dancing Tango: Embodying Argentina in Movement, Style and Identity

Eduardo P. Archetti

In this book one of the key assumptions is that sport is a ritual and a game at the same time, and is, as such, a cultural and social construction that makes bodily and symbolic communication among its participants possible. The content of the communication may vary according to the degree of formality, rigidity, concentration of meaning and redundancy. But the ritual is also a performance in the sense that saying something is also doing something: hence, the ritual action makes possible a connection between the meanings and values mobilized by the participants. In every ritual, various types of participants can be distinguished: the experts in knowledge, the central participants, and the peripheral participants or audience. This approach will permit the consideration of discourses, practices and identities by the various kinds of participants: players, journalists and public. A historical analysis of the impact of sports situates these narratives and practices within specific periods of time and place, and, consequently, enables us to follow their transformations. At the centre is the apprehension of the significance of bodily exploits. The anthropological analysis of sport is not a reflection of society, but a means of reflecting on society. I will try to demonstrate that football and tango are connected historically and socially in Argentina. Sport and dance are privileged arenas for understanding liminality and cultural creativity. Let me give as an introduction two Latin American examples.

DaMatta (1982) has argued that Brazil is a society articulated by the sharp division between the 'home' and the 'street', and between the family – a system of hierarchical social relations and persons – and the market and free individuals. According to him the role of football is paramount in Brazil because the personalized social world of the home and the impersonal universe of the street are combined in a public ritual. Impersonal rules regulating the game make an opening for the expression of individual qualities: 'football, in the Brazilian society, is a source of individualisation . . . much more than an instrument of collectivisation at the personal level ' (1982: 27). The male players escape from fate – the fate of class or race – and construct their own successful biographies in a public arena. Football makes it possible to experience equality and freedom, important values of nationhood, in hierarchical contexts. In order to triumph, a football player (like a *samba* dancer) must have *jogo de cintura*, the capacity to use the body to provoke confusion and fascination in the public and in their adversaries. The European identification of a Brazilian style of playing relating football and samba dancing, manifested in the expression '*samba*-football', is therefore not an arbitrary creation: it is rooted in Brazilian self-imagery and identity (Leite Lopes 1997). This ident-ification establishes important cultural differences, because the existence and development of European styles of playing are not automatically linked to music and dance.

Brazil is not unique. In Cuba the ritual of playing baseball, the national sport, has been associated with dancing: 'each baseball match culminated in a magnif-icent dinner and dancing, for which orchestras were hired for playing *danzones*' (González Echeverría 1994: 74). As in the case of football, baseball during the first two decades of the twentieth century was perceived as a democratic and modern game that made it possible for young male players of modest origins to experience social mobility. As in the case of Brazil with samba, the *danzón* was also exported to other Latin American countries, and in its continuous transformations over time became *salsa*.

Argentinian tango was first exported to Europe in the 1910s, and then to the rest of Latin America and North America, becoming a 'universal' dance to express eroticism and modernity. Argentinian football players were exported to Europe as early as in the 1920s. Over the years, tango and football have become represent-ative of performing Argentinians and a pervasive global image of 'genuine' Argentinian cultural products. Today, very few Argentinians will deny that they play the double role of public mirrors and models of identity. As in the cases of Brazil and Cuba, Argentinian performing bodies – those of dancers, musicians, singers and football players – became highly visible in the world arena of leisure (Archetti 1999). This chapter explores this historical connection in a rather eclectic perspective. My many years of research on football and tango in Buenos Aires, Argentina, has combined traditional fieldwork and orality – stories and histories told by the informants – with textual analysis – historical essays, ideological writings of the nationalist authors, journals, magazines and tango lyrics. A central concern is the process by which meaning, images, identities and performances are produced. I try to combine what my informants said, did or commented on, with what I read or saw. This approach makes it possible, in principle, to capture the complexities of football and tango.

Thinking the National

One of my informants, in a passionate exchange of views on Argentinian male performances, in a cafe of Boedo, a *barrio* of Buenos Aires, said to me:

> We exported, as you know, beef and cereals, and we were known due to these merch-andises, but we have been exporting men and women all the time during this century. We exported football players by hundreds and hundreds, to Europe, to South America and to Mexico, but also we have been exporting music, tango, our national music, since 1900, and of course musicians, singers and dancers. We are seen and we think of ourselves, as a country exporting beef, cereals and human performers of all kind.

Andrés was right. In 1928 Borocotó, a writer, sport journalist and the founder of Argentinian football mythologies, wrote:

> Football is the collective sport of the *criollo* [Argentinian Creole], tango his music. Do these two predilections differ so much? The first constitutes an aesthetic pleasure associated with affections, traditions of clubs and neighbourhoods; the second clearly speaks to sentiments with a dose of sensuality . . . When tango is played . . . we can see the woman (*milonguita*) with her head on the chest of the dancer . . . dreaming of a past love or with something vague and melancholic while the male dancer draws on the floor the most elegant and complicated figures. Perhaps increasing cosmopolitanism will condition these predilections, but now there is nothing that indicates possible changes. The tango and football will continue in their privileged position during many, many years, or perhaps for ever (*El Gráfico*, 467 (16/6-28): 8).

Borocotó associated the popularity of tango and football in Argentina with their global expansion and consecration in Europe:

> The tango has been accepted in Paris. It comes out from the suburbs of Buenos Aires, the places were the footballers were formed; it was introduced into society and later expanded its reign to the City of Lights . . . The same destiny was waiting for football, the popular sport of the River Plate basin. Football brought to Europe something unknown. Against strong adversaries, the *criollo* player dribbled and scored goals. Their physical strength was smashed by the ability and the class of *criollo* players, and in front of thousands and thousands of spectators, Argentinians and Uruguayans played the final of Amsterdam (in 1928) . . . The same players dribbling in the tango dribbled the Europeans in the field of football (*El Gráfico* , 467 (16/6-28): 8).

José Manuel Moreno, a charismatic River Plate player in the 1940s and, accord-ing to many journalists, one of the best players Argentina ever produced, expressed vividly the symbiosis at that time between tango and football:

Many people blamed my nights devoted to dancing, but they did not know how important the tango was for football players. You see, you get rhythm, you learn how to change rhythm in a *milonga* dance, you learn how to control your body profiles, how to work with the waist and the legs while doing figures. You see, perhaps I was so good in football because I was dancing tango every night (*Clarin*, 11/1-98: 69).

Iglesias, a Spanish sport journalist, characterized the performances of Fernando Redondo, the Argentinian mid-fielder of Real Madrid, in the two semi-finals of the European Cup played against the German team of Borussia Dortmund, in the following way: '. . . and suddenly Redondo appeared with his hairdo with a middle parting, asked for the floor and induced the other twenty-one players to dance tango: in two nights he injected in their veins Gardel, Piazzola, Bochini, Beto Alonso and Adolfo Pedernera; an Argentinian century of music and football' (*El País*, 20/4-98:51). The connection made by Iglesias between tango – Redondo with his hairdo in the Valentino style, Gardel, the mythical singer of the Golden Age of tango in the 1920s and 1930s, and Piazzola, the contemporary avant-garde composer and bandoneon player – and football – Adolfo Pedernera, representing the famous 'machine' team of River Plate in the 1940s, and Bochini and Beto Alonso, two famous number ten players who never succeeded outside Argentina and who represented, more than other players of international fame, the Argentinian technical and baroque style of playing – is not random. It is not an arbitrary abuse of analogy by a professional journalist, but the reproduction of a historical construction.

It is clear that today Argentinian professional players will hesitate to accept the existence of a deep bodily connection between technical ability and tango. I am quite sure that Redondo is not a good tango dancer like Moreno, and maybe he prefers rock and international pop music to tango. The connections are made at a different level, in a kind of historical semantic extension so well articulated by Iglesias and so clearly experienced by Moreno during his life as an active player.

Very few Argentinians will disagree with Iglesias' argument that tango and football certainly played, and still play, the double role of public mirrors and models of Argentinian imageries. However, the world of tango, both in choreography and lyrics, is made of the complex relations between men and women. In contrast, the world of football is exclusively male, an encounter in the stadium (and in the history of clubs, nations and competitions) between competing groups of male players and supporters. Consequently, analyses of tango and football must reflect the complexities of models and idioms of gender and nationhood.

It has been consistently argued that the nation is an 'imagined political community' in the sense that its members share a sovereign boundary and have a strong feeling of communion. Hence, the ideology of nationalism must be integrated in social practices that can create, over time, the image of 'people' having 'something' in common. Therefore it is crucial to identify social practices that appear to reflect ideas of nationalism and to investigate the 'content' of these practices with respect to the actors involved and the meaning of the values conveyed. The case of Argentina makes it possible to examine how certain given bodily practices and associated discourses are involved in the formation of national imageries. As was pointed out by Borocotó, football was perceived as a democratic and modern game that makes it possible for young players of modest origins to experience social mobility. It is quite interesting that football in Brazil, Uruguay and Argentina, baseball in Cuba and the Dominican Republic, and cricket in the West Indies, sports which originated outside the Latin American countries, were integrated into the construction of the 'national'. 'Thinking the national' was, thus, a typical modernist project, because it was fabricated by the introduction of foreign cultural practices and not by the revival or invention of traditions. This strategy of research is not focused on the official ideology of nationalism and the nation-state, but on the margins of the national, the fields where the national can be perceived and related to specific individual features, cultural creativity and public performances. Argentinians can see themselves in football and tango, and the 'others' can see them. A complex interplay of mirrors and masks is thus created and re-created over time. Tango and football as arenas for 'national' identities reveal the complexity of these kinds of 'free' zones in relation to 'otherness'.

The National Imageries of Football and Tango

Argentina received, between 1869 and 1930, more immigrants in relation to its native population than any other modern country, and there was a perfect mirror of this historical pattern in the growth and development of the capital city of Buenos Aires, the city where tango was invented and football developed. The city grew rapidly from 180,000 inhabitants in 1869 to 1,576,000 in 1914. The percentage of foreigners was 13.8 in 1869, 14.0 in 1895 and 42.7 in 1914. In the nineteenth century British immigrants brought to the country their modern sports – together with industrial capital, new technology in agriculture and livestock, and financial institutions. The first football match was played in Buenos Aires in 1867, only four years after the creation of the Football Association in London. In the park of Palermo, a modest monument with the name of the British players commemorates this important event in the history of the nation. The first league, and, until 1911, the dominating clubs, sprang out of British Schools. Not only was the game a British export, but so too were the standards and the quality of play. The importance of the British colony transformed the city into a privileged place to be visited by famous English first-division teams. From 1904, Argentinian football grew under the influence of the excellent professional teams that came to play in Buenos

Aires: Southampton, Tottenham, Everton and Nottingham Forest. They played several matches against the British local teams and, in all cases, returned to England undefeated.

The majority of the new sports clubs rapidly incorporated non-British, European immigrants and their sons, or were directly founded by them. The intense competition in football between British local teams and the new 'mixed' clubs, created outside the boarding schools, was a growth point for inventive creolization, the creation of the Argentinian style of playing football. The British were the founders of football; they codified the rules; they developed a morality based on fair play; they constructed a style of playing and exported it all over the world. The native Argentinians and the immigrants accepted and incorporated football as an important bodily practice in their leisure time and as a ritual context for competition and the emotional display of loyalty and engagement. The emergence of a truly creole foundation began in 1913 when Racing Club, a football club started in 1903 by Argentinian natives and Italian immigrants, without a single player of British origin, won the first-division championship for the first time. From that moment the British clubs declined in importance and their players disappeared from the Argentinian national teams. This process was accompanied by the ideological construction of an opposition between the British (or English) style and the creole. 'Britishness' was identified with being phlegmatic, disciplined and methodical, and concentrated around elements of the collective, of force and of physical power. These virtues helped to create a repetitive style, similar to that of a 'machine'. In this way, British football was conceptualized as 'perfect', that is, industrially perfect. The creole (*criollo*), owing to the Latin influence, was exactly the opposite: restless, individualistic, undisciplined, based on personal effort, agile and skilful (see Archetti 1996).

The conceptual oppositions between British and *criollo* physical virtues have become encrusted in common perceptions of football. The British physical virtues are still associated with 'force and physical power', while the virtues of the *criollos* are those of agility and virtuoso movement. The metaphor of the 'machine', as opposed to individual creativity, is constant in contemporary Argentinian football imagery. 'Britishness' is still associated with the industrial, and the *criollo* with the pre-industrial social system. During a game, when faced with the British machine or repetitive play, the typical *criollo* response would be the 'dribble'. This manifestation of style is eminently individual and cannot be programmed. It is the opposite of the industrial, collective game of the machine. The masculine imagery is, thus, related to powerful ideas of individual creativity and freedom. The creativity of Argentinian players is a victory against pure collective discipline and training (see Archetti 1995 and 1996).

Tango as a dance evolved gradually from the confluence of the Cuban *habanera*, the urban *milonga* and the African *candombe* (see Collier 1995). The *habanera*, a

Cuban transformation of the Spanish *contradanza*, was very popular and was danced to the African rhythms best remembered today from its appearance in Georges Bizet's opera *Carmen*. The *habanera* and the polka stimulated the emergence of the local couple dance known as the *milonga*. The *candombe* was a group dance of the black population of Buenos Aires that at some points included an embrace. It is assumed that the *candombe* influenced the *milonga* in the way bodies moved. The *milonga* was an 'embrace' dance, and, in this sense, close to the way tango developed. By 1880 it comprised a gradual crystallization of the choreography of the tango after two decades of improvisations, experiment, trial and error. By the end of the nineteenth century and the beginning of the twentieth century, urban life in Buenos Aires was being rapidly transformed. Luxury hotels, restaurants, bistros, hundreds of cafés, a world-famous opera and theatres were built by European architects. This prompted changes in the use of leisure time and created a new environment outside the walls of privacy and the home. This period, as I just pointed out, was also characterized by a rapid expansion of sports and social clubs. The appearance of public arenas created new conditions for public participation and enjoyment, where cultural life, sports and sexual concerns dominated. Three institutions, in particular, provided the public with new excitement and opportunities for the deployment of sexual fantasies: the modern legal brothel, the 'dancing academies' (*academias de baile*) or 'cafés with waitresses' (*café de camareras*), and the cabaret. These arenas provided a space of freedom for men and women, albeit of a special kind (see Archetti 1994).

The tango was directly related to these public contexts: in the last two decades of the nineteenth century, the brothel and the 'dancing academies' were the places where the original tango dance was created. Later, at the beginning of the twentieth century, the cabaret became a privileged public space for dancing and singing. The playing of the first orchestras took the form of a kind of dialogue between the orchestra and the dancers in which the musical improvisations were closely related to a rich and complex 'erotic' choreography. It has been rightly observed that the rapid expansion of the tango in Europe in the 1910s was a product of the eroticism of the dance. Savigliano explains the European acceptance in the following way:

> Tango did not perform 'instinctive' sensuality (like the dances of the 'primitives'), rowdy excitement (like the dances of the peasants), or overt impropriety, cynicism, or defiant aggression toward the upper classes (like the dances of the urban marginals). Nor did it focus solely on the erotic powers of the female body, like other 'traditional' exotic dances. Tango's sexual politics were centered in the process of seduction. A fatal man and a *femme fatale* who, despite their proximity, kept their erotic impulses under control, measuring each other's powers. In its choreography, the tango resembled a game of chess, where deadly contenders took turns moving invisible pieces with their dragging feet. Their mutual attraction and repulsion were prolonged into an unbearable, endless tension. And everything took place, apparently, under male control (1995: 110).

At the beginning, then, the tango was for dancing and not for listening. The texts accompanying the music were direct, insolent, imprudent, and, in many ways, reflected a kind of male 'primitive' exhibitionism.

The 'new' tango developed in the 1920s and 1930s – and coincided with the consolidation of the creole style in football. The musical composition became more sophisticated, drastically reducing the degree of improvisation. The conductors became more concerned with details and nuances in the orchestration than with performances of improvised solos. We can say that tango evolved in the opposite direction to the Argentinian style of playing football. The most important change, however, can be observed in the lyrics. The new authors of the tango, Celedonio Flores, Enrique Cadicamo, Enrique Santos Discepolo, Francisco García Jiménez or Homero Manzi, tell compressed, moving stories concerning characters and moral dilemmas that were easily understood and identified by vast, heterogeneous social audiences. Thus, the tango shifted from being first and foremost a musical expression to being primarily a 'narrative' interpreted by a plethora of extraordinary singers, both male and female (see Archetti 1994).

Tango poetics relate not only to 'universal' emotions, like sadness, happiness, fear, and anxiety, but also to those of love, pride, guilt, shame, and honour. All are fundamental in the articulation of individual identity and sociocultural processes. The tango, dispossessed of its history and particularities, has been transformed in the Argentine society of today into the 'mythical' language of gendered emotions. It is, in spite of different attempts to transform its authoritative framework, a kind of 'frozen' universe of meanings reflecting different types of love: love as duty, passion, deep friendship, and, finally, as romantic love. The lyrics revalorize (hetero-)sexuality, sexual relations and sensual love. The modernity of tango lyrics lies precisely in their presentation of uncertainties related to the exercise of romantic choice. In this type of lyric the basic elements in the cultural construction of romantic love are intimacy, companionship or friendship, the existence of mutual empathy and the search for sexual pleasure. The distortion of one of these, such as too much emphasis on sexual pleasure, creates an emotional imbalance leading to unhappiness, loneliness, and nostalgia. The universalization of romantic love in these texts is highly dependent on a definition of a 'self' that can choose in accordance with deep emotions and thus achieve a full realization of him/herself (see Archetti 1994).

The globalization of tango took place during this period with the help of modern technology: radio, movies and records. Some of the singers, like Carlos Gardel, and the orchestras (Canaro, D'Arienzo, De Caro, Troilo, Pugliese and Di Sarli) became famous worldwide. This very process of globalization served to invent a 'tradition', a mirror in which Argentinians could see themselves precisely because 'others' began to see them in terms of these images. The narrative of the tango became a key element in the creation of a 'typical' Argentinian cultural product.

The texts as a written discourse became a popular poetics. However, the impact of the words without the power of the music would probably have been quite different. The forceful combination of text and music gave the written emotional stories a special dimension, because they were both sung and danced. During this period, the dance lost the aggression of the first epoch, and many of the choreographic figures disappeared. As a dance, the tango became more sophisticated, but, at the same time, the lyrics became increasingly important in the constitution of a national 'musical narrative'.

The transformation of the dance in the 1920s and 1930s coincided with the consolidation of a football playing style. Andrés, and other informants too, expressed the view that 'dribbling' in football and 'dancing' were related. Manucho said that '*cortes y quebradas* in the dancing are figures invoking the great dribblers in our football'. In this way he gave support to Moreno on the importance of dancing for playing football. Andrés defined *cortes* and *quebradas* in the following way:

> The *corte* is a sudden pause, an unexpected break in the dancing and in the figures; it is not a movement. Much dribbling in football is a *corte*, a player stopping and at the same time controlling the ball. A *corte* can eliminate a defender and can help to change direction, as in tango. On the contrary, a *quebrada* is an athletic contortion, a dramatic movement, and a rapid improvisation with the legs and the waist, avoiding physical contact with the opponents. The essence of tango dancing was a combination of *cortes* and *quebradas*. The best Argentinian players, and Maradona is the most fantastic example, based their way of playing on *cortes* and *quebradas*.

The fact that tango in Buenos Aires is not a massive and popular dance as it was in the past, and in this way is not like samba or *salsa* for Brazil or Cuba, was not seen as an impediment to imagining the close relation between football and dancing. My informants emphasized the analogies between steps and figures in tango and dribbling in football. When confronted with the fact that the Argentinian style, at least in Europe, is not known as tango-football, they attributed this fact to lack of historical knowledge. Manucho expressed this in a vivid way: 'in the tango we find the roots of the Argentinian way of playing football'. I will not deny this analogy. I would like, in the next section, to present the interconnections between tango and football that transcend dancing.

Football in the World of Tango Music and Lyrics

From 1910 onwards tangos were composed in tribute to football clubs and players. Emilio Sassenus composed the first tango devoted to football in 1910, with the title *Football porteño*. In 1911, Vicente Greco, an outstanding director of orchestras and a bandoneon-player, composed the tango *Racing Club* that is still played today. These tangos had no lyrics. A number of tangos have been written in honour of football clubs. Four are dedicated to San Lorenzo de Almagro, five to Boca Juniors, two to Independiente, one to Huracán, two to Estudiantes de la Plata, one to Banfield, one to Gimnasia y Esgrima de La Plata, and one to Newell's Old Boys. The majority of them were composed in the 1920s and 1930s. During the same period, when Argentinian football appeared on the international scene, a series of tangos were composed and dedicated to great players – Botasso, Monti, Nolo Ferreira, Tarascone, Onzari, Varallo, Sastre, Bernabé Ferreyra and Orsi – and to great teams. Examples are: *Bravo nuestros campeones* – to the team that won the South American Cup in 1927, *Olímpicos* – to the team obtaining the silver medal in the Olympic Games of 1928 in Amsterdam, and *Argentina campeón* – to the team that won the South American Cup in 1955 (see Archetti 2001). The majority of these tangos were musically rather mediocre, and the lyrics simple and marginal in relation to the main themes developed in the 'new guard' tradition. More tangos were composed in the 1930s and 1940s, but only two tangos have survived the dust of time and the filter of historical quality. Let me present both.

El sueño del pibe ('The *pibe*'s dream' or 'The young boy's dream') was composed in 1943 and recorded in 1945 with two of the most important singers of the time: Roberto Chanel and Ricardo Tanturi. This tango has become closely associated with the life and success of Maradona, who knows the text very well and has sung it twice on different television programmes. These events, triggered by a rich imagery, were commented upon by my informants. Sergio, a man in his late twenties and a devoted follower of Maradona's exploits, remembered well a 'historical television programme with Maradona, a real *pibe* at that time'. A real *pibe* in the cultural imagery of Argentina is associated with creativity and spontaneity. The best players are always *pibes*, and Maradona is, by extension, nicknamed *el pibe de oro* ('the golden boy'). Sergio told me that when Maradona was twelve years old, Pipo Mancera, a famous television entertainer, showed Maradona juggling with a ball, doing incredible things that even a worshipped professional player would have enormous difficulty imitating. After a minute of juggling, 'a minute that was eternal' according to Sergio, Mancera asked Maradona what were his future dreams as a football player. Without hesitation, the boy answered that he had three dreams: to play in the first division league, to wear the shirt of the Argentinian national team in a World Cup, and to win the Cup. Sergio explained to me:

> It was like in the famous tango *El sueño del pibe*, you remember? But Maradona was more aspiring and conscious of his capacity. Well, the lyrics narrate the story of a talented *pibe* who, while crying with joy, shows his mother a letter from his club telling him that he has been accepted as a player in the junior team. That night, he dreams, like so many crack Argentinian players, that he reaches the First Division and that in his début he

scores the winning goal. Look, in this tango the *pibe* is a forward, and he scores after dribbling past all the defenders of the opposing team. It is Maradona. It is incredible, but this tango was composed for him more than thirty years before he started to play.

This image has been used on countless occasions in Argentina and in international television programmes devoted to the life of Maradona. The perfect synchronism of the performance, the age of the performer and his future career parallel real life with the flavour and melodrama of a soap opera with tango music and text. A nation needs heroes even in times of peace, and sports can provide them. The history of concrete individuals, like Maradona, is transformed into social models through which paradoxes and dramas in society are perceived, and key values are recognized and eventually questioned (see Archetti 1997).

Professionalism in sport has produced marginal participants, 'shallow players' in Geertzian terminology: the supporters following athletes and sport events as spectators, and the passive watchers of television or listeners to radio. The chants of Argentinian football supporters are concerned with the importance of sexuality and masculinity – real against dubious men. They defend their teams and attack the opponents, and in this they are no different from other engaged supporters. However, alongside the dramatization of sexuality there is a set of chants that refer to the elusiveness of the 'world', to a sort of disenchantment and loss of hope, and consequently stress the importance of loyalty to a club. In this difficult world what remains as something 'pure' is the love of the colours, the passion of the strip, the nostalgia for a glorious past and the pride in what was and what can become. The tango *Desde el tablón* ('From the pitch'), composed in 1971, when the negative sides of professionalism were perceived and discussed in Argentina, deals with these kinds of emotions. The narrator tells us the passion ('fever pitch') that is associated with his loyalty, moments of happiness, profound sorrow, and moral indignation towards the team and the club. He left the stadium many times telling himself that this match was his last, and in order to convince himself he tore his club membership card to pieces (and in an exaggerated Argentinian way he tells us that he did it 'forty times'). But in spite of all these experiences, he is always back, at the pitch, and 'in each cry of support he sets free the best parts of his soul, which he has saved (for the club)'. One might conclude by saying that in a world with so many things to be 'endured', among them the risk of losing illusions, the fans affirm the importance of the continuity deriving from positive self-identification with the clubs.

By Way of Conclusion

Tango and football are central in the 'imagining of the national' in Argentina. However, football is today a marginal theme in the world of tango. What has survived, the two tangos referred to above, is important because it puts voice and sound to key aspects of football in Argentina: the homage to *pibes*-players, the essence of creativity and freedom, and the loyalty of the supporters. Without the supporters, football as a complex ritual would enter into a deep crisis. One of my main arguments is that dominant national imageries work primarily through the transformation of meanings, semantic extensions and analogical uses (and abuses). Consequently, national narratives are constructed and reconstructed in different fields of activities and in the interplay between internal and external forces. Notions of Argentinian identity are not exclusively constructed internally, within given boundaries. They can also be conceptualized in contraposition to other identities, recognized or not by the natives themselves. The ideas and images of the 'national' are quite often a mirror in which the glance of others is as crucial as the glance of the natives themselves.

The bodily images produced in tango were transferred to Argentinian football. I have shown that the individual style of great players was based on the 'dribble'. Many of my informants too related tango figures, the *cortes* and *quebradas*, to the great dribblers in Argentinian football. Some even insisted that Maradona's dribbling is better seen accompanied with the music of some classical tango. The historical confluence of tango and football is without any doubt a powerful factor in creating a world of images and narratives in which the interconnections between these embodied practices make it possible to perceive football as a way of dancing.

References

Archetti, E. P. (1994), 'Models of Masculinity in the Poetics of the Argentinian Tango', in E. P. Archetti (ed.), *Exploring the Written. Anthropology and the Multiplicity of Writing*, Oslo: Scandinavian University Press.

—— (1995), 'Estilo y virtudes masculinas en *El Gráfico*: La creación del imaginario del fútbol argentino', *Desarrollo Económico*, vol. 35 (139): 419–42.

—— (1996), 'Playing Styles and Masculine Virtues in Argentine Football', in M. Melhuus and K. A. Stølen (eds), *Machos, Mistresses, Madonnas. Contesting the Power of Latin American Gender Imagery*, London: Verso.

—— (1997), '"And Give Joy to my Heart". Ideology and Emotions in the Argentinian Cult of Maradona', in G. Armstrong and R. Giulianotti (eds), *Entering the Field. New Perspectives on World Football*, Oxford/New York: Berg.

—— (1999), *Masculinities. Football, Polo and the Tango in Argentina*, Oxford: Berg.

—— (2001), *El potrero, la pista y el ring. Las patrias del deporte argentino*, Buenos Aires: Fondo de Cultura Económica.

Collier, S. (1995), 'The Tango is Born: 1880s–1920s', in S. Collier, A. Cooper, M. S. Azzi and R. Martin, *Tango*, London: Thames and Hudson.

DaMatta, R. (1982), 'Esporte na Sociedade: Um Ensaio sobre o Futebol Brasileiro', in R. DaMatta *et al.*, *Universo do Futebol: Esporte e Sociedade Brasileira*, Rio de Janeiro: Ediçoes Pinakotheke.

González Echeverría, R. (1994), 'Literatura, baile y beisból en el (último) fin de Siglo cubano', in J. Ludmer (ed.), *Las culturas de fin de siglo en América Latina*, Rosario: Beatriz Viterbo Editora.

Leite Lopes, J. S. (1997), 'Successes and Contradictions in 'Multiracial' Brazilian Football', in G. Armstrong and R. Giulianotti (eds), *Entering the Field, New Perspectives on World Football*, Oxford/New York: Berg.

Savigliano, M. (1995), *Tango and the Political Economy of Passion*, Boulder, CO: Westview Press.

12

Michezo:[1] **Dance, Sport and Politics in Dar-es-Salaam, Tanzania**

Anne Leseth

This chapter seeks to demonstrate the manner in which body practices both reflect and, in turn, subtly shape the political contexts and purposes within which they occur. While governments may pay particular attention to how different body practices, such as sport and dance, could be employed as means to advance their political objectives, they can never readily control the ambiguity, complexity and irony that are generated by the performing bodies of social actors. The ethnographic context for this discussion consists of performing practices and discourses on sports and dance in Dar-es-Salaam in Tanzania.[2]

In my previous work on sports and culture in Dar-es-Salaam (Leseth 1995, 1997) the Kiswahili concept for sport, *michezo,* has been of crucial importance in providing an alternative approach for studying body practices. Literally, *michezo* stems from the verb *kucheza,* which has the following meanings: 'play, sport, play a game, make a move in a game, waste time, trifle, act, work, move, drill and be loose'. Its noun *mchezo* (plural *michezo*) is translated to mean 'a game, pastime, amusement, sport or a mockery' (F. Johnson 1990). *Michezo* is not differentiated into concepts such as competitive sports, mass sports, leisure and play. Playing cards, playing football or basketball or skipping rope are all *michezo.* Thus the concept is very broad compared to the Western notion of 'sports'. In trying to grasp the ambiguity and complexity of performing, whether it is within fields of sport, dance or everyday practices, I found the concept of *michezo* a 'door opener'.

In this essay, I suggest that the concept of *michezo* provides vital ethnographic support for grasping the workings of the performing bodies of social actors. I will add further depth and detail to this concept and its practice as the chapter proceeds. Implicit in my presentation is a critique of the conventional and evolutionary tendencies within social science writing on sports. I want to move beyond conventional categorical definitions and boundaries that isolate fields such as dance, sport, play, work and everyday practices from each other. The word *michezo* has served as a 'key' in illuminating this point, as people's experiences of *michezo* in different ways link fields of activities that are for Westerners isolated from one another.

I also disagree with 'evolutionary tendencies' in the treatment of sport in scientific writings, especially the treatment of sports in non-European societies. 'Traditional sports' (Baker and Mangan 1987), 'indigenous sports' (Ndee 1996), 'pre-colonial sports' (Nkongo 1979) or 'sport in developing countries' (Heinemann 1993) are all categories applied to non-Western sport-like activities and games. The way these categories are applied implicitly indicates both a temporal and spatial difference between 'modern' and 'traditional' sports. First, the application of categories of 'tradition' at the same time as 'modernity' illustrates, from the perspectives of Osborne (1992) and Latour (1996), that modernity is a qualitative, not a quantitative concept. Second, time is spatialized in terms of the well-used terms of 'First World' and 'Third World' ('developing countries').[3] However, my aim is to demonstrate that people do not necessarily experience a rupture between, for example, traditional dances and modern fitness or between unorganized games and field sports. Rather than referring to different 'authentic' practices, these categories are, in the words of Ranger (1983), a product of the 'politics of trad-ition'. However, as this essay will show, performances and performers are always sited and contextual (Werbner 2001).

The analytical perspective on which I build my interpretations draws on Paul Connerton's (1989) concept of 'incorporating practice' as a way societies remember as well as Michael Taussig's (1993) concept of 'mimesis' as entailing a capacity to be like and to be different. Incorporating practices refers to bodily practices where the transmission occurs only during the time bodies are present to sustain that particular activity. According to Connerton, much of our cultural knowledge is reproduced through our bodily practices, through 'living models' of people walking, sitting and working. Our bodies keep the past in an entirely effective form in their continuing ability to perform certain skilled actions. While Connerton stresses the cultural and social continuity created through body practices, Taussig's concept of 'mimesis' is fruitful for grasping continuity as well as transformation through performing bodies. According to Taussig (1993) imitation, or what he calls 'mimesis', is not a blueprint of an action, but rather the ability to cope with change and continuity at the same time. An important point made by Taussig is that mimesis is explicitly tied to the body, and through mimesis people can dramatize and negotiate understandings of themselves and of others. It is in this tension between continuity through body memory and transformation through imitation of 'the other' that the complexity, ambiguity and creativity of the performer will be illuminated and hopefully further explained in this chapter.

Performers and Politics

Sport and dance have played important parts in the nation-building process in Tanzania since liberation (or independence) in 1961. Traditional dances were revitalized as a symbol of national identity, and the practice of sport and physical activity were encouraged in order to provide people with healthy bodies and minds. The National Stadium in Dar-es-Salaam was finished in 1962 in order to improve the infrastructure of sport, and it became an important stage for performers of sport and dance, hosting both national and international events (Nkongo 1979; Tenga 2000). The liberation politics conducted by Julius Nyerere, the leader of Tanzania after independence, was founded on a form of African socialism that favoured pure national-cultural ideals such as anti-imperialism, self-help and the breaking down of tribal, religious, ethnic, gender and class barriers. Heterogeneity was to be prevented, while equality and homogeneity were ideal-ized. Today, it might seem as though Tanzania, at least in its urban areas, has turned out completely opposite to what had been the intention of liberation politics. A multi-party system has replaced the single-party political system. There is inequality instead of equality, privatization of schools and hospitals at the expense of education and health for all and the rising of a powerful elite without economic restrictions instead of equal distribution of resources.

While social differences between people were under-communicated during the period of socialism, today one registers various kinds of class-differentiated practices such as fitness, golf, rugby, bodybuilding and traditional and modern dance. In a city like Dar-es-Salaam, a melting-pot of people from all over the world, with nearly 3 million inhabitants, one might sense this expansion of plur-ality and multiplicity merely by walking through the city centre. In the last ten years, the city has been faced with major cultural, technological and political changes. In terms of cultural politics, there are continuous debates about what kind of 'new' practices and habits are to be incorporated as Tanzanian culture. In 1997, the bodybuilding contest, Mr Dar-es-Salaam, and a beauty contest, Miss Tanzania, were postponed several times owing to disagreement among politicians when it came to classifying the events. Was bodybuilding a kind of 'sport', and were beauty competitions 'culture'? While politicians operate with categories such as 'dance', 'sports', 'art' or 'traditional' and 'modern' in classifying body practices, people might incorporate all kinds of practices into one concept such as *michezo,* or they may note distinctions between practices according to the experience of performing them. *Michezo* (in the sense of 'sports') and *ngoma*[4] (in the sense of 'traditional dance') are politically separated between different government depart-ments. *Michezo* 'belongs' to the sports section, while *ngoma* 'belongs' to the arts.

However, interviews conducted with residents of Dar-es-Salaam on their ways of conceptualizing activities indicate that many made distinctions or connections between *michezo* and *ngoma* dance by pointing at the experience of engaging in these activities. Asking whether *michezo* and *ngoma* were the same or different, I got answers such as: '*Michezo* is like *ngoma,* it is the same, but it is different'; '*michezo* is *michezo* and *ngoma* is *ngoma,* they are different'; or '*michezo* and *ngoma* are the same' (Leseth 1995). Pursuing these matters further, I learned that *michezo* and *ngoma* are highly embodied and non-discursive phenomena; people knew them by practice, not by speaking. *Michezo* and *ngoma* included not only many activities, but also many different experiences. Some started to explain differences or similarities between them by drawing on a piece of paper or demonstrating with their bodies. In *ngoma*, you had the drums placed in specific positions, while in a football match there were no drums or they were placed outside the football field. One woman said: '*Michezo* and *ngoma* are different. In *ngoma* there is lots of noise, lots of dust and not any special structure. *Michezo* like ball games has a specific number of participants and the playing-ground is often better than in *ngoma*.' Others pointed to the experience of performing the activities as being different; '*Ngoma* is jumping up and down, while *michezo*, like running, is to move forward.' Others stressed the similarities: '*Ngoma* and *michezo* are the same, you use your body and your joints and you sweat.' Hence the Tanzanian performer transgresses, so to speak, conventional categorical definitions and boundaries that isolate fields such as sports, dance, work and play, and breaks with distinctions such as 'modern' and 'traditional'.

In 1992 I talked to Mr Comba in the Ministry of Sports and Culture in Dar-es-Salaam, who claimed that: 'Most Tanzanians don't yet see the meaning in doing sports.' I was surprised, and wondered what had happened, taking into account the assumed importance of sports after liberation and the fact that I actually observed many people moving, playing and dancing. Mr Comba continued:

'Sport' is science. To be able to do sports in the modern way it is necessary to understand its meaning, like that sports give you better health and better morals and increases co-operation. The problem is that sports in Kiswahili, *michezo*, might imply activities without any specific meaning, like play, while 'sport' is organized, meaningful activities which have an important place in the development of a country. Our aim in this Department is to develop modern sports like football, basketball, volleyball and athletics. To see the point in these sports, one has to learn them in a scientific way. This is different from how people learn *michezo* from birth. This discrepancy between 'sports' and *michezo*, is the reason why most Tanzanians don't relate sports to a perspective of health and development.

According to Mr Comba, there is a discrepancy between people's conception of *michezo* and politicians' promotion of 'sports' as development. I will try to explain this statement further by giving a short historical overview of how *michezo* and sports have been used in political discourse as a means to obtain political objectives. It is interesting to note that even if the word *michezo* is translated to 'sports' in contemporary language, the words are treated as representing two different phenomena in historical writings on sports in Tanzania. While *michezo* often refers to 'pre-colonial', 'traditional' activities, 'sports' seem to represent 'modernization', 'colonialism' and 'internationalization'.

Michezo as Pre-colonial Activities[5]

The practice of sport and dance in Tanzania dates back as early as the time before the coming of the Portuguese, the Arabs, the Germans and the British[6] (Johnson 1980; Baker and Mangan 1987; Tenga 2000). The practising of local dances, archery, wrestling, and singing games played by children indicates that these games have been handed down from generation to generation through various local institutions. *Michezo* (sports and games) and *ngoma* (traditional dances, singing and drumming) were naturally differentiated by tribe, geography, gender and age. People living close to a lake or a river usually had good swimmers, while people living up in the mountains had good long-distance runners and athletes.

The style of the dances also differed. While members of the Masai tribe did more jumping with less hip movement, the dances of the coastal tribes were characterized by wild movements of the hips (Lange 2002). The teaching of dance and sport was linked to initiation ceremonies, such as those marking a change from childhood to adulthood. There were activities that children and adults engaged in for amusement and also as necessary skills to be acquired for individual or tribal defence and prestige. Children exercised by throwing items at targets, fencing with sticks, running and jumping, distance and target spear-throwing and jumping for height (Ndee 1996). Both men and women participated and competed in *ngoma* (traditional dances). The group of dancers that attracted most spectators was deemed to have won. Men competed in different forms of *michezo*, like tug-of-war contests, wrestling, running, throwing the javelin and swimming. As a good sportsman, you obtained prestige among your peers. For a man, it was important to be strong and to train hard, or else it would take him a long time to acquire the recognized status of manhood. Women had other *michezo*, like running with a bottle on the head or skipping a rope (Leseth 1995).

From *Michezo* to Sports

Modern sports that developed in European industrial societies were introduced to Africa as part of European colonization. This process began with the introduction of formal education through the infusion of European missionary societies (Tenga 2000). The missionaries viewed many of the traditional games and dances as pagan, and they argued that Western sports were morally better.[7] During the German occupation of East Africa, physical education existed in the form of military training, often featuring marching parades. Two guiding factors characterized the British influence upon physical education: the military and the British public school. Later on, military gymnastics seem to have developed within military barracks, and became part of training programmes for sport and exercise.[8]

Women and girls were not encouraged in the same way as men to participate in sport. Netball, a ball game for women that is also played in England and Australia, was introduced to Tanzania in the 1940s and 1950s. The colonizers argued that netball fitted the female shape. A crucial point made by Ranger (1975) is that, in the colonizers' attempt to record African 'tradition', their invented 'custom' was based on descriptions obtained from male informants. 'Men's dominance in society, that is their control over religious activities and political organisation, was expressed even more clearly in colonial invented custom than it had ever been before' (1975: 258) The idea of 'tradition' was provided with a feminine identity, while 'modern' was designated a male domain. This might further explain women's exclusion from 'modern sports'.

The model of Victorian public schools also played a crucial role as a colonizing strategy. School sport aggregated dominance and difference, because it promoted loyalty and obedience. It was, hence, a useful instrument for colonial purposes, as it promoted in athletes the confidence to lead and the compulsion to follow (Mangan 1986). By means of the moralistic ideology of athleticism, schoolboys would learn the basic tools of imperial command: courage, endurance, assertion, control and self-control. As was reported by the East African Committee for Education in 1924:

> The improvement of many tribes in Africa is impossible until the degrading influences of their pleasures are corrected or eliminated . . . All concerned with colonial welfare, whether European or native . . . will find their efforts hampered by the demoralising results of games and pleasures that are physically or emotionally enervating . . . It is therefore imperative in the interests of Africans and Europeans alike that Native amusements shall be corrected and improved (cited in Nkongo 1979: 23).

Modern sport, defined as 'civilising games' (Ndee 1996), was the pathway to this improvement. The colonial way of doing sports required a different way of structuring time and space than did many of the traditional games. Running had usually been conducted without territorial limits; now the sportsman should run in a stadium, measuring the distance in metres and seconds. An interesting paradox, however, was that on the one hand 'athletes' should become civilized, while on the other hand they were expected to remain 'natural'.[9] The traditional dances were, according to Ranger (1975), the only activities that were not hampered by colonialism. The emergence of different dance societies in colonial Tanzania, such as *beni*, *mganda* and *dansi,* incorporating ideas of modernity and multitribalism in their styles, indicates that the colonization of body practices wasn't a straightforward process in which people responded without resistance (see also Lange 1995). In 1948 there was a change of colonial policy in which the importance of 'traditional' dances in preparing Tanzanians for Independence was recognized. Traditional dance was again invented to serve the purpose of a national culture.

Nation-building through Sports

After colonialism, there was a widely shared belief among African leaders concerning the efficacy of sport for developing national unity. The potential value of sport and education was accepted in newly independent African states as an indispensable strategy for the integration of ethnic groups and as a means of diminishing tribalism (Tenga 2000). Sports, such as athletics, football and gymnastics, along with traditional dance were 're-constructed' as national activities that bore important images in the Tanzanian self-representation of the nation. The Ministry of National Culture and Youth was formed in 1962, in order to effectuate a cultural campaign. Nyerere, along with other African leaders, held that the culture and traditions of a nation could only be preserved through the re-introduction of indigenous activities, including traditional sports and games, into the new education system.

As did many other African countries, Tanzania engaged in an Africanization project that was intended to restore the cultural heritage and pride of African people (Tenga 2000). This meant, among other things, that British or European names for sports clubs were replaced with African names, explicitly stating their African identity. The two largest football clubs in the country, Sunderland and Young African Sports Club, changed to *Simba* and *Yanga* Sports Clubs (ibid.). Traditional dances that had been discouraged during colonial times for fear of encouraging tribalism and possible revolt, were now revitalized, not as activities claiming tribal identity, but as 'symbols of the Nation'. Performing in the traditional *khanga* in the colours of the Tanzanian flag (black, white and yellow), dancers were collected from all over Tanzania to create national dancing troupes. Today, performances of traditional dances are also very popular among tourists. However, many tourists react to the nationalization of the dances, pointing to the widespread political use of *ngoma*-songs in performances (Lange 1995). They come to see traditional dances at the tourist hotels or at the museum. But what they see and hear is political propaganda (for example, singing about the president or the party while dancing) and a praising of the nation, instead of the 'original folklore' that they expect.

Nyerere, who was educated at Oxford, has been criticized for his direction of the process of nation-building and his use of European ideas of nationalism: projecting them on to Tanzania without taking into account the fact that Tanzania didn't have one tradition on which to build a nation. Nyerere wanted to create a national culture, but he didn't take into account differences in power-relations among the tribes. As Lange puts it (1995), even today people don't seem to know what a 'national dance' is. Traditional dance (*ngoma*), like *michezo,* is still differentiated by tribe and geography. While Nyerere wanted to make a break with the colonial period, he was himself an athlete, brought up under colonial practices and

– 237 –

British influence. National development also implied assistance in the form of 'foreign aid'. Sports aid has been, and still is, part of this arrangement (Leseth 1995; Tenga 2000). The belief in the efficacy of sport for the development of the nation has been hampered by the economic difficulties Tanzania has experienced. There has been an overall lack of a defined cultural policy in Tanzania since independence. The cultural undertakings of the state have been based on speeches and statements about culture issued by government leaders. No specific direction has been given to sport, as part of culture, in the development of society (Tenga 2000). This might be attributed to the general lack of direction for the nation as a whole (ibid.).

Living Models at the National Stadium

In 1997, more than thirty years after the liberation of Tanzania, I was present at the reopening of the National Stadium in Dar-es-Salaam. The guest of honour was the former president, Julius Nyerere, followed by the sitting president, Mkapa. Performances of football, dance and running played a central part in the ceremony. The National Stadium had played an important role in the nation-building process in Tanzania, and every year Liberation Day (9 December) was celebrated with a ceremony at the Stadium and the staging of sporting events. The rehabilitation of the Stadium was meant to revitalize the importance of sport in developing national unity, just as it was promoted after independence. Yet the Stadium and other local spaces were declining owing to negligence on the part of the government in protecting such areas against demolition and new building projects.

As body models for the nation, the two presidents, Nyerere and Mkapa, might symbolize a shift of interest and evaluation from active involvement in sports to sport watching. Compared to Nyerere's fit body, which had encouraged people to involve themselves in sports, President Mkapa was not an athletic figure. As modelled by Nyerere, the body image of the nation was that of a working body that represented solidarity through a decent lifestyle and robust physical effort. President Mkapa is rather fat and rich, symbolizing the wealthy and vigorous man. Mkapa's belly is a sign of wealth.[10] His regime also represents a shift in Tanzanian politics, from single-party to multi-party politics, from socialism to capitalism and an increasing degree of class differentiation.

Here I will recount the ceremony at the National Stadium and use this event as a frame for describing *michezo* in post-colonial Dar-es-Salaam. My point is neither to explain a 'decline' of sports in Tanzania, nor to point to the need for 'sport-development'. As was argued earlier, this way of thinking makes it too easy to define 'needs' and 'what is lacking' when considering body practices, instead of describing what people are actually doing. I will therefore point at the power of performing bodies, of 'living models' (Connerton 1989), in reproducing and transforming political contexts in Tanzania today.

I arrived at the Stadium together with a Tanzanian friend, Tunu, a 22-year-old woman living in Dar-es-Salaam. There were lots of people outside the Stadium, waiting to get a ticket for the event. Entering the Stadium an hour and a half before the football match between Zambia and Tanzania was scheduled to begin, we were met with loud music and a marching brass band performing music on the field. People kept pouring in, filling up the space. Men and boys definitely outnumbered women in the audience. Men, who could be characterized as having a potbelly like Mkapa and wearing a mobile telephone, took the most expensive seats. Two of the most popular commercial dancing groups in Dar-es-Salaam at that moment (TOT and Diamond Sound) started to perform. The female dancers performed in white tights and tight upper garments, while the male performers who were singing and dancing were dressed in suits. The female dancers in the first group were also quite thin, while in the other group they were rather plump. The dancers in this group also each wore a *khanga* wrapped around the waist, emphasizing the wriggling movements of the hips. One of the dancers had a totally bleached face, probably as a result of the use of chemicals. The audience was shouting and standing upright as the dancers started to perform, and some of the female dancers moved away from the scene and among the audience at the tribune.

The different body shapes of the female dancers illustrate two dominating body ideals among young women in Dar es Salaam. The first is labelled *English Figure* while the second is labelled *Bantu figure*.[11] It is an obvious yet often ambiguous evaluation of those shapes, that the *English figure* represents imperial ideals, while the *Bantu figure* is the more authentic. To bleach the skin is another 'imperial' practice that, despite being widespread, is condemned by the government. It is commented upon by people with respect to those who follow this practice, to whom are attached nicknames such as *mkorogo* (this is also the name of the chemicals used), *fanta-cocacola* (illustrating the colour patches you get when the bleaching fails) and *Half-London* ('you are becoming half-European'). The outfits of the performers in commercial dance have also changed dramatically in the last few years. Now the female dancers are wearing miniskirts and tights, compared to 1993, when most female dancers were dressed in *khangas* or long dresses. The interesting point here is that when performed through dancing, those critical aspects of appearance seem to be incorporated into known patterns. As is remarked by the artist Songoyi (1988) in his description of the nationalization of songs in traditional dance: 'To most people, movement is all that matters' (1988: 37).

The new dancing styles popularly called *Kwasakwasa* and *Ikibinda Nkoi* have obtained an enormous popularity among ordinary people as well as among politicians. People run to see these erotic dances, which are like modern versions of the traditional initiation dances, *Sindimba* or *Mdundiko*,[12] with impulses from other African countries such as Zaire. The movements are similar to those of traditional dances: the waist and the hips rolling, the feet flat on the ground, the wriggling of upper parts of the body. But the movements are maybe more explicit in challenging the erotic and sexual parts of the body, and the body-parts, such as the hips, legs and breasts, are more undressed. In Dar-es-Salaam, hip-movements and 'wild' behaviour have become very popular, which again makes the invention of new dances flourish. The fact that the audience enjoys erotic movements makes some groups not only prefer dances that 'naturally' have this, but also add such movements into dances that originally did not have them. In this way, these dances are presenting hybrid forms of the traditional culture.

> The guests of honour and Julius Nyerere, followed by President Mkapa, arrived in one Mercedes each that drove into the Stadium. When the guests were seated, a female dancer, dressed in black, started to perform together with a snake at the stage at the front of the field. 'She is a *mchawi*' (a witch), said Tunu. People were shouting and clapping, and at the same time football players were entering the pitch and starting to warm up. An old man was running around on the field. 'That's a *mchawi* too', people commented.

These performers were relating the fields of football and dance more or less implicitly, since in both dance and football the belief in and practice of witchcraft (*juju*) is common, even if it has been officially abandoned as 'traditional belief' (Leseth 1997; Mesaki 1992). Victory in a football match or between groups of competing dancers is credited not only to actual performances in themselves, but also to the medicine used by the medicine man. Thus, witchcraft is a way to handle the element of unpredictability in sports and dancing competitions, and the practice of witchcraft is reproduced through performing bodies, transgressing limits of 'traditional' and 'modern' practices.

> The warming-up exercises consisted of stretching the joints, gymnastics and short spells of running with a military look, like a parade. Simultaneously with the warming up, the dancers were still performing and there were competitions in 100 and 200-metre races around the field. The running took place without any announcement. Tunu didn't show much interest in the running; she did at least find the exercises surprising. When I informed her that now they were competing in the100 metres, she replied 'How do you know it is exactly 100 metres?'

It is interesting to observe how today athletes in Tanzania are reproducing a myth of the 'natural athlete' who is brought up in the mountains and who ran to and from school since childhood.[13] At the same time, athleticism seems to decrease in popularity and athletes do not perform with impressive results in international competitions, in contrast with the Kenyans, for example. The idea of the 'natural athlete' might also be part of a political discourse that justifies the government's lack of funding in athletics, because 'natural athletes' do not need 'scientific training' or expensive equipment (Leseth 1995).

Then at last it is time for the match. The two football teams re-enter the field, while the band is playing the respective national anthems. The atmosphere is for a short while ceremonious, despite the songs played by the brass band being completely out of tune and, to me, a bad copy of British military brass band music. The football play obviously does not impress the audience, as they are constantly criticizing the Tanzanian players. The trainer is a European (*mzungu*) and people laugh and say that there is no use in sending experts from Europe, when all he can do is to beautify the players with good equipment, not make them better at playing football. The match ends 0–0, and we are escorted out, trying to avoid the fighting that usually follows after a football match.

The event at the Stadium is an illuminating example of how performing bodies both reflect and shape the political contexts in which they occur. The multiple embodied practices at the Stadium reflect the change to multi-party politics in Tanzania and increasing internationalization and globalization. At the same time, the idea of *michezo* is reproduced and transformed through performing bodies, through imitation of new styles and images and reproduction of old ones that transgress conventional boundaries and categories of body practices such as sports, dance, work and play. In a free listing exercise[14] among people in Dar-es-Salaam in 1997, I found eighty different activities associated with the word *michezo*. Football was the activity mentioned most often, followed by other ball games such as netball, volleyball and basketball, and then athletics. Music and dance, often named as *ngoma*, were among other activities frequently listed as *michezo*. At the same time 'traditional' activities such as archery, wrestling, and spear-throwing were mentioned, as well as 'modern' practices such as bodybuilding and aerobics. The high number of activities associated with the word *michezo* makes it interesting to ask how people make sense of and learn to view as *michezo* 'modern' body practices such as bodybuilding and fitness practices that in the political discourse are defined as 'foreign' and non-cultural.

Moving beyond *Michezo* – The Importance of Movement

Most people told me that they learned by imitating (*kuiga*), whether from 'living models' on the street, on TV, at the cinema or in a magazine. To imitate (*kuiga*) was an expression incorporated in everyday discourse as a way of indicating whether it was a skill, an action or a way of moving. Models representing both body-building and fitness and beauty competitions were highly visualized in the media. These models could be imitated. An important point, however, is that this imitation was not, as stated by Taussig (1993), a blueprint. People seemed to be conscious about what they wanted to copy, but at the same time they built on previous patterns of performing. Tino, a bodybuilder, didn't imitate this practice only by looking at photographs of American bodybuilders in magazines. He also drew on experiences both from *ngoma* (traditional dance) and football in his performance as a bodybuilder. He explained:

> For the time being I am dancing and doing weightlifting. When doing exercises in bodybuilding it reminds me of the rhythm from the drum. The dance has provided me with endurance and I am able to do several exercises lifting weights. I have also played football. I use to be the keeper. I like to jump, like I do in the dance. I fetch the ball, but people laugh at me and say I am better in jumping than in fetching the ball!

Hence, from the performer's point of view, the skill you use in your performance is not only related to that attached to the role, in this case that of Mr Bodybuilder. Rather, one exploits the accumulated embodied experience of a lifetime in the performance.

Accordingly, the bodybuilder is not only 'imitating' a Western body image, but is also drawing on his own experiences as a performer. In contrast to Europe, where body ideals, such as being slim or muscular, are presented as static and detached from the moving body, people in Dar-es-Salaam talked about ideals of the moving body. Betty, a 25-year-old woman living in a squatter area of the city, explained: 'You know, Anne, it is not important whether you have a body shape like a bodybuilder, a beauty queen or a traditional figure. The crux of the matter is how this person moves, both when it comes to speed and style.'

Starting to collect words on walking-styles among people in Dar-es-Salaam, I found around twenty different words for styles of walking. The metaphors used for naming different ways of walking (also implying an element of speed – i.e. fast or slow) indicated imitation. Names of animals were often used. *Mwendo ya twiga* (move like a giraffe) or *mwendo ya kiboko* (move like a hippopotamus) were common expressions. *Kulinga* refers to walking slowly, wriggling your buttocks (for women) and waving your right hand. This way of walking is both attractive and dangerous. It is the way a hyena moves when looking for meat. Betty told me that people, especially the youth, continuously created expressions for walking-styles and copied new ways of moving. *Kutembea kwa mbwembwe* (walking with style, showing off) refers to the walking style of a bodybuilder, while *kujyata* refers to walking like a model, like Miss Tanzania.

People imitate ways of moving like a bodybuilder or a beauty queen. However, people incorporate new experiences into established patterns and thus create an embodied continuity with the past, which escapes the invocation of official political discourses. The bodybuilder and the beauty queen, representing Western body images, are incorporated not primarily in the concept of *michezo*, but in a general pattern of everyday practices, like walking. Yet what is being copied is the movement ideal as an already known image, and not the body ideal. The selection of how and what people copy further stresses the difference between the European static body image and the Tanzanian moving body image. Youth continuously invent words for new beauty-ideals, and the terms are incorporated with already known practices, such as walking. Hence, through imitation performers are able to transform and move beyond official political discourses on culture and at the same time create continuity with the past through their body memory. Thus, the power of imitation, as a way of being like and being other, is crucial not only for explaining the malleability and tranformative character of *michezo*, but also for explaining the character of performers in general, of moving bodies as social actors and cultural producers.

By Way of Conclusion

Nyerere sought to foster national uniformity and a common culture through promotion of a set of ostensibly pan-Tanzanian emphases in physical culture that nonetheless readily accommodated and still accommodates lingering colonial, tribal and post-colonial dimensions. Attempts by politicians to exercise control over politics and public displays and uses of the body run up against the stubborn but unspoken manner in which body practices resist simple regimentation. The process of building a nation, as conducted by Nyerere, also built on principles of imitation, though quite implicitly. Nyerere used his background of 'being like' Europeans, to become 'the Other'. His experiences of being educated in Oxford and of being an athlete were important in creating a 'capacity' to become different, to promote national identity. The multiplicity of practices and traditions in Dar-es-Salaam today might be interpreted as an outcome of ongoing processes of imitation, invention and reproduction of this multiple heritage. Moreover, in all embodied performances, these elements must be taken into account in creating and reproducing culture. Within processes of continuity, performing actors work in a constant process of hybridization and challenge conventional and political categorical definitions of and boundaries between activities such as sport, dance and art, as well as established theoretical notions of modernity, tradition, culture and nationalism. In this regard the concept of *michezo* provides us with new and valuable insights.

Notes

1. *Michezo* is the Swahili word for 'sports'. In Tanzania, English and Swahili are the official languages, and, in that Tanzanian political rhetoric that deals with sports issues, the words *michezo* and sports are interchangeable. However,

the word *michezo* includes a range of activities that Westerners do not label sports, such as dance, play, games and cinema. The English concept 'sport' is often too narrow in describing the non-differentiated aspects of *michezo* and the meaning-content incorporated in the word.

2. This chapter draws on material from two periods of fieldwork in Dar-es-Salaam, in 1992–93 and 1997, as well as a preliminary visit in 1988, when I was engaged for a period at the Norwegian sports project 'Sports for All'. My field of research has been focused upon a squatter area on the outskirts of Dar-es-Salaam, but has also included frequent visits in company with sports groups such as football teams, and athletics, aerobics, bodybuilding and dance groups. The historical part of this chapter is necessarily incomplete, but my main concern is to give a brief image of post-liberation politics and to show how sports and dance were employed as means for obtaining political objectives. All the names used in this text are fictive, except for those of major leaders (e.g. Nyerere).

3. This point is taken up by the anthropologist Johannes Fabian in his book *On Time and the Other* (1983). Fabian calls this spatialization of time 'the scandal of anthropology'. This evolutionary tendency can be further related to the development of evolutionary thought, anthropology and modernity in nineteenth-century Europe. According to the British philosopher Peter Osborne (1992), modernity emerged in this period not as a moment in time, but as an abstract, qualitative idea. Modernity referred only to Western Europe and America, while 'tradition' became descriptive of the rest of the world. According to Jean and John Comaroff (1992), anthropologists still tend to 'preserve "zones" of traditions' in their writings on 'the Other' (1992: 5). I develop this point further in Leseth (forthcoming).

4. Like the word *michezo*, the word *ngoma* includes several aspects of an activity, such as 'a drum', 'any kind of dance', 'music in general' (F. Johnson 1990).

5. On the one hand, the hybrid background of Tanzanian history might bring into question the idea of any 'pure' Tanzanian/East African culture in the past without any 'encounters' or 'borrowings'. On the other hand, the writings on pre-colonial Africa often 'invent' such an image of an authentic culture.

6. The eastern part of Africa was 'discovered' by the Portuguese in 1505. In 1698 the Arabs conquered Mombasa in Kenya and ended the Portuguese power in East Africa. From 1890 to 1919, the Germans ruled East Africa. German East Africa was divided into Tanganyika, Rwanda and Burundi. Following their defeat in the First World War, the Germans lost their colonies and Tanganyika became a British mandate in 1919. The British ruled Tanganyika until independence in 1961, when the Republic of Tanzania was formed.

7. There are several examples of similar 'civilizing missions' through sport in societies in Africa, Asia and South America. See for example Jean and John

Comaroff's (1992) account of body politics in colonial South Africa, Gael Graham's writing on American mission schools in China (Graham 1994), and Archetti's account of two models of bodily and moral care, based on German gymnastics and English games and team sports, which were imported to Argentina in the 1860s (Archetti 2002).

8. 'Parade' is still a *michezo*, practised in the military service and in schools. During my fieldwork in Tanzania, I often participated in warm-up sessions in football and athletics at the National Stadium, and I remember being surprised by the practising of military-style gymnastics that were rather old-fashioned. Furthermore, fitness training also combined a mixture of movements from gymnastic exercises, marching drills based upon the German model and Jane Fonda-inspired exercises from America.

9. This points to what Homi Bhabha (1994) labels 'the ironic compromise of mimicry' in characterizing the colonial discourse: the desire for a reformed recognizable Other that is 'almost the same, but not quite' (1994: 86).

10. The male potbelly is a characteristic part of the typical male body ideal in Dar-es-Salaam. This belly is in popular street language given names such as *kee-freezer* and *kitambi*. *Kee-freeze*, a Swahili word mixed up with English, refers to an image of a fridge; it can melt any time.

11. This way of incorporating hybrid elements into nicknames in the Swahili language is an example of the malleability of this language, which cont-inuously incorporates changes and globalizing trends, yet at the same time builds on previous patterns and represents 'Tanzanian identity' in international contexts. The Swahili language, spoken in Tanzania, Kenya and parts of Uganda, is originally a hybrid, building on elements from English, German, Arab and Bantu languages. The language is still expanding, incorporating new and modern words and expressions. Old people today complain that they hardly understand the Swahili spoken by the youth, which is a mixture of English and 'old Swahili'.

12. *Mdundiko* is the name of an initiation-dance from the *Zaramo* tribe in Dar-es-Salaam. The dance contains many erotic and sexual elements. The *Sindimba* is a similar dance, from the *Makonde* tribe.

13. From a sample of fifteen athletes I interviewed in 1992 in Dar-es-Salaam and Arusha, thirteen of them stated that the fact that they had been running 5–10 kilometres to school when they were kids was the basic reason why they had become good athletes (Leseth 1995).

14. 'Free listing' is a systematic interview technique and a powerful way of studying cultural domains, such as understandings of diseases, plants, occup-ations, animals and sports. You ask people to list all the 'X' they know. After collecting 15–20, you already have a picture of certain domains (see Russell Bernard 1995).

References

Archetti, E. P. (2002), 'Transforming Argentina: Sport, Modernity and Nation Building in the Periphery', Unpublished manuscript.
Baker, J. W. and J. A. Mangan (eds) (1987), *Sport in Africa. Essays in Social History*, London: Africana Publishing Company.
Bernard, Russell H. (1995), *Research Methods in Anthropology*, Walnut Creek/ London: Alta Mira.
Bhabha, H. K. (1994), *The Location of Culture*. London: Routledge.
Comaroff, J. and J. Comaroff (1992), *Ethnography and the Historical Imagination*, Boulder, CO: Westview Press.
Connerton, P. (1989), *How Societies Remember*, Cambridge/New York: Cambridge University Press.
Fabian, Johannes (1983), *Time and the Other: How Anthropology Makes Its Object*. New York: Columbia University Press.
Graham, G. (1994), 'Exercising Control: Sports and Physical Education in American Protestant Mission Schools in China, 1880–1930', *Signs. Journal of Women in Culture and Society*, vol. 20: pp. 23–48
Heinemann, K. (1993), 'Sport in Developing Countries', in E. Dunning, J. Maguire and K. Pearton (eds), *The Sport Process: A Comparative and Developmental Approach*, Champaign, IL: Human Kinetics Press.
Johnson, F. (1990 [1939]), *A Standard Swahili–English Dictionary*, Dar-es-Salaam/ Nairobi: Oxford University Press.
Johnson, W. (ed.) (1980), *Sport and Physical Education Around the World*, Champaign, IL: Stipes Publishing Company.
Lange, S. (2002), 'Managing Modernity. Gender, State, and Nation in the Popular Drama of Dar es Salaam, Tanzania', Thesis submitted for the degree Dr.Polit., Department of Social Anthropology, University of Bergen 2002.
Latour, B. (1996), *Vi har aldri vært moderne*, Oslo: Spartacus Forlag.
Leseth, A. (1995), 'Bevegelseskultur', Thesis submitted to the Cand. Polit. degree, Social Anthropological Institute, University of Oslo, 1995.
—— (1997), 'The Use of *Juju* in Football: Sports and Witchcraft in Tanzania', in G. Armstrong and R. Giulianotti (eds), *Entering the Field. New Perspectives on World Football*, Oxford/New York: Berg.
—— (forthcoming), *Culture of Movement in a Postcolonial Context: A Critical Approach to the Study of Body Practices*.
Mangan, J. A. (1986), *The Games Ethic and Imperialism*, Harmondsworth: Viking/ Penguin Books Ltd.
Mesaki, S. (1992), *Witch-killings in Sukumaland, Tanzania*. Dar-es-Salaam: Department of Sociology, University of Dar-es-Salaam.

Ndee, H.S. (1996), 'Sport, Culture and Society from an African Perspective: A Study in Historical Revisionism', *The International Journal of the History of Sport*, Vol. 13, No. 2 (Aug.1996), Frank Cass: England.

Nkongo, J. M. (1979), 'Factors Influencing the Development of Physical Education in Tanzania as Compared with Other African Countries'. Unpublished M.Ed. Thesis, University of Manchester.

Osborne, P. (1992), 'Modernity is a Qualitative, Not a Chronological, Category', *New Left Review*, 1992: 65–84.

Ranger, T. (1975), *Dance and Society in Eastern Africa 1890–1970*. London: Heinemann.

—— (1983), 'The Invention of Tradition in Colonial Africa', in E. Hobsbawm and T. Ranger (eds), *The Invention of Tradition*, Cambridge: Cambridge University Press.

Songoyi, M. E. (1988), *Commercialization. Its impact on Traditional Dances*, Trondheim, Norway: University of Dar-es-Salaam/Rådet for folkemusikk og dans.

Taussig, M. (1993), *Mimesis and Alterity*, London: Routledge.

Tenga, T. S. M. (2000), 'Globalisation and Olympic Sport in Tanzania', Doctoral Dissertation, The Norwegian University of Sport and Physical Education, Oslo.

Werbner, P. (2001), 'The Limits of Cultural Hybridity: On Ritual Monsters, Poetic License and Contested Postcolonial Purifications', *Journal of Royal Anthropological Institute*, 2001, Vol. 7.

Index

as communication 116
competition 180, 190
national, 180
learn to, 126
liturgical 180, 189, 190
macho, 127
practice 10, 116, 126
traditional 132, 136–7, 239–140
Da Matta, R. 217
*de*construction142
Dobson, T. 144
Donnelly, P. 141
Donohue, J. J. 145
Dyck, Noel 186

Eggen, Nils Arne 100–1, 110
elite 1, 4–5, 25,37, 60–1, 67–8, 83, 86–7, 91,
    160, 133
ethnography
    of male 158
    of masculinity 4, 158
    of performance 71
    regional, 158–160
embodied
    acticity 2,11, 70
    identity/ies 1, 2, 15, 158, 161, 171
    experiences 4, 13, 110, 145
    performances 7, 63, 65, 70–1, 77, 228, 243,
    practices 1–2, 5–6, 11, 13, 17, 228,
explanatory system 132

fans
    German, 15, 18
    English, 107, 110
    long-distance 98–9, 105, 109
    Norwegian, 3, 17, 103, 105–6, 108, 110
FIFA 210,
Football
    Argentina 219, 227–8
    British, 3, 15
    broadcasting rights 212
    Denmark 44
    El Salvordor 157
    English 98, 100, 103–6, 108–110
    German 5, 16, 197, 199, 203–4, 207, 209–11
    Latin-American 158
    modern, 97
    Norway 3, 78, 81, 99, 107–8,
    practice of, 4, 158, 171

samba, 218
Foucault, Michel 182
Free Presbyterian Church of Ulster
    Government 5, 179, 182–3,
fun 27, 29–31, 37, 39, 41, 44, 55, 58, 60, 63–4,
    68–9, 78–80, 85, 129, 141
fællesskab 28–9, 39, 49–50,

gender
    entrepreneurs 91
    eqality 1, 17, 130–1,
    identity 3–4, 78–9, 90–1
    ideology 3, 77, 130–1
    roles 75, 79, 91–2, 128
    sexuality and, 187
    stereotypes 77, 81, 90, 123, 128, 130, 132
German Football Association 199, 201
    GFA 199, 201–4, 206, 210–12
Geertzian terminology 227
Giddens, Anthony 100
Gibbons, Luke 181–2
Giulianotti, Richard 100
globalization 2, 105, 116, 212, 241
Gose, Peter 161–2
Greer, Robin 179
gym 1, 29, 32, 43–44, 46,48, 81

habitus 8, 141, 152, 188
    see also Pierre Bourdieu
Hall, Frank 182, 184, 186
handball
    associations 83
    activity/ies 75
    children´s, 3, 77, 84
    communication 82
    and leadership 80
    Norwegian 86
    practice(s) 81
    techniques 83
Hanks, W. F. 42–3
Hanna, Judith L. 116
historical analysis 217
Horn, John 13, 141,
Howell, Signe 181–2, 189
hybrid 6, 240

ice hockey
    see also 'pond hockey'
    understanding of, 62

Index